Phenomenology: Continuation and Criticism

PHAENOMENOLOGICA

COLLECTION PUBLIÉE SOUS LE PATRONAGE DES CENTRES
D'ARCHIVES-HUSSERL

50

F. KERSTEN AND R. ZANER

Phenomenology: Continuation and Criticism

ESSAYS IN MEMORY OF DORION CAIRNS

DORION CAIRNS

Photograph courtesy Michael Schrayer

F. KERSTEN AND R. ZANER

Phenomenology: Continuation and Criticism

ESSAYS IN MEMORY OF DORION CAIRNS

MARTINUS NIJHOFF / THE HAGUE / 1973

ISBN 90 247 1302 1

EDITORS' FOREWORD

Under the title of "Phenomenology: Continuation and Criticism," the group of essays in this volume are presented in honor of Dorion Cairns on his 70th birthday. The contributors comprise friends, colleagues and former students of Dorion Cairns who, each in his own way, share the interest of Dorion Cairns in Husserlian phenomenology. That interest itself may be best defined by these words of Edmund Husserl: "Philosophy – wisdom (*sagesse*) – is the philosopher's quite personal affair. It must arise as *his* wisdom, as *his* self-acquired knowledge tending toward universality, a knowledge for which he can answer from the beginning ..." [1] It is our belief that only in the light of these words can phenomenology and phenomenological philosophy be continued, but always reflexively, critically. For over forty years Dorion Cairns has, through his teaching and writing, selflessly worked to bring the idea expressed by Husserl's words into self-conscious exercise. In so doing he has, to the benefit of those who share his interest, confirmed Husserl's judgement of him that he is "among the rare ones who have penetrated into the deepest sense of my phenomenology, ... who had the energy and persistence not to desist until he had arrived at real understanding." [2]

In presenting this volume to Dorion Cairns we not only wish to acknowledge his work but also our indebtedness to him for his generosity in sharing that real understanding in such a way that Husserlian phenomenology remains a living philosophy for which one can answer from the beginning.

It is perhaps not inappropriate here to speak of that sharing with others, especially with his students, in a somewhat more personal way. For beyond being a superb scholar intimately conversant with the history of philosophy, as well as phenomenology,

[1] Edmund Husserl, *Cartesian Meditations*, translated by Dorion Cairns (The Hague: Martinus Nijhoff, 1960), p. 2.
[2] See below, p. 181.

Dorion Cairns is unquestionably among the very few philosophers whose presence as a teacher is equally remarkable. Whoever has had the opportunity of talking with him, and of listening to him, has come away with that unmistakable sense of having been with a truly great teacher and an uncommon human being. Whether one's encounter was brief or more prolonged, the impact of his integrity, skill, concern and rigorousness has been deep and lasting. Certainly, for those who have been fortunate enough to have worked at length with him, Dorion Cairns has been and continues to be an exceptional model of philosopher and teacher, and a man of great warmth and dignity. The editors in particular wish here publicly to acknowledge their profound gratitude for their years of study and friendship with him; without them, their lives and understanding of philosophy, and Husserlian phenomenology, would be poorer indeed.

In addition to the essays by contributors to this volume, we are especially pleased to include the publication of three essays by Dorion Cairns: "A Husserlian Approach to Phenomenology," "The Ideality of Verbal Expressions," and "Perceiving, Remembering, Image-Awareness, Feigning Awareness." The first two essays are thoroughly revised versions of works previously published; the third essay is published here for the first time. We wish to thank the Harvard University Press for their kind permission to reprint the first-mentioned essay, which appeared in its original version in *Essays in Memory of Edmund Husserl* (1940), edited by Marvin Farber; similarly, we wish to thank Marvin Farber, editor of *Philosophy and Phenomenological Research*, for his kind permission to reprint the second-mentioned essay which appeared, in its original version, in *Philosophy and Phenomenological Research*, I (1940). In addition, we gratefully acknowledge the kindness of Prof. Gerhart Husserl in permitting us to publish his father's letter to E. Parl Welch.

We are indeed deeply grateful to those whose contributions have made this volume possible. Above all we must express our debt to Dorion Cairns for his kind permission to reprint, in revised form, his two essays published previously, to publish the third essay for the first time along with his autobiographical sketch. The dedication of this volume to him is, accordingly, equally its dedication to the cause of philosophy to which he has committed himself: "the attempt to understand and criticize the philosophy of Edmund Husserl."

* *
*

After the volume of essays here were completed and in the hands of the publisher, Dorion Cairns died, after having undergone major heart surgery at the Beekman Downtown Hospital in New York City, on January 4, 1973. In recognition of this sad event, the Editors decided to alter the sub-title of the volume: *Essays in Memory of Dorion Cairns*, and to append this brief note, prepared by Aron Gurwitsch, his close friend and colleague, and Richard M. Zaner, one of his former students and now literary executor of Dorion Cairns' estate.

After graduating Phi Beta Kappa from Harvard College, in 1923, Cairns received the Sheldon Traveling Fellowship two times, enabling him to go to Freiburg and study with Husserl. A close personal as well as intellectual connection developed between the two men, which lasted until Husserl's death in 1938. Husserl repeatedly expressed the very high esteem in which he held Dorion Cairns, as have many others, of different generations, since then.

Cairns was a man of a great variety of interests and of a very broad general culture. He spoke French, German and Italian fluently, and read Latin and Greek. Although his main interest was in Husserlian phenomenology, his penetrating and original understanding extended much further, both within the phenomonological thematic and in other philosophical periods. He was perfectly at home in classical philosophy, especially the modern period: Descartes, classical British empiricism, the Scotish School, Kant, Lotze, Brentano, the early history of modern logic. His contributions to phenomenological literature, too, indicate his wide and penetrating range of interests: among the manuscripts he left behind are extensive studies of Husserl's theory of mind (including a theory of thinking, intentionality, evidence, judgment, and other central topics), a complete value theory with a developed ethics as well, and major significant commentaries on all the major works published by Husserl in his lifetime, as well as extensive studies of the major works of Descartes, Locke, Berkeley, Kant, Oswald, Reid, the nineteenth-century logicians, Brentano, and many, many others. Beyond this, are lengthy studies in phenomenological epistemology, and horizonal problems of phenomenology. His knowledge, too, extended beyond the confines of philosophy to other disciplines. It is hoped that these seminal studies will be able to be prepared for publication.

His natural environment was among his students, upon whom he exerted a profound influence and to whom he generously gave of his energy and time, going far beyond the call of duty. His explanations of philosophical texts and his expositions of philosophical theories were masterful in their sobriety and thoroughness. Devoid though his presentations were of rhetorical embellishments and momentary "brilliance," one felt a philosophical passion pulsating in them. By his devotion and conscientiousness he gave a living example to his students who responded to him, both as a scholar and a man, with affection, love, and a loyalty which has become very rare in these times. His collaborators were deeply attached to him and he enjoyed the general respect of the phenomenological community. He was one of the founders of the *International Phenomenological Society*, a member of its Council and also a member of the Editorial Board of *Philosophy and Phenomenological Research*.

His loss is mourned by all who had the privilege of having come into contact with him, in any capacity, and they will forever cherish the memory of a genuine scholar, one of the finest philosophical minds ever to emerge from the culture of the United States, and a noble gentleman and friend.

Frederick Kersten
Richard Zaner

PREFACE

For any scholar interested in phenomenology, a discussion with Dorion Cairns became a dialogue with a *Socrates redivivus*. A few quiet questions from him, and the searcher was led straight to the heart of the matter. Such dialogue never failed to produce new and profound depths of meaning as, unconsciously, one gave birth to new and exciting insights under his gentle probing. Indeed, his was the true maieutic art of delivering one's mind, or heart, of never-suspected hidden visions. In him worked a spiritual mentor, the socratic δαίμων, which uncovered rewarding ideas even at a first glance. Many were the talents unearthed by his words.

H. L. Van Breda
President,
"Phaenomenologica Editorial Committee"

Leuven (Louvain), March 1973

TABLE OF CONTENTS

DORION CAIRNS

MY OWN LIFE[1]

I was born July 4th, 1901, in the village of Contoocook, in the
town of Hopkinton, New Hampshire. My father, James George
Cairns, was the pastor of the Methodist Church in Contoocook,
and I was the first child of my parents. During my first three and
a half years of life, my father moved from one place to another
as pastor of Methodist Churches in New Hampshire and Massachusetts. My brother, Stewart Scott Cairns, currently Professor
of Mathematics at the University of Illinois, was born May 8th,
1904.

My father felt that there was no future for a young minister
in New England, and he decided to move his family – which
consisted of my mother, my brother and me – to California. He
shipped all of our family goods, all of our furniture and things,
to California on the very day of the San Francisco Earthquake,
or "Fire," as they like to call it in San Francisco.

The California Conference of the Methodist Episcopal Church
at that time controlled what was called the "Utah Mission." This
was a mission to Mormon Territory, needless to say. My father,
since there were so many people of longer standing in the California Conference who had no churches left owing to the earthquake, was given a church in Utah Mission, in Salt Lake City
itself. It was there in 1907 that my sister Mary, who is the wife

[1] On two evenings in July, 1969, Dr. Lester Embree visited Professor Cairns to
collect information with a tape recorder for a sketch of Professor Cairns' life to be
written by the editors. However, as Professor Cairns told about his life it became
apparent that a transcription of his own words was possible and indeed preferable
to anything the editors might make from them. In collaboration with Dr. Embree,
the editors have added punctuation, emphasis and paragraph divisions where necessary. Where it seemed called for, some rearrangement of the material has been made.
The title was added by Dr. Embree.

of James Wilkinson Miller, currently Professor of Philosophy at McGill University in Montreal, was born.

When they wanted to transfer my father from this little church in Salt Lake City to a church or mission in Provo, Utah, my father went and looked at the set-up in Provo, and he came back, and it was the first time I had seen a grown man cry. He lay on the couch there, and he said to my mother: "Laure, I just can't take you there." They had packed all our goods for a short trip to Provo from Salt Lake City, and I can clearly remember that night – I was six years old – they began unpacking and repacking the things to go into storage or for a longer move.

My mother, brother and baby sister and I went to live with my mother's sister in Cleveland, Ohio. My father went down to Cincinnati and started working at his trade. Before he had decided to become a minister of the gospel, he was what is called a "metal spinner," and there was a metal spinning concern there. By this time it was not lamps for carriages but lamps for this newfangled thing the automobile. So father went there and worked, meantime looking around for some opening to go back into the ministry.

After a few months or maybe a year, I can't say, he found a chance to have a church in the so-called Holston Conference in Tennessee. This was a church in an industrial suburb of Chattanooga, Tennessee, and he picked up his family and was for some years minister of the Methodist Church in Alton Park near Chattanooga. He got promoted to District Superintendent, which then was the novel title for what used to be called a Presiding Elder in a conference, and travelled extensively, even far up into the mountains, to visit churches in the Chattanooga District of Holston Conference.

He took me with him on one of these trips because he wanted me to see how people up there lived. I happen to remember clearly that in the house where we stayed the night there were no windows. There were shutters that you could raise to let the air in. There wasn't a privy in the whole community. People – men, women, and children – when they had to relieve themselves went out into the woods and hid. As I learned later, these people were mostly Scotch-Irish whose ancestors had emigrated to the United States very early, in the Seventeenth Century, I would judge. I've never seen a Negro community in the South that approached in primitiveness and poverty the condition of that place.

I had schooling, first in Alton Park and then in Chattanooga itself, through the eighth grade, when one normally went into high school in those days. I started high school at Central High School in Chattanooga. My father, for reasons that are too complicated to explain, wanted to live in New England. And so once again there was a big transition for him and his wife and three children, this time to the town of Westboro, Massachusetts. This is in the New England Conference of the Methodist Church. Before I had gone to more than perhaps a couple of months more of high school there, my father was transferred to a church in Cliftondale, which is part of Saugus, Massachussetts, and I continued high school there through the fourth year and was graduated.

My first interest in philosophy, to come at long last to this point, was aroused by the lady who was principal of the high school in Saugus, a Mrs. Lucy Mears Norris. She did so in the following manner. Among the things that she had us read in Senior English were Emerson's *Essays*. That was the first philosophical book that I read. And I think that my interest in philosophy was aroused because I thought that *I* could understand it and that the other kids *could not* understand it. I thought – although I was a good student all around – "This is for me. Philosophy is the thing for me."

A lady who lived in Cliftondale – I must tell you by the way that my father's salary was extremely small even then – gave a one hundred dollar scholarship to the most promising student who graduated from Saugus High School every year. That year I got the scholarship. I took the College Entrance Board Examination, which existed even in that time, 1919, and I applied for admission to Harvard. My scores on the College Entrance Examination must have been *bad*. But the high school I had gone to was also by ordinary standards bad. So that Fall I was admitted to Harvard College as a Freshman-on-trial.

In those days at Harvard anyone who was concentrating in philosophy had from his very inception of work in his freshman year a tutor. And my first tutors, because they alternated semester by semester, were the late Ralph Eaton and the late Raphael

Demos. I got good enough marks, so that by the beginning of the second semester I had a full scholarship covering all tuition at Harvard and was no longer on trial.

Ralph Eaton was my first tutor and I went around to his room – he was a proctor in one of the dormitories then – for my first tutorial. Ralph had on his desk a plaster of Paris reproduction of the Venus de Milo. He also smoked, lighting his pipe with old-fashioned kitchen matches, and it was his habit to light the match on the Venus de Milo's belly, so that scarified ... it was practically eliminated! I had grown up with such a reverence for art that I was shocked at this irreverence on Eaton's part.

I can't say just what I got in the way of philosophy from Ralph Eaton. But while I was still his "tutee," as we say, I ran into Raphael Demos in the Harvard Yard, and I started talking with him, or he started talking with me, and I talked about something, what it was, I've forgotten. And Raphael, who had nothing to do with me – I was somebody else's tutee – said: "Write me a paper on that and bring it around to me." Well, I worked harder on that paper than I did in any of my courses. (I no longer know what the subject was.) I brought that around to Raphael and even before I became his tutee we were plunged in philosophical discussions.

Raphael Demos was a poor Greek from Smyrna and had his B.A. from Anatolia College in Asia Minor. He got this Ph.D. from Harvard in 1916 and had shown such promise that he got the Sheldon Traveling Fellowship in philosophy from Harvard to England in 1917–1918 and 1918–19. During the First World War Bertrand Russell, as you know, was put in jail for his pacifist anti-war pronouncements. Among the people who did go and see him in jail and learn philosophy from him was Raphael Demos.

The strongest influence on Raphael was the influence of Arthur William, the man that Whitehead always used to refer to as "Bertie." (When speaking of Russell they would always refer to him as Arthur William; his name was Bertrand Arthur William Russell. In one of Whitehead's lectures, a formal lecture, he was about to criticize some of Russell's things, and he said "Russell has said such and such, and such and such, but, you know," he said, "Bertie is wrong!") The earliest influence on me in philosophy came from Raphael Demos or it came from Russell by way of Raphael Demos. Early Whitehead – *The Concept of Nature*, those early works of Whitehead – came to me the same way. I doubt that I have read more than two or three of Emerson's *Essays* in my life since I graduated from high school!

Russell had written an article that appeared in *Mind* which was primarily concerned with Meinong but also mentioned and said something favorable about Husserl. It was common in those days for people in the English speaking world to construe Husserl as a realist and in consequence of Russell's highly favorable remarks on Husserl for me to think that I would like to learn more about Husserl. My German, although I had passed the reading examination, which was required for the doctorate at Harvard, was extremely bad. I thought: "Well, if I get a chance I will go to hear Edmund Husserl" – among others, of course.

During my first year of graduate work at Harvard a young lecturer was having his first year in the philosophy department, a man by the name of Winthrop Bell. Winthrop Bell was a Canadian, actually a Nova Scotian, and he had been a student of Edmund Husserl's at Göttingen. Bell had finished his doctoral dissertation, submitted it, and it had been approved by three members of the Göttingen philosophy department when World War I broke out. As a Canadian Bell was interned. Edmund Husserl persuaded his two colleagues to go with him to the internment camp and have Winthrop Bell, technically a prisoner there, defend his thesis. And they did. Winthrop Bell got his doctor's degree from Göttingen in the earliest year of the war because, after all, the university stands independent of the state. Those were the days!

Bell had written his dissertation on Josiah Royce. Not because he was interested in Josiah Royce but because Husserl told this young graduate student to write on someone in the American tradition and he had complied. The first year that Winthrop Bell taught at Harvard was the year 1923–1924. I was one of a handful of students who attended his main course, which was on general theory of value, and was indeed from a phenomenological point of view.

I went on struggling through Husserl in the original – there was no translation at that time – doing my best, which was very bad.

The end of my first year of graduate study, I was awarded the
Sheldon Fellowship in philosophy for study abroad. The current
holder of the Sheldon Fellowship was then Marvin Farber, and I
can't remember whether I ran into Farber again in Freiburg or
he had already left Freiburg before I got there. At all events, in
time for the beginning of the Fall semester of 1924 I was in
Freiburg equipped with two letters of introduction to Herr Ge-
heimrat Professor Doktor Edmund Husserl – one of them from
William Ernest Hocking, who had also studied a short time with
Husserl at Göttingen,[2] and the other was from Winthrop Bell.

At first I had intended to follow the pattern of my predecessors
as Sheldon Fellows, such as George Santayana and William
Ernest Hocking, and so to speak make a grand tour of European
universities. So many weeks here, so many weeks there, so many
weeks some place else. And in Germany, France, England, and in
that way – well – spend the time. I decided that the first philosopher to look up and visit was Paul Natorp. Inconveniently but
fortunately for me, Natorp died while I was on my way to
Europe, and number two man on my list for this quick run-
around was Edmund Husserl.

So I went around to Edmund Husserl's apartment and I did
not realize that the proper time for making a formal call in Freiburg – at least in those days and, I think, throughout Germany –
was exactly twelve o'clock noon. I got there at about three o'clock
in the afternoon, and rang the doorbell. A young man who looked
like a prematurely aged Emmanuel Kant answered the door. His
name was Ludwig Landgrebe and he was Husserl's assistant at
the time. I said as best I could, because my German was still
pretty bad, that I'd like to speak to Professor Husserl. He took
my letters and asked me: "Wen darf ich melden?" "Whom shall
I announce?" I no more understood "Wen darf ich melden?"
than nothing at all! I made a big guess and said "Herr Cairns."
Apparently that was all right; he went in and I waited in an
anteroom. The doors to Husserl's study were closed.

<hr />

[2] Dr. Bell's recollections of his work under Husserl have been published in Herbert
Spiegelberg, *The Phenomenological Movement. A Historical Introduction* (The Hague:
Martinus Nijhoff, 1960), Vol. I, p. 145. Dr. Hocking's recollections have been publish-
ed in *Edmund Husserl 1859–1959* (La Haye: Martinus Nijhoff, 1959), edited by H. L.
van Breda and J. Taminiaux, under the title of "From the early days of the 'Logische
Untersuchungen'," pp. 1–11. – Ed.

There came out from the study a little man who introduced himself in a light, calm voice as Edmund Husserl; incidentally, he had taken the time to read the letters. He then took me into his study, and though I can't reproduce everything he said in that first conversation, part of what he said was, to translate into English: "You have come to Freiburg at a time which is most dangerous for phenomenology." The gist of what he said from there on was, I shan't say a diatribe, but a very acerbic criticism of Martin Heidegger.

This was 1924-1925. Heidegger, then professor at Marburg, was exerting what the Germans would call a "colossal" influence on students. I can remember students during that first year coming back to Freiburg and lending me their notes on Heidegger. Husserl told me, probably at a later time with reference to *Sein und Zeit*, "I thought he was with me and that I simply could not understand his language." This "I thought he was with me" attitude must have lasted into 1929 when Husserl became Emeritus and Heidegger moved from Marburg to Freiburg to take over Husserl's chair.

To go back to my first meeting with Husserl, he asked me what I had read of his work and I said, "Well, my German as you see is not very good, but I have attempted to read the *Logische Untersuchungen*." He turned around in his desk chair, took down the first part of the second volume of the *Logische Untersuchungen*, and said: "Study this. Study it pen in hand. If you don't understand or if you object, write down your question or objection. Come to me next week with what you have done and we shall discuss it together."

My plan to do the grand tour of all the universities of Germany, France, and the United Kingdom went completely by the board. Soon I became immersed in studying Husserl, and talking with him, and I decided to remain and study with Husserl. The first thing that made me believe he had something that nobody else had was his analysis of perception, imagination and memory. I had never seen anything like it before. I felt: "The guy is right! and nobody else. He's right, at least about these things, and I'm going to stick with him. Who cares about a grand tour," etc.

I spent my first year as Sheldon Fellow with Husserl. Husserl must have written a very adulatory letter to Harvard about me, because, for the first time since Raphael Demos had been Sheldon Fellow, I was awarded the Sheldon Fellowship for a second year. So I stayed a second year in Freiburg, working with Husserl. I heard, of course, the lectures of every philosopher on the faculty there, but I worked with Husserl on Husserl's work.

At that time I had a letter from the then chairman, Ralph Barton Perry, in quasi-humorous vein: "I hope when you come back after having studied two years with Edmund Husserl that you won't tell us that phenomenology is the only true philosophy." I came back and told him that the only true philosophy, or, rather, that the only valid philosophical method was Husserl's phenomenological method! I then continued at Harvard for two years as what we used to call a "section hand." It was during this time that I made the acquaintance, and more than the acquaintance, of Alfred North Whitehead, who had come to Harvard during the time that I was in Germany. I attended all of his lectures and seminars, but apparently the phenomenological virus had bitten me so deeply that I must say that the philosophical influence of Whitehead on me was minimal. I still went on studying Husserl and started writing a dissertation. At this moment I cannot remember even the theme of that dissertation, but I worked very hard on it, and then, eventually, destroyed it.

On the second occasion of my stay in Freiburg I studied with Husserl from the early Fall of 1931 through November 1932. At that time Husserl was Professor Emeritus and Martin Heidegger had succeeded to Husserl's chair. Husserl was most generous in allowing me to read his unpublished manuscripts and several times a week I would go with Husserl and Eugen Fink on Husserl's walk around the Lorretoberg, during which time we discussed or, more exactly, Husserl held forth on whatever problems were uppermost in his mind at that time.[3] I also attended the lectures and the seminars of Martin Heidegger, but social relations between Heidegger and Husserl were already, to say the least, estranged, and academic life in Germany being what it was in those days, I never met Martin Heidegger personally, to say nothing of being a guest in his house as I was frequently with my new wife a guest at the Husserls'.

[3] See Dorion Cairns, *Conversation with Husserl and Fink* (The Hague: Martinus Nijhoff, in hands of publisher). – Ed.

During this time I made the acquaintance of Eugen Fink who was then Husserl's assistant. My conversations with Fink, whom I saw frequently without seeing Husserl, were also of great advantage in making known to me some of the later developments in Husserl's phenomenology not touched upon in the manuscripts which Husserl lent me, and indeed allowed me to take home to study. As a consequence I can say in fact that Eugen Fink was indeed the second most important personal source of whatever acquaintance I acquired with the phenomenology of Edmund Husserl. I might add that during this time that Husserl gave me access to unpublished material I began not just listening to Husserl but actually on occasion I was able to discuss various points in phenomenology with him.

The *Ideen* had been translated into English and that translation had appeared – I'm speaking of what is today called *Ideen, I*.[4] I read it critically and told Husserl some of my objections to the published translation, and Husserl said (translating almost literally): "If that's the way that translation runs, instead of being a bridge to an understanding of my philosophy it will prove to be a wall against such understanding." The French translation of the *Cartesianische Meditationen* had come out shortly after my arrival in Freiburg,[5] and that translation is a comparatively good one. From that translation I gained insights into further aspects of the phenomenology of Edmund Husserl in addition to those I had acquired from Husserl himself and from Eugen Fink.

As regards the so-called *Ideen, II* and *Ideen, III*, there was extant among Husserl's unpublished manuscripts one that had been put together for Husserl by Miss Stein as a basis for the announced second and third volumes of the *Ideen*.[6] Parts of Miss Stein's manuscripts were used by Husserl as a basis for continuing what would have been *Ideen, II*, but he dropped this work of completing the *Ideen* and turned to writing a logic. Among his manuscripts assembled by Fink there was one small manuscript

---

[4] The translation is by W. R. Boyce Gibson, 1931. The rights for a new translation by Dorion Cairns have been secured by Martinus Nijhoff, The Hague. – Ed.

[5] The translation is by J. Pfeiffer and E. Levinas, 1931.

[6] See the posthumously published *Ideen zu einer reinen Phänomenologie und phänomenologischen Philosophie*, Zweites Buch, and *ibid.*, Drittes Buch (Den Haag: Martinus Nijhoff, 1952). *Husserliana* Bd. IV, V. Herausgegeben von Marly Biemel. Cf. "Einleitung des Herausgebers," pp. XVIff.

which Husserl thought could be used, elaborated, as a preface or introduction to this logic which he expected to write. He took this small manuscript and, he told me, in the course of six weeks wrote on the basis of his manuscript the volume called *Formale und transzendentale Logik*.

Husserl once told me that the desire to write a book was something that came over him now and then and that when that desire came over him he shoved aside all of this work – which consisted in his daily meditations – and wrote a book at a furious pace, like someone in a trance, that he would write a page and put it to one side on his desk, another page and put it to the side on his desk, without numbering any of these pages. He would just throw them aside and leave to himself or his assistant the later task of going through them to find the order of the pages for the book he had finished. Incidentally, this can hardly apply to the *Logische Untersuchungen*. It applies, however, to the *Ideen*, "Einleitung", and Band I, the *Formale und transzendentale Logik* and the manuscript for the *Cartesianische Meditationen*, as the context of what Husserl was saying indicates.

His daily work, however, which was thus interrupted, consisted in daily meditations, *Meditationen* as he called them. And he said to me once: "When I go back to what I have written in an earlier meditation, I always go back to that which is most obscure to me and I wrestle with that problem. I never go on and leave a problem unsolved and that is why I shall never write a philosophy. My work is not that of building but of digging, of digging in that which is most obscure and of uncovering problems that have not been seen or if seen have not been solved." All of his works are, therefore, *introductions* to phenomenology, introductions with the aim of uncovering and, if possible, solving the most profound problems. On my second visit to Freiburg, and in one of my first talks with him after I returned, Husserl said: "Herr Cairns, I am writing two introductions to philosophy, one is for philosophers and one is for non-philosophers and, you know, it is harder to write introductions to phenomenology for philosophers than it is to write an introduction to phenomenology for laymen." These two introductions, of course, never saw the light of day. Even *Die Krisis der europäischen Wissenschaften und die transzendentale Phänomenologie* bears the subtitle "an introduction to phenomenology." Everything was an introduction.

At the time that I left Freiburg in November, 1932, Husserl's main objective was to go on with the *Cartesianische Meditationen* and supplement those that had been translated into French by additional meditations. Shortly after I left, however, he turned his attention to a completely new work, the *Krisis der europäischen Wissenschaften und die transzendentale Phänomenologie*. And although Fink had written out a full outline of what topics were to be dealt with in the additional Cartesian Meditations, Husserl pushed these matters aside and became immersed in the writing of the *Krisis*.

My interest at that time was a naively ambitious one. It was to master the whole of the philosophy of Edmund Husserl, and I had already chosen as the title of my doctoral dissertation eventually to be presented at Harvard: *The Philosophy of Edmund Husserl*.

I left Freiburg in November, 1932, because I felt the necessity of completing my doctoral dissertation and at last getting my doctor's degree because almost ten years had elapsed since I had been graduated from Harvard College in 1923. I went to Cambridge, Massachusetts, and worked unremittingly on my doctoral thesis. I completed the thesis and turned it in to Professor Ralph Barton Perry, the chairman of the philosophy department at Harvard at the time, at five minutes to twelve midnight on the last day when theses were accepted. I then had the usual oral examination on the thesis and received my degree in June, 1933.

My wife's family, more particularly her father and sister, were living in New York, and I came to New York with her accordingly to look for a job. 1933 was at the depths of the Great Depression. I was able to get three jobs, all of them part-time: a part-time job in the evening session at Hunter College, another at New York University at Washington Square, and a third at New York University in the Bronx. The consequence was that I spent a large proportion of my time familiarizing myself more intimately with the New York subway system.

All the while I was, of course, looking for some sort of permanent position. A permanent position did turn up and I was, chiefly on the recommendation of Professor William Ernest Hocking, appointed Professor of Philosophy and Psychology at

Rockford College in Rockford, Illinois, a college for young women. I remained Professor there until 1950.

In the meantime, the Second World War had drawn the United States into itself, and I applied for and received a commission in the Army Air Corps. At first I was an instructor in navigation at an air station near Waco, Texas. I had no desire to fight the war in Texas, however, and I pulled various strings. Eventually one of the strings got me into the Air Corps Intelligence School at Harrisburg, where I completed the regular course for Intelligence Officers and the course for Prisoner of War Interrogators, more particularly the course as it was given for persons who were going to interrogate German prisoners. After this schooling at Harrisburg, I was sent over to the Mediterranean Theatre and was a prisoner of war interrogator in Africa and later in Italy, first in the Naples area and then in Rome after its fall to the allied troops. Between these two assignments I was prisoner of war interrogator on the island of Corsica. Toward the end of my activity as a prisoner of war interrogator I began to have various symptoms which were at first diagnosed as symptoms of virus pneumonia. I was in and out of several hospitals in Italy, in Rome, in Naples and eventually in Leghorn where I had been sent to be returned to the United States. A doctor at the hospital in Leghorn eventually diagnosed my ailment not as recurrent pneumonia, but as tuberculosis. I was returned to the United States on a stretcher and spent the next two years first in Army hospitals and then during the final six months of the two years in a civilian sanatorium for the tubercular. I was a year and a half at bedrest.

Upon being discharged from the sanatorium, I resumed my job teaching at Rockford College. At that time Rockford College was undergoing great financial difficulties and was having to make drastic cuts in salaries. Eventually it was told me by the president of Rockford College that my salary for the following year would be approximately what I was paying the college for a place to live. This seemed rather the opposite of feasible and I returned to New York without a job, was supported by my wife, who was a psychiatric social worker, and eventually I was invited by my friend Alfred Schutz to teach at the New School, on the Graduate Faculty – which I was more than happy to do. I was there at first as a Visiting Professor, 1954-1960, then as Full Professor of Philosophy, 1960-1969. I retired from the Graduate Faculty in September, 1969.

The course that I developed and gave parts of at various times at the New School for Social Research under the title of "Husserl's Theory of Intentionality" is a development from that first over-ambitious and very bad doctoral dissertation of mine. I also took parts of the work in progress and used them as the basis for three other systematic courses that I gave at the New School. In addition to "Husserl's Theory of Intentionality," my course on the "Phenomenology of Thinking," my course on "General Theory of Value," and my course on "Advanced Theoretical Ethics" are really parts of the complete systematic exposition and criticism of the philosophy of Edmund Husserl, which I may say has been my life's work.

I am leaving out the historical and critical work that I did for courses that I offered at the New School on each of the British Empiricists, Locke, Berkeley, and Hume, on the Scottish School and Hamilton, on the History of Philosophy in the Nineteenth Century, and the expository and critical work that I did for my course on Emmanuel Kant.

My life has been the attempt to understand and criticize the philosophy of Edmund Husserl, and as I went further and further in this enterprise my criticisms of certain aspects of Husserl's philosophy, in particular his account of intersubjectivity, became more and more radical, so that as a matter of fact the title of my course "Husserl's Theory of Intentionality" has become a misno-mer. At most I could call it directly "A Husserlian Account of Intentionality" because it contains perhaps as much criticism as exposition of the great man's work.

HARMON CHAPMAN

THE PHENOMENON OF LANGUAGE

In an article entitled "The Ideality of Verbal Expressions" [1]
Dorion Cairns has shown that there are "cultural" objects such
as the words of a language which are neither "real individuals"
nor "ideal universals," but rather "ideal individuals" sharing
with real things individuation in time and the vicissitudes of
change, and with changeless universals the character of being
ideal, not real. Distinct both from the sounds or visual signs
which embody them and from the sense or meaning which they
express, words are historical individuals of a distinct type, which
come to be, develop or change, and – in many cases – pass away
playing all the while an important role in the lives and fortunes
of men. But unlike the many artificial implements and edifices
of a civilization they are wholly lacking in physical reality and
are never exhumed as archeological remains. Other instances of
"cultural" objects combining ideality and change are such things
as folklore and dances, songs and ballads, religions and litera-
tures, science and knowledge, and a host of similar entities all of
which go to make up a culture. Like words they are all historical
yet ideal individuals.

But the arch example is language itself. It is the most inclusive
of all and the most ubiquitous; for language is the matrix, as it
were, of all human culture. In it we find most strikingly displayed
this singular quality of ideal individuality. In it too we find displayed an intimate interplay between ideal and real individuals,
for example, between words on the one hand and on the other
hand sounds by which the words are spoken or ideographs by

[1] Dorion Cairns, "The Ideality of Verbal Expressions," *Philosophy and Phenomenological Research*, I (1941), pp. 453–462. (In a revised version, this essay has been
reprinted below, pp. 239–250. – Ed.)

which they are written. This interplay may be described as a consortium of "ideal" and "real." It were better described, however, as a consortium of "ideal" and "sensible" (ideal individuals and sensible individuals). For if the consortium itself is "real,' i.e., a real or empirical phenomenon, then its components too are "real." "Real," accordingly, would include both ideal and sensible – and, of course, whatsoever else experience may reveal. It is in this sense that language is "real" and in this sense that I speak of it as a phenomenon.

My inquiry into the phenomenon of language will begin by noting, as Cairns pointed out, that in every actual linguistic situation at least five things are involved:

1. Psychic activity on the part of both speaker and hearer.

2. Audible sounds (or visual signs) which are sensible objects common to both parties.

3. The words and sentences of a language with which both are acquainted.

4. The sense or meaning thus linguistically expressed.

5. The meant things or events which the meaning means or is about.

I shall consider these five components in the order of mention and endeavor to make clear the phenomenal nature of each and the role each plays in the complex whole which is the phenomenon of language.

1. Usually the psychic activity involved is not overtly or verbally expressed, but only covertly expressed or "manifested." In the present instance, for example, my aim to communicate with you, whether you be reader or hearer, is certainly manifest, even though previously unexpressed, as is also your willingness to let me hold forth. This much at least is simply taken for granted on the part of both of us without any explicit mention. None is needed. For explicit mention could only presuppose it as already manifested. This indicates quite clearly that discourse between us can occur only in a "social" situation wherein each of us is aware of psychic activity on the part of the other, i.e., wherein each of us is implicitly aware of the other as a psyche or self. Since this awareness of the other, be it ever so vague and inarticulate, is clearly a prius, not a result, of discourse, we may conclude that language is by nature a social phenomenon and hence that a private language is all but unthinkable. We may also conclude, although a bit tentatively, that this awareness of the other is the source of what is often called "our knowledge of other minds." For it would seem to be here that we gain our most direct access to the presence and inner workings of another mind or psyche. This access, to be sure, is not immediate in exactly the same way as that of introspection or reflection on our own psychic activities. But it is probably the most direct access possible under the circumstances, the only way in which one psyche can reveal its inwardness directly to another. And this revealing is direct, for it has the immediacy of intuition; it is not inferential, and certainly not discursive. Only as such can it be the prius of discourse. It is thus quite literally that I speak of language as "manifesting" psychic activity.

This manifesting of psychic activity is the ground level of language. I call it a "manifesting" in order to distinguish it as a preverbal or covert mode of expression from the verbal or overt mode of expression by means of words, thereby implying that both modes are but species of the genus "expression."

2. Within this social situation – again considering the present instance – I am making audible sounds or visual signs all of which are physical objects accessible to our senses, public things or events in the natural world. They are, however, not merely natural objects, but artificial objects, that is, objects with a natural basis, but made or framed in accordance with rules of skill. This skill, whether of speaking or writing, is an integral part of the great convention of language and can be acquired only by training and practice, as every learner of a foreign tongue is painfully aware. Only by means of these artificial sense objects can I communicate with you or you with me. I do not mean by this to deny extra-sensory perception. I mean only that being unaware of possessing any such power, I am unable to exercise it and hence must resort to ordinary sensuous means.

3. These artificial sounds or signs are for both of us the physico-sensuous embodiments of the English words which I am uttering. They serve as common carriers or conveyers from me to you of ideal entities quite other than themselves. They serve in this capacity by being conventional symbols which "call to mind," on being perceived, the English words which they "stand for" and

which themselves cannot be perceived. In this consortium of ideal word and sensuous symbol there is an intimate relation which binds the two together. For it is the nature of a word to be pronounced or spelled and through this embodiment to become flesh, as it were, just as it is the conventional nature of the physical symbol, by its very artificiality, to symbolize or stand for the word. For all its ideality, therefore, the word is bound by its own nature to the sensuous symbolism which is its proper vehicle.

But if their togetherness is unmistakable, so too is their difference. For every physical embodiment of a word is a unique sensuous individual different from all other embodiments of the same word. The one English word "book," for example, may be spoken numberless times, each time with a different inflection of voice, a different accent, and so on. Or, it may be written or printed with varying handwritings or kinds of type, properly or improperly spelled, and so on. Each embodiment is a distinct sensuous individual, a unique physical object different from all the rest. They all, however, equally embody or symbolize the one word "book," which retains its ideal identity throughout the whole manifold of its incorporations, actual and possible. Plainly, the relation between ideal word and its sensuous symbols – whatever else it may be – is in this respect at least that of one-to-many.

4. By the English words thus brought to utterance I am expressing meanings, most of them propositions, which in themselves are not English at all, but beyond English, for they could just as well be expressed in German or French or Italian or Russian sentences. Meanings or propositions are in this sense "trans-linguistic," which is to say that any meaning can be expressed in any language (tongue) – ideally speaking, of course – as the fact of translation makes evident. Thus just as one and the same word or sentence can be symbolized in countless sensuous embodiments, so one and the same meaning or proposition can be expressed in many different tongues; the same one-many relation holds between meaning and sentence as holds between sentence and symbol.

To the extent that meanings are trans-linguistic – that is, beyond any given tongue and *a fortiori* beyond the sensuous symbols of that tongue – they would seem to be also beyond the reach of time and change and to enjoy a kind of eternal repose. This aloofness from time and change, however, is only relative, not absolute, as we shall see. Still, it will suffice to distinguish propositions from sentences, to reveal why it is that although sentences may come and go, propositions go on forever, accessible at all times and expressible in all languages. Meanings would thus seem to constitute a kind of timeless and universal realm of Parmenidean being, like that of the Platonic forms. If this realm of meanings be that of the classical *logos*, we may apply to it the adjective "logical" – with the express understanding, however, that this adjective is as wide in its extension as the substantive *logos*, and hence is not to be restricted to "logical" in the sense of logic as a formal discipline. In this sense we may speak of meanings as the logical components of language.

So far, then, discourse appears to be a kind of laminated phenomenon made up of three distinguishable layers, not counting the ground level of manifestation: *1.* a sensuous layer of physical symbols, *2.* a linguistic layer of words and sentences, and *3.* a logical layer of meanings (concepts and propositions). The relations between these three layers are extremely tight, for they weld the three into one phenomenon. For the present these relations may be indicated by saying *1* that the sensuous symbolizes the linguistic, and *2* that the linguistic *expresses* the logical.

The difference between symbolizing and expressing should now be made clear. In a former paragraph I distinguished two modes or species of expression, *1* a preverbal mode of manifestation, and *2* a verbal mode of explicit utterance. I am now talking about the latter mode, but only in part, not in its fullness. The part in question is that phase of verbal expression which binds the linguistic to the logical layer of language, word to concept, sentence to proposition – that phase which comes to the fore when we ask after the meaning of a sentence of a phrase or a term. It is in this sense – mode *2* of expression – that words, singly or in groups, express meanings.

Symbols by way of contrast express nothing, they merely symbolize, i.e., "stand for" entities other than themselves. But symbols can express in mode *1*, i.e., they can manifest psychic activity; for as artificial or conventional entities they bear intrinsic marks of their conventional origin and the psychic activity therein involved. In this respect symbols, or artificial signs are quite different from natural signs which can neither symbolize nor manifest, but only signify – and this only adventitiously, because natural signs become such (i.e., come to function as signs) only as a consequence of being so "taken" by a perceiving subject. Apart from being so "taken" natural signs are not signs at all, but simply natural phenomena, empirical things or events like all the rest, connected to be sure in natural ways with other phenomena, but containing nothing in themselves that makes them "stand for," "refer to," or "signify" anything else. This latter is solely the work of consciousness, a work which in the case of natural signs is extrinsic to the given phenomena, but which in the case of artificial signs is intrinsic to their very formation. We may say accordingly that the signifying function, being a product of consciousness, is extrinsic to natural signs, but intrinsic to artificial signs or symbols.

But not all symbols stand for words or sentences. The symbols of mathematics and of many roadside markers symbolize directly what they stand for without invoking the intermediary of language. The symbol "2" for example stands not for the English word "two" or for the German word "zwei," but simply and directly for the number two. Similarly words are not symbolized by the sign indicating a crossroad. Such symbols are conventional ideographs without any auditory counterpart, i.e., pronunciation. Or, if they be auditory symbols, like the fire siren, they have no visual counterpart, i.e., orthography or spelling. Such symbols lack most of the complications of word symbols: in particular, they are free of any involvement with a given tongue. As a result they can be simple, economic, precise, and hence exceedingly useful for certain limited purposes. Language however is not one of these purposes, for in every instance it is precisely language, with its "ambiguities," flexibilities, and varieties, that is to be avoided. There is therefore a sharp distinction to be drawn between linguistic and non-linguistic symbols.

One further point. Symbols, like signs generally, are perceived objects wholly distinct and separate from what they signify, which may be anything whatsoever – deity, numbers, crossroads, or oranges. Expression and what is expressed, on the other hand, are not thus distinct and separate entities, the one a perceived object and the other a second object, perceptible or imperceptible, to which the mind is directed, by inference or association, on perceiving the former. Quite the contrary, an expression is so wedded to the expressed as to be virtually one with it. And this oneness is such that the mind on perceiving the expression grasps at once and directly (not by inference or association) the expressed as immanent in the expression as that inner presence without which the expression could not be. This is to say that awareness of the expression is also and inseparably awareness of the expressed; only by a subsequent analysis can the two be distinguished as expression and expressed. Thus it is that language manifests (expresses) psychic activity. And so it is that words express meanings – (but only so far as words, being themselves ideal individuals, receive sensuous embodiment in sensuous individuals or symbols).

There is, then, this radical difference between the two relations: symbol-symbolized and expression-expressed. There is also, as the above parenthesis indicates, a radical connection between the two, inasmuch as words can become expressions only to the extent that they are symbolized, or uttered. That this connection should be radical is hardly surprising in view of the oneness of the language phenomenon.

5. There is yet another, a fourth, level of discourse beyond the previous three, again not counting the ground level of manifestation. I refer to that which we are discoursing or talking about, that which in or through our meanings is meant. In the present instance, of course, we are talking about discourse itself and its various levels, one of which is meaning. But this is quite unusual. Usually we converse about other things, the election, taxes, the weather, almost anything under the sun. If I may call the object or topic of our conversation the "meant," simply to distinguish it from the meanings we employ in conversing about it, then plainly the range of the meant is illimitable; for there is literally nothing we cannot talk about.

Plainly, too, the meant – embracing as it does all things, including language – cannot possibly be a level of discourse in the same sense as the other three. For these latter are actual constituents of discourse, whereas the meant, ordinarily at least, is not. But if it is not strictly a level of discourse, the meant is nonetheless an indispensable accompaniment of discourse, if only because we cannot discourse without discoursing about something, or because, more precisely, it is the nature of a meaning to mean ("refer to," "be about," "intend," etc.) something as its meant. This brings us face to face with the delicate question as to the relation between meaning and meant, a question which cannot be taken up here. For the present let it suffice to say that beyond the level of meaning is the meant with which the meaning is inseparably bound up, in a manner yet to be discerned.

This completes our inventory of the components of discourse. They are five in number: *1* the ground level of manifestation, *2* the physico-sensuous level, *3* the linguistic level, *4* the logical level, and *5* the meant. To these five taken singly, we must now add that taken together they fuse into a single whole, the single phenomenon of language or discourse. This fusing into one is not a sixth component or factor and cannot be otherwise described than as the original unity within which alone the five components occur and from which alone they can be excised by analysis. It is imperative that we keep in mind this living unity of language, for it is only by virtue of this unity that we can speak meaningfully of language and its many-layered structure.

With this admonition let me return to the first feature of discourse with which this analysis began, the ground level of manifestation. In pointing out that psychic activity is manifested in every use of language I made but scant reference to the range of activity involved. Now, however, having noted the complex structure of language, we may well anticipate that this psychic activity is far more intricate and varied than my initial remarks could indicate.

Consider this psychic activity from your side, the side of the listener or reader. From the beginning you have been perceiving sounds or letters and grasping, through these, the English words they symbolize. Only occasionally have you paid these sensuous symbols any particular heed. Perhaps a slovenly pronunciation or a misspelled word momentarily deflected your attention. For the most part you were hearing or reading, not sounds or letters, but the symbolized words and sentences.

But even my English words and sentences did not stay your attention. You were – and still are – intent on my meanings, on what I am trying to say. Here, too, you may have been caught up momentarily by an unwonted word or unfelicitous phrase; but in the main it is my meanings that you are following, not merely my words.

But even my meanings are not your quarry; you are after something further. My meanings are but ideal entities vastly different from the things and events we usually talk about. In this paper, to be sure, I am talking about discourse and its constituent meanings. But, again, this is unusual. Usually we talk about matters other than meanings, all but oblivious of the meanings involved in our concern with the topic in question. In these instances our meanings are functioning normally as instruments for focusing our attention on the meant, not as objects intruding themselves between us and the meant. It is on the meant, then, that your attention finally comes to rest, on the meant as it is alleged to be in the meanings I have expressed, on the meant as you perceive it to be, and on the accord or lack of accord between my meanings and the meant itself.

Clearly the psychic activity which you have been carrying on as you hear or read my words is of amazing complexity. Perceiving sounds or letters you have grasped words and sentences, framing to yourselves the meanings, statements and inferences which the words express, and focusing thereby on the meant as thus depicted. Your attention, like a beam of light – or ray of intentionality, as Husserl spoke of it – has traversed, penetrated the several layers of discourse and come to rest on the meant. This optical analogy is inadequate; for no beam of light can make its own medium. You, however, have done just that; on the slender basis of what you have heard or seen you have made (framed or constituted) the linguistic and logical media through which the meant has been brought to view. Only in doing this have you "followed" my words, caught their "sense," and fixed your gaze on what I am talking about.

This, I repeat, is an amazing performance on your part. No wonder there is such a thing as "language disability!" My own performance is no less complicated. In the main it parallels yours. But it may notably exceed yours. For, especially as speaker, I may also manifest a whole range of feeling or emotion, my utterance, as we say, may be impassioned. Without actually saying that I am excited or pleased or annoyed or angry or whatnot, I may yet reveal or display these emotions by my mere manner of speaking, by the choice of words, by intonation, inflection, gesture, facial expression, and the like. The context alone may at times betray me. This kind of manifestation is obviously not preverbal. But neither is it strictly verbal. It is non-verbal and as such but an extension of the ground level of manifestation.

It is now sufficiently clear, I think, that psychic activity is present at every level of language. Psychic activity is involved in forming and grasping the artificial sounds and signs of language. It is by psychic activity that these sensuous symbols come to symbolize ideal words and sentences. It is also by psychic activity that words and sentences express meanings and that meanings refer to their meants. All of these relations – sign-signified, symbol-symbolized, expression-expressed, meaning-meant – are supplied by consciousness alone and hence cannot obtain apart from psychic activity.

And so it is that the ground level of manifestation pervades and suffuses the whole structure of language giving it the quality of a "living" tongue. When psychic activity ceases the language is no longer living, but dead. In a way, then, language as a living phenomenon *is* the very psychic activity which it manifests. But only in a way. For insofar as it manifests, language is also more than bare psychic activity. Hence it were more accurate to say – remembering that manifestation is mode *1* of expression – that language is the expression *par excellence* of psychic activity, the hallmark, as the ancients held, of man's rational humanity.

But if language is psychic activity, it is also physical activity, physiological and neurological activity, and perhaps other kinds of activity as well. Within the phenomenon of language are fused in an original and organic whole many disparate facets of the real, psychical and physical, mental and material, ideal and real, inner and outer, consciousness and object, thought and thing, and so on. Plainly these pairs of opposites are not to be construed as shattering dichotomies, but as complementary features of a single empirical whole. This remarkable togetherness of so many seemingly uncongenial factors is one of the most intriguing aspects of language.[2]

[2] Dr. Chapman's essay, "The Phenomenon of Language," makes up the first chapter in a work in progress dealing with the phenomenology of language.

LESTER E. EMBREE

AN INTERPRETATION OF THE DOCTRINE OF
THE EGO IN HUSSERL'S *IDEEN*

Husserl's *Ideen zu einer reinen Phänomenologie und phänomeno-logischen Philosophie* (1913) [1] contains relatively few statements about the Ego. However, if these statements are taken together and considered within the context of the whole work, the outlines of a fairly large and coherent doctrine appear. In the present interpretation I refer to the *Ideen* by sections. For the sake of verbal distinctness I adopt Dorion Cairns's translation practices of expressing the concept Husserl usually expressed with the German word *Ich* with the English word *Ego* (spelled with a capital) and of referring to the Ego pronominally in the masculine gender. Husserl usually refers to the Ego in the third person singular, a mode of expression I shall use here exclusively. I shall not use the adjectives "pure," "transcendental," "empirical," etc. because they have occasioned much misunderstanding and because what Husserl basically means by Ego can be grasped without them.

"Consciousness" is defined in the *Ideen* as something which consists of mental processes, intentional objects, and the Ego. Some mental processes are called "acts" in that they can be seen reflectively to "radiate" from the Ego (§ 33). Acts are also called "spontaneous activities" and include perceptual mental processes in which the Ego grasps objects in his surroundings, distinguishes and compares them, believes and doubts them, likes and dislikes them, and choses and decides them. All such acts are included under the Cartesian title *cogito*. Such acts have the fundamental form of what is called "actual" living, regardless of whether

[1] Edmund Husserl, "Ideen zu einer reinen Phänomenologie und phänomenologischen Philosophie," *Jahrbuch für Philosophie und phänomenologische Forschung* (Halle: Max Niemeyer, 1913), Bd. I.

reflected upon or not. An act of reflective observing, however, would also be a cogitatio (§ 28). In reflecting, the Ego not only grasps his mental processes, including those of the form cogito, but also himself as the subject to whom all mental processes relate as he who lives in them in various manners, who is active, passive, spontaneous, who behaves in a receptive or in another manner (§ 34).

In his general exposition, Husserl next characterizes the cogito in distinguishing it from what he calls the "cogitatum." The cogitatum for an observational cogitatio, for instance, is something which detaches itself from the perceptual field as the thing perceived, the perceptum, one might say. The modification that a mental process undergoes when it becomes a cogitatio can be characterized as a free conversion of the look or gaze, the mental regard which moves from one object to another within the field of consciousness, such objects being at one time "implicit" and at another time, when regarded, "explicit." There are thus in correlation to changes in the cogitatum two modes of mental process, one called "actual" or "explicit" – the cogito – and the other called "implicit" or "potential." In the explicit or actual mental process, the Ego is "directed toward" or "busied with" the object (§ 35).

But this modification is not the same as attention. It is broader and comprises all the cogitationes in the Cartesian enumeration, thinking, feeling, willing, and so on. Each actual mental process, each cogito, is surrounded with a horizon of inactual or potential mental processes. The Ego is the one who *actualizes* cogitationes and he is called the "vigilant Ego" when he does this (§ 35). When a mental process is actual a subject directs himself through it toward the cogitatum. There is a regard which is immanent in the cogito and, on the other hand, this regard is said to shoot out of the Ego. This "regard" is not a distinct act, but instead is something which differs with the different sorts of cogitationes. Attention, as has been said, is not the mode of actuality itself, not the cogito form that mental processes can take, but one mode among others of actuality. Acts of observation always include attention, but in valuational acts and in volitional acts the Ego is turned toward the value and the use. Nevertheless, the value and the use can be objects of attention, and in every complex act the attentional mode of actuality dominates (§ 37). The life of a vigilant Ego is one of constant perception, be it actual or inactual (§ 39).

For the most part I am following Husserl's order of exposition in the *Ideen*. What I have just related would seem to amount to a first characterization of the situation of the Ego, the cogito, and to some extent the cogitatum. Some forty pages further along, Husserl has occasion to touch on the matter of the Ego again.

The Ego is not a mental process, nor is he an original part of a mental process. Yet he appears to be there along with mental life constantly and even necessarily. He somehow belongs to every mental process as it emerges and fades away. The Ego's regard passes through and bears upon the object of a mental process. Such a mental process penetrated by a regard is, as has been seen, an actual cogitatio. The ray of this regard, as Husserl calls it, varies with each cogitatio, arising and fading away with it. The ray is part and parcel of the cogito. But over and against the streaming multiplicity of cogitationes the Ego remains identical. He cannot, therefore, be considered as a really inherent part of a mental process. Here, although Husserl nowhere says so in the *Ideen* that I have noticed, because the opposite of a really inherent part is an intentional part, one is tempted to say that the Ego is in some sense an "intentional part" of a mental process. (In § 82 he does say that the stream of mental life and the Ego are "correlates.") In the present connection the Ego is said to be an original transcendence, what is called, awkwardly, a "transcendence in immanence." As such, the Ego can be observed and described as a phenomenological datum given conjointly with consciousness. The stream belongs, somehow, to him and he belongs to the stream, his stream (§ 57). But once again Husserl drops the matter of the Ego, saying that Vol. II of the Ideen will deal fully with him. This volume was not written by Husserl.

A remark is in order at this point concerning the distinction between immanence and transcendence. Mental processes can be intentive to things in the same mental life, namely other mental processes intended to in protendings as future and coming later and retrotended to in retrotendings as past and coming earlier, not to speak of the more obvious example of reflecting on the past, present, or future mental processes in a mental life. Mental processes can thus be the intentional objects of other mental processes in the same stream. The totality of mental processes making up a stream of mental life is called "immanence." By contrast, there are mental processes which are intentive to things *beyond* the mental stream, *beyond* the immanence in which they go on. Such mental processes thus have "transcendencies" as their intentional objects, e.g., real objects, ideal objects, other Egos, the mental lives of others, etc. Thus when the Ego is said to be transcendent, he is said to be in some way intentively *beyond* the immanent stream. It may be useful to speak of "outward" and "inward" transcendencies in order to avoid the confusion or at least awkwardness of an "immanent transcendency."

Yet another forty-odd pages along in the *Ideen*, Husserl takes up the matter of the Ego once more. Through acts of reflecting, the Ego experiences his stream of mental life and its necessary reference to the Ego. This stream is then seen to be the field in which cogitationes are performed by a single and same Ego. And this stream belongs to the Ego insofar as he can regard the mental processes in it and bring his regard to bear through them upon something alien to the Ego (§ 78). Further along he says that mental processes located in the background or horizon of the Ego are at different "distances" from him as he who is living in his cogitationes as the center of reference (§ 84).

The "relation" of mental processes to the Ego is one of the foremost traits of mental life. Each cogito is an act of the Ego, it goes out from him, he lives in it actually. He can participate in his acts and by reflection he can grasp himself as participant. The Ego himself has certain traits: he "directs himself at" something, he is "busied with" this or that, he "takes positions in relation to" things, he "construes" experiences, he "suffers"; all of these things are meant when it is said that there is a ray which emanates from the Ego or is directed to the Ego. But inactual or potential mental processes do not have the characteristic relation to the Ego that actual mental processes, cogitationes, have. They relate, we might say, *indirectly*, in being the field of his freedom to actualize them (§ 80).

The Ego himself cannot be taken as an object of study because if we abstract from his manners of relating, his manners of behaving, there is nothing to describe. But insofar as the Ego lives in various sorts of cogitationes, he is open to a vast number of descriptions of his particular manners of living in them. We have a situation, then, where on the one hand there is the mental process itself and on the other hand the Ego in his manners of behaving. There is thus on the subjective side of mental life a sort of content turned toward the Ego. Mental life, it seems has two sides, one "subjectively oriented" (presumably toward the inwardly transcendent) and the other "objectively oriented." Accordingly, phenomenological investigation necessarily has two lines of inquiry. But here once again Husserl says that the question of the Ego and the various ways in which he participates in his mental life can be ignored and therefore Husserl turns to other matters (§ 80).

A dozen sections later, Husserl repeats how there is a ray emitted by the Ego which traverses mental processes, but this ray is itself a moment of the mental process. Not only does this ray, mental regard, or ray of the regard – here Husserl admits to using figurative language – radiate from the Ego, but it also terminates at the object. Apparently, the ray can be figuratively conceived of as going either way, from the Ego to the object and from the object to the Ego, for the Ego is said to suffer as well as to act. We have seen that the Ego is said to "live in" his acts. What is called *living in* is not a superadded content, but rather a matter of describable multiplicities which are manners in which the Ego engages in his cogitationes. The Ego himself is a free being, he goes out of himself, comes back to himself, acts spontaneously, affirms, suffers, etc. The rays, regards, or cogitationes are beyond the intrinsic actuality of the Ego, but they still belong to him as parts of his field of freedom (§ 92).

The most distinct manner of behaving of the Ego treated by Husserl in the *Ideen* is that in which the Ego is said to "operate" his acts. All mental processes are intentional, each consciousness is a consciousness of something. If all mental processes are intentive to things, then processes of the form cogito are also intentive to things. They are manners of being-busied-with and of being-directed-to things. Among potential or inactual mental processes some can be reflectively recognized which are initiations or stirrings of actual processes. These are said to be at various distances from the Ego, who is their center of reference. When the Ego is actually living in a cogitatio, that cogitatio is said to be an "operated act" and the Ego is the "operative subject"; this includes when he is, for example, sufferingly engaged in a cogitatio of grieving. But when acts are not quite operated, Husserl calls them "initiations of acts," in contrast to "operated acts." When potential and then stirring, the mental process can be intentive to the same thing that it is when it is actual, operated (§ 84). This is how it is when acts go from their potential condition of initiation to their actuality as operated. But an act can also cease to be operated, as when the Ego turns to operate another act and, as it were, drops the first. The previously operated act fades away. Yet although the Ego no longer lives in it as an operative subject and although the former act fades into the past, the formerly operated mental process continues to be intentive to what it was intentive to as initiated and as operated (§ 115). These statements about the Ego as he who operates his acts will be seen to have greater significance when we see how he operates what Husserl calls "synthesis."

Whether actual or potential, mental living is in the broad sense positional or "thetic." Theses include doxic theses, affective or emotional theses, and volitive theses. In thetic mental processes, new object-determinations are constituted, a belief-character for doxic processes or believings, valuedness for valuings, and uses for willings. Thus statuses are imputed to objects in theses (§ 117). Now, as we have seen, a mental process can be intentive to something when the process is initiated, operated, or abandoned by the Ego and all along it can be intentive to it as the same thing. When several thetic mental processes have the same object, they are said to make up a "synthesis." We can sometimes reflect and see a segmented consciousness, a consciousness with several discrete phases, as constitutive of an object. In such a case, we can speak of an "articulated" synthesis and we can investigate how discontinuous thetic acts combine in being intentive to the same object. Articulated syntheses are also called "polythetic acts." They occur in the doxic, the emotional, and the volitive dimensions of positionality. A good example of a polythetic act is a collective synthesis, one in which a collection is constituted (§ 118).

An articulated synthesis or polythetic act has a whole object. For each simple thesis comprised in the articulated synthesis there is a correlative positedness in the object which that simple thesis posits. When a polythetic act is converted into a "mono-thetic" act the whole object is posited as a unity. If we consider the articulated synthetic cogitatio on the subjectively oriented side, on the side facing the Ego, we can see that it has several rays that emanate from the Ego; a simple thesis has one ray. We can also say that the synthetic operation of collecting is a "plural" consciousness. It proceeds by positing unity after unity, "this *and* this *and* this." The synthetic object arises as intended to in the synthetic consciousness. When this synthesis is convert-ed properly, the object which was posited in each of its parts with a plurality of rays can be posited as one in an act of a single ray. Thus from "this *and* this *and* this" we go over to *"all this";* a plural consciousness is made singular (§ 119).

The conversion of polythetic acts into a monothetic act applies in the case of affective theses, including acts of loving. Husserl speaks of a mother who regards her several children with love. This can involve a collective affective synthesis that is articulated and then converted from polythetic to monothetic. She loves each child with a simple affective thesis and then all of them together monothetically. The group as object of love is a collective object. In it each child has the character of being loved. Ego-rays branch out from the Ego to each child in the group lovingly. The conver-sion is from "this loved child *and* this loved child *and* this loved child" to "the loved children" (§ 121).

Finally, the Ego is said to *operate* his articulated synthesis, step by step. He lives in one thesis and then goes on to the next thesis. The Ego is free, of course, to pose, counterpose, compose, etc. The theses are rays that emanate from him. In a thesis we can say that the Ego has something in his grip. He can also let go, as it were. Most important for our present concern, however, he can also continue to keep something in his grip as he goes on to grasp something else. Thus there can be many theses operated in an articulated synthesis. And when the things collected are posit-ed as a collection, the Ego *operates* the monothesis (§ 122).

To understand this most fully, we must refer to the structure of the object in the broad sense. Where the situation of the in-

tentive mental process and the thing intended to in it is concerned, there is a distinction to be made between the thing which is
intended and the thing as it is intended. The thing as it is intended is called the "noema" and the intending to it is the "noesis."
Cogitatum and cogito would seem to be the actual noema and
noesis. The object in the narrow sense is the thing which is intended to. *Apart* from the noemata in which it is intended, which are
how the thing is intended, the object, what is intended, is said to
be nothing; Husserl calls it an "X." Like the Ego apart from his
manners of behaving, it is indescribable.

When a thing is intended to in several ways, perhaps as seen,
touched, and smelled, or as expected, presented, and remembered, or as believed, valued, and willed, or as grasped either clearly
or obscurely or grasped distinctly or confusedly, etc., the thing
is still intended to as a unitary and identical thing over and
against not only a multiplicity of intending noeses for each noema
but also as identical over and against a multiplicity of noemata.
That which remains identical within the multiplicity and variation of noemata is the "object" or X.

Now in processes of thetic consciousness, the mental regard or
ray that has been mentioned so often is said by Husserl not only
to come out of the Ego and to go through the cogito or noetic
actuality, but also to penetrate the noema or cogitatum as well,
terminating at the X or object in the narrow sense (§ 129). A
thesis is a positing of an object. In synthetic or polythetic acts,
each thesis has its X and the X's each have a determinate content
of noemata, and the synthesis is intentive to the synthetised X
as an X of X's and its noematic content. The Ego-ray branches
out into many rays and then, through the X of each thesis, con-
verges upon the X of the synthesis. This X of the synthesis can
then be posited as a unity monothetically.

If we now take this account and *transpose it from* the objectively
oriented side of mental life *to* the subjectively oriented side, we
may be able to construe the various things that we have seen
Husserl says about the Ego more amply. Where Husserl said that
the Ego was indescribable apart from his manners of behaving
or relating, I believe that he meant that these manners were
related to the Ego or subject in the narrow sense in the same
way that noemata as how an object is intended are related to the

object in the narrow sense. Manners of the Ego's behaving would then seem to be analogous in correlation to the subjective side of the mental stream to noemata in correlation to the objective side of the mental stream, noemata being manners in which the thing that is intended to is intended. The vigilant Ego-mode probably then corresponds to the intuitedness of a thing intuited, the intuitum. Where positionality is concerned, there are processes in which the Ego takes positions; hence he has his manners of being a believer, a valuer, and a willer. In this way the Ego is the subject of each thesis and more deeply the subject of all theses, monothetic or polythetic. Indeed, he may ultimately be the subject-X of X's just as there are object-X's of their X's. However, the relation of the Ego to his modes of behavior is something that I have supposed interpretively to be the same as that of the object to its noemata; there are indications, but this is neither explicit nor directly implied in the doctrine of the Ego in Husserl's *Ideen*.

MARVIN FARBER

THE PHILOSOPHIC IMPACT OF
THE FACTS THEMSELVES

1. On Philosophy as the Basic Science

If philosophy is to have the status of the most rigorous science, or if it is to be regarded simply as a science, it must earn the right to the designation. Every science has a special function, and a selective domain for inquiry. Although a discipline which applies to all special sciences – logic – has been called the science of sciences, it would be fatuous to portray logic as resting upon a throne and as governing all that exists or could possibly exist. The special sciences function as fields for work in a primary sense, and they grow out of the need to enable human beings to maintain themselves and to further their interests by understanding and changing the world. With conflicting social classes, this need has been satisfied one-sidedly, in accordance with the dominant interests of the social system. The logic which is implicit in the nascent and developing sciences receives fresh impetus when it is treated as a special discipline, even though it has unrestricted application. It develops further with the growth of the sciences, and it is also an aid to that development. But there should be no talk or image of a logic "governing" the sciences.

The transcendental philosopher who ascribes to transcendental logic and phenomenology such a universal regulative function is really seeking an absolute key to the riddles of the universe, contained in a kind of philosophical Pandora's Box of pure subjectivity. How can that be accomplished? By instituting a new form of subjective science, free from all the uncertainties and vicissitudes of natural existence? Can it then be shown that the detached pure science really conditions the natural world? But if the realm for inquiry is concerned with experiences which are treated as disengaged from their natural setting, the transcendentalist never gets beyond idealities and fictions in his ontology. The methodological restriction of the objects of reality to a relationship with an experiencing subject – the subject-object limitation – serves as a wheelhorse for idealistic arguments at crucial points. The philosophical Pandora's Box is one more fairy tale, as a matter of fact. It is, however, a fairy tale with socio-historical linkage and consequences; for it is an ingenious philosophy of renunciation which leaves the *status quo* unexamined and unchallenged, and which may even be accommodated to reactionary ideas. This has in fact occurred in the larger aura of influence of subjectivism, as illustrated by Scheler, who has added to the arsenal of philosophical apologetics serving the existing social system.[1]

The methods of establishing knowledge and explanations in all the sciences, including the progressive growth of synthetic chemistry, the effort to achieve a unified physical theory, and the study of human behavior and social relationships, are primary sources of the positive knowledge underlying philosophic thought. These sources must be treated critically because of the historically conditioned motives leading to falsification and the defense of the established social order. They, and the motivations derived from the social system, determine the course of philosophy by presenting the decisive problems and the opportunity for direction-giving thought. The transcendental view which seeks to provide the principles and structures for historical change is itself a historical phenomenon, to be explained in relationship to the interests it serves, directly or indirectly, and not alone by a systematic analysis.

2. The Ego and the World

The so-called problem of the existence of the world, and of the existence of the "external" world, results from an assumed standpoint and method – in the present case, from the transcendental approach. The traditional problem, engaging the attention of idealists and realists, involved protracted discussion with no generally accepted solution. The lively idealism-realism contro-

---

[1] Cf. M. Farber, *Naturalism and Subjectivism* (Albany: State University of New York Press, 2nd ed., 1968), pp. 297ff.

versy early in the twentieth century antedated the rise and spread of a new form of subjectivism, with the problem of existence the most crucial challenge to be met.

The early Husserl admonished philosophers to go "back to the things themselves," which meant attending to what is given in and to experience. That was much more promising in its time than the slogan, "Back to Kant," as expressed by O. Liebmann in *Kant und die Epigonen* (1865). The late Husserl developed a philosophy of pan-subjectivism programmatically, with a "world-problem" resulting. It proved necessary to accept a "pre-given" world of experience; and the assimilation of that world to the transcendental-subjective realm of pure experience remained an unsolved problem.[2] The provisional "egology," amounting to an individualistic subjectivism, was an initial stage of the operation, and it was to be overcome and absorbed in a larger subjective framework, universal in its scope.

It may be noted that no mere subjectivity ever caused a war or committed rape and robbery. The subjectivist of the latest vintage must acknowledge an order of events independent of all human processes of experience. He can only resort to an absolute being to encompass the order of independent existence; and such a being has not been instated descriptively in experience.

Has something been missed in the examination of this issue? Have the facts themselves been insufficiently considered? What may well be most obvious may for that very reason be neglected. The appeal to the facts themselves (which is to be distinguished from the Husserlian slogan "Back to the things themselves") involves a reexamination of the ontology which unavoidably underlies all epistemology. It may break what has been embalmed as a perennial deadlock and consign it to its rightful place among the discarded curiosities of history. The implications of established knowledge, based upon adequate evidence, must be fully and frankly recognized. A broad definition of facts, allowing for the many types of fact, formal and ideal as well as real, is called for.[3] Exponents of subjectivism must be forced to state

[2] Cf. M. Farber, *Phenomenology and Existence* (New York: Harper & Row, 1967), pp. 113ff.

[3] Cf. M. Farber, "Humanistic Ethics and the Conflict of Interests," in P. Kurtz, ed., *Moral Problems in Contemporary Society* (Englewood Cliffs, N.J.: Prentice-Hall, Inc., 1969), pp. 256ff.

their case precisely on all essential points: on the nature of man; on the mind and consciousness, the self, ego or egos, including the transcendental ego; on the nature of the world and man's actual place in the world.

It is not to be supposed that questions about the relationship of an ego to the world or to passing circumstances of social standing and opportunity, or to genes, etc., would be disconcerting to a subjectivist. For the subjectivist is ever ready to admit the influences bearing upon the development of the mind, self, or ego, while being equally well prepared to transmogrify the influences and the entire world in subjective terms. The operation is a simple one, even if less simple than the traditional theology, for which it was sufficient for a deity, blessed with aseity, to take a handful of nothing and produce something – the world and man. For the philosophical operation an intricate process of thought is required, in order to provide a semblance of plausibility, but only by disregarding some of the most pertinent facts about knowing and being. The promise of pure subjectivism, that a universal suspension of beliefs and a retirement to immanent experience would bring to light all influences and all conditions bearing on experience, is not fulfilled. For a larger realm is needed, in which the mind and all experiences are contained – the infinite realm of existence, antedating the relatively recent development of human beings, and continuing after the possible disappearance of life as we know it from the cosmos. The transmogrification of real existence to accommodate the central position accorded to minds, selves, or egos, is a methodological achievement of philosophical subjectivism, which is at times concealed linguistically by describing its determinations as "objective."

One must look to sociohistorical factors for the explanation of the receptivity and persistent adherence to this position. Accommodation to the social order, the influence of factors of personal and class interest, and religious motives are prominent in the explanation, along with personal factors such as fidelity to past teachers and faulty or confused reasoning.

The underlying conditions of pure subjectivism, like pure or formal logic, are to be found in the natural and cultural world. Both types of discipline are derivative, presupposing the existing world; and they have only a restricted, relative autonomy, as special systems of thought and modes of inquiry. The idea of a pure life-world as featured in phenomenology is similarly a derivative of the real world of existence. It is a nameless realm, unaffected by the troublesome world in which we live. But there is still more to attract many persons in our time: it offers a way to avoid taking a stand on the pressing practical issues affecting mankind. For there is a widespread *search for an alternative*, often unconsciously motivated, on the part of all those not wishing to take a stand on the burning issues of our time, many of them related to the basic issue of socialism vs. capitalism in any of its forms.

Since it is the real world of existence which is presupposed by any thought of a pure life-world, let us take a look at our actual life-world; and also at the procedure by which the ideal structures of phenomenology are obtained – above all, the *epoché* or suspension of beliefs and judgments. The *epoché* which is required in order to delimit the realm of pure experience can only be partial as a matter of fact. As a methodological device it still presupposes the infinite realm of nature and the sociohistorical world. The professed aim can be viewed constructively: everything is to be examined for its evidence in direct experience, beginning with my own experience as a supposedly solitary knowing being. Since a solitary knowing being cannot exist in fact, the very beginning is artificial, and the whole procedure must be regarded as ancillary to natural beings. There has been no real flight from nature, and no real breach in nature has been effected; nor has the existence of the world been disposed of by the process of suspension or questioning. On the contrary, it was a matter of ordinary observation that even pure phenomenologists defended their special privileges and property interests despite any suspension, so that they always maintained the independence of the natural world in practice. It is a curious fact that they did not acknowledge the priority of that world. This applies to the life-world as well, for it presupposes the physical universe, and also the cultural world in all its forms of development.

The nature of the solitary ego which is to perform the *epoché* presents us with a group of questions. Is my *epoché*-performing ego the same as your *epoché*-performing ego? And what is its nature? How is it related to my body, to other human beings, to my environment, social system, and historical tradition, with regard to physical, biological, and cultural factors? Is there one unchanging ego, or does a person have a plurality of egos, differing from one another in at least one respect? Is this ego a part of nature, or does it have a special ontological status, elevating it above nature?

Real egos are always concrete, historically conditioned individuals. They are bodies in action, and they provide a unity of reference and ascription to experience. Biologically and socially they owe their existence to other egos. The pure ego, or the class of pure egos, cannot escape such conditions, however transformed they may seem to be.

It is easy to lapse into the view that an ego or self is an independent agent, an isolated unity of existence, out of which social aggregates are compounded. The indebtedness of an ego to the prevailing social group is the primary fact; and if the ego in turn contributes novelty and helps to sustain the activities of the group, the fact of indebtedness to the group is still primary. His language and the chief influences upon his thought are derived from the social group. That group is not to be thought of as an undifferentiated unity, however, for there are individual and class differences to be noted. Egos differ not only individually, with differences due to capacities, desires, and bodily features; they also differ because of their places in the social system. A social system dominated by property interests is made up of economic classes which are in conflict. Ancient slavery, medieval feudalism, and modern capitalism register both similar and distinctive patterns of social conflict. It is always necessary to make the framework of reference clear, and to indicate the areas of conflicting interests. One ego may be frankly aligned with a dominant economic class; and another ego may challenge the entire *status quo*, and criticize all existing socioeconomic relations. He may do so as a representative of those that work, and in opposition to those that largely own the means of production. Again, in a given case he may resort to a framework of reference reaching beyond his own national boundaries. In any case, it should be borne in mind that an ego is always a historical product; and that is also true of the actual cases of philosophically prepared, abstractive egos, which should always be dated and located geographically for identification and understanding.

3. On Structures and Reality

If experience is taken to be the subject matter for philosophic thought, the domain of existence must be accounted for, and its relationship to experience established. Is it correct to say that the actual world is an exemplification of ideal structures, discerned in and through experience? That may be a convenient formulation, but it also proves to be a misleading way of stating the relationship of cognitive devices to the existing world. A dogmatic idealist may proceed from ideal structures as the true and basic reality, the problem then being to make connection with the real world of passing events. But the truth is just the reverse: what is called the world of contingent events is the reality, and the structures are to be discovered there, using any and all cognitive devices, including the artificial devices designated as "ideal." This is not to deny that there are objective structures; for every event embodies relationships and can be described in terms of ideal relations, which are constituted in keeping with the variable events in natural experience.

From one perspective, P', concerned with the growth of knowledge and experience, it is seen that structures are discovered in the analysis of real events. From another perspective, P'', presupposing the achievements of natural and cultural experience, one can operate "freely" with "pure thought" and its constructive activities. Fictions play an important role in such activities. The point is then to determine how the conceptual patterns of construction – the ideal structures – are realized in the world of experience. For P', the "discovery" may be mistaken, totally or in part, and confirmation is required. For P'', the likelihood of error is reduced in practice, because of the greater degree of control by the knower over his materials; but error is never eliminated completely. "Pure" structures with no application to real existence may still be of theoretical interest to us. But they do not have basic practical importance until there is an application to the natural or social world. They may however have secondary or derivative importance through application to other ideal constructions; and the latter may eventually have a realization in the world and therewith practical importance. It can also be said that there is a value in understanding, in the satisfaction of any human interests, including those which are most abstract and remote from the practical world.

The term structure is useful; as a general term it is broadly synonymous with "relational pattern" or "relational organization." One may speak of formal structures, as well as of nonformal or material structures (or, as is frequently the case, of material and formal components of structures). Formal structures are illustrated in the ideal systems of formal logic and pure mathematics, which in turn are indebted to the cognitive activities and motivations of human beings and the natural-social world. On the other hand, material structures always have formal components.

All real things or events have space-time relations; and space-time has formal characteristics. To be sure, a skeptic might challenge this statement, for as a universal statement it goes beyond that which has been actually observed. But such an objection merely illustrates the trivial and empty truth that the field of the observed is the observed, and that what has not been observed is not to be treated as observed. The universality of space-time relations is rooted in the basic fact of existence which underlies science and philosophy. That our experience progressively demonstrates the success of our predictions of the future would still not convince the persistent skeptic, for whom it is possible in a vacuous sense that the entire realm of existence might cease to be, and, indeed, "might not be at all." This kind of skeptical reservation would not be enough to undermine our confidence in the reaches of empirical knowledge, for there is no evidence to support it and very much evidence against it.

Some philosophers have endeavored to discern structures intuitively in the stream of experience. Such intuitive discernment (whether as *Wesensschau* or by another name) was supposed to be emancipated from the difficulties of empirical knowledge and the natural world. It would have to be shown that the structures, allegedly nontemporal and eternal in a sense, could be justified by intuitive experience, whether "pure" or "impure." A reflectively observed structure is there as that which is meant or referred to by the experience. If the entire realm of experience is viewed in isolation from its natural setting, with all positing of real existence suspended, and only essential structures of experience and its meant objects are considered, it is misleading to ask whether the meant objects are continuous existents. It should not be said that they are eternal, any more than they could be said to last three hundred years. Strictly speaking, all suggestions of actual reality, whether temporal or spatial, should be avoided. The structures discerned in pure experience belong to an ideal order, and have the ontological status of fictions. Just as the pure-reflective (alias transcendental) knower is a child of the natural-cultural world, who must breathe and derive his sustenance from that world, so does he owe his speech, thought, and fund of knowledge to that world. Furthermore, it is the actual natural-social world which provides the real basis and the motivation for all thought, including the turning to subjectivism of so many philosophers. The difficulties of naturalistic thought are not overcome by a subjective philosophy. The belief that in the transcendental realm the basis has been provided on which all conceivable philosophical and scientific problems of the past are to be put and decided, simply reverses the real order of events. The order is, first, the natural-social world, with man as an active agent in it, affecting that world; and, then, as a late development, the turning to subjectivity.

It is not true that the ideal truths found subjectively are "first in themselves," so that they have a privileged status with respect to the real order of the natural-cultural world. To maintain that would simply be to give expression to wishful thinking. The term "first" must be clarified, when one mentions the difference between that which is "first for us" and that which is "first in itself." In other words, is structure prior to natural-social events; or are the latter events prior to structure – which is "first"? If one wishes to understand (or to "see" in an extended sense) the structure of capital, or of capitalist production, there must first have been an actual case of social and economic organization in existence; or one may proceed from a past case of actual existence. The structure would otherwise be a matter of ideal imagination, without any known application to the real world. The determination of ideal structures, as illustrated in purely formal science, may precede any application to the existing world by a considerable amount of time, or there may never be an application. In that case, the determination of structures is first in a qualified sense which must be carefully indicated. In a real, primary sense, the sociohistorical and the natural events are first. There was an indefinitely long evolutionary process and a long historical process before the sciences began to determine structures of real existence and of ideal possibilities which might be illustrated by the real world, thus adding to the humanly directive elements in the process of change.

Marx's thought has been examined for an illustration of the role of structures, with special reference to his economic analysis. The distinction between structure and superstructure is pertinent here. The terms structure and superstructure refer to the relationship between basic economic factors producing change, and the cultural factors (intellectual, religious, moral, etc.) which presuppose the economic activities. Since this relationship was clarified by Marx, to allow for the effects of cultural factors upon the economic process, it would be unwarranted to portray the structure-superstructure relationship as operating in a fixed, one-way direction. Marx's economic analysis can be viewed as showing the structure of production and distribution. But it must also be viewed as based upon a most detailed factual knowledge of changing historical events. Thus real workers and employers are seen in their actual roles in their social system. The intellectual devices for analysis employed by Marx represent an important development of scientific and philosophic method.

The issue recently raised by structuralists has been complicated by the reference to Marx's economic analysis. Hence one does not say enough about the method of structuralism until he indicates the type involved, whether pure phenomenological, or phenomenological in a mixed or extended "existential" sense, or Marxist in any one of its versions, including its forms of revisionism.

It is possible to find structures everywhere. That is the case if all events and collocations of events are regarded as containing arrangements of parts. Thus there are unique passing structures, for every event embodies a relational pattern. The real world, which is always changing, has a variable structure. Each event, such as laughter, a sigh, a meeting of workers, or a musical concert has its structure, which is disclosed by analysis. The structure of "a meeting as such" is to be distinguished from "this particular meeting, with its individual characteristics." Similarly, the structure of "a musical concert as such" is to be distinguished from "this concert by the New York Philharmonic Orchestra"; and similarly for the other cases.

The general abstractive determination of the structure of "a meeting as such" selects relationships present in all events of that kind, without allowing for the individual factors peculiar to one particular case. How much is established thereby? A structure-philosopher may believe that he then has absolutely secure knowledge of the conditions of real existence, that he has knowledge of relationships which must be present in all future events of that kind, and that, furthermore, such findings are valid for all possible knowers. Expressed in the language of phenomenology, this is one instance of a universal eidetic or essential science, which Husserl envisaged in its most generalized form; and the eidetic structures fit into an *a priori* framework underlying the natural-social world, which was said to exhibit a remarkable teleology. It must be admitted that the examples of such *a priori* knowledge did not progress beyond the obvious and the trivial, with an understandable paucity of results. The desired "geometry of experience" (to express it analogically) was not realized, and all attempts to determine the conditions of future realities remained nugatory. It does not help much to assert that the principle of noncontradiction is a negative condition of possible existence; and it is not very helpful to know that there must be a space-time structure, a meeting-place, various individuals with a reason for their collocation, etc., in order to have a meeting.

This is to be distinguished from questions about the structure of matter – of genes, for example – with which scientific inquiry is concerned, and which are often fruitful and important. In such cases, there is no effort to oppose one type of knowledge to other types, and all available sources of experience are used collectively. The field for inquiry is not cut off "radically" from the real source of all experience by an artifice of method which then presents the methodogenic problem of real existence. Scientific inquiry is motivated and influenced by the prevailing social system, and it is indebted to the previous development of scientific knowledge. Its problems are largely forced upon scholars by the nature of the world and man in all his activities.

A partial suspension of beliefs is illustrated by each special science as a matter of procedure, and the ideal of a universal suspension of beliefs of pure philosophy remains in the background as an ideal warning against obscurity and dogmatism. The universal suspension of beliefs is thus an ancillary device with a practical function. It may however also become a mode of retreat from the world and its problems. Those who seek a more permanent realm of being, after devaluing and "bracketing" the natural world as a contingent realm, are apt to forget the most pressing problems of contemporary society, highlighted by frustration and suffering due to unequal opportunities and the threat to human existence resulting from the profit system and pollution of the environment. The quest for structures may simply go along with the process of renunciation of the real world, for which the turning to subjectivity is a preparation. The disregard of the most important human problems is not limited to pure philosophers, to be sure, for many specialized scientists are also far removed from them. In such cases, the specialization itself may be a large part of the reason. But there are also other reasons which may be traced to influences of the social system, to explain the disregard of major human problems; and this applies to philosophers as well. A philosopher can also be viewed as reacting to his social system, either actively or passively as a beneficiary of that system, and not only as an exponent of pure thought. If he lives and acts in accordance with a dominant social group, he can be regarded as a member of that group. No methodological device is likely to overcome the habits of thought of his social class, unless it is effectively based upon a dimension of radical reflection going far beyond the presumed radicalism of transcendental analysis. This applies equally well to scholars in general.

4. The Priority of Historical Event-Structures

Proceeding from the static analysis of familiar structures to the emergence of new events, one sees the priority of historical

event-structures. The fact that every event is an embodied structure has been obscured by the abstract treatment of structures
as though they were independent of events. Let us consider some
historically conditioned examples of older and more recent
standing.

"Pollupolis" is a term presupposing a certain historical stage
of our industrial society featuring pollution; the historical conditions leading to the function of a foreman in a factory or to the
need and place for such a worker antedates the conceptual determination and definition of a foreman; and real, malfunctioning
organic beings are prior conditions for determining the essence or
structure of obstipation. Further examples include the ice age
and Niagara Falls as antecedent natural events, and events involving human beings such as computers, time-loans, poverty,
inflation, imperialism, bankruptcy, and rascal in its various
senses, one of which includes an element of approval. It is not a
timeless or supertemporal tornado that is first, either in time or
in some "in itself" sense. Examples such as exploitation, black-
mail, revolution, and radicalism have overflowing boundaries,
defying neat little essence-determinations and depending upon
the so-called contingent historical events. The essence-determiner
or describer must be wary lest the natural backs upon which he
rests should unseat him. His "inner" region for analysis is not as
completely self-contained as he had believed it to be; it is a
derivative domain, as artificial and confining in its way as any
formal system. Although conceptual determinations may be
proposed for which there are still no examples, it is nevertheless
true that there is always an antecedently existing world, including a cultural tradition, as a basis for thought. In general, any
number of actual events, more or less uniquely individual,
precede the essential-structural determinations.

Most of the examples which have been adduced show the active
interaction of sentient organic beings, socially conditioned and
motivated, with the natural-social world. This is also seen in the
extreme case of meanings and structures discerned by subjectivists, which can be attributed to real, effective human agents
who add something to experience. The description and evalua-
tion of those additions are precisely what is in question. The
subjective analyst calls attention to subtle distinctions and rela-

tionships which show many of the creative activities of the human mind. But he fails to do justice to whole regions of experience because of his failure to subordinate his restricted method to the basic facts of ontology and human existence. The method of phenomenological description as such requires and presupposes the results of ordinary experience and the sciences. Human experience is the resultant of natural, social, and individual factors; temporal priority is to be ascribed to nature and cultural conditions in the first place, and only in a carefully qualified sense to the activities of an individual or group of individuals.

The real, unique event-structures are at the basis of the abstractive determination of variable conceptual or ideal structures. The universe at a given time would be the most general natural event-structure. There are micro-event-structures as well as intermediate types, illustrated by human beings and their activities, which include constructions of thought with their idealities. The existing social system is itself an event, a changing historical organization, a passing event-structure. To idealize that structure might mean in effect to attempt to eternalize the existing social relations, based upon the institution of private property and the profit motive – in short, the capitalist system in any one of its stages of development. Depending upon the standards selected for judgment, that development may be described as progressive or as retrograde. The degree of satisfaction of the needs of all human beings would be the most defensible ultimate standard for judgment. That this ultimate standard must be modified temporarily in order to make progress toward the goal of universal human equality is a practical consideration of tactics, which does not signify an abandonment of the final standard.

5. Subjectivism and the Nonparticipating Observer

A historical explanation must be included in the attempt to understand the significance of the subjectivism which has been so prominent in the philosophy of the recent past. It may be viewed historically as a later phase of the development of idealism as opposed to materialism. The influence of religion, and the complex interest in preserving the existing form of society, have important bearing upon the emergence and development of subjectivism. That historical function would mark it as destined to a limited period in cultural history. But that is not the whole truth about subjectivism. Marx, for example, called attention to the merit of idealism in recognizing the active, contributive function of human knowing, in opposition to the comparatively passive role assigned to it by many other philosophers. Even though every sound and positive finding of subjective procedures may be restated in another, science-oriented framework in which the activities of thought are located in accordance with the factual knowledge of man's place in the cosmos, it remains true that in its best examples, subjectivism has added to the understanding of experience and knowledge. Only that addition must be critically reexamined from a larger methodological perspective.

In medieval thought, even mysticism was at times one of the means for combatting the authoritarianism of the Church, whose mediation was unnecessary for the salvation of the mystic; for the mystic claimed to make direct contact with the highest reality. In the recent past, the clamor for freedom of the individual was also expressed at times by a turning to subjectivity. As in the case of the mystics, however, the supporting philosophy was untenable in important respects. But it is desirable to undertake to salvage all that is sound in it, in a more complete framework of thought, in keeping with logical principles and the scientific level of the time. It is also necessary to revise the terminology of subjectivism, so that there are no assumptive terms claiming more than the methods can accomplish. The chief claim for the value of subjectivism has been based upon the results of its descriptive procedure.

The difficulties in the way of empirical description are well known. Empirical description may be influenced by psychological, social, economic, and physical factors; there may be bias and dishonesty, or there may be simple mistakes. The evil effects of biased testimony purporting to be descriptive, in cases of industrial and political conflict, or where private interests are threatened, are graphic illustrations of the problem. Are such difficulties obviated by subjective inquiry? Does the retirement to the "inner" realm free the investigator from error and prejudice? It is undeniable that even pure subjectivists can make faulty reports or commit mistakes. The question is whether they are sufficiently free from their natural and social entanglements to make correct descriptions. The restriction of subjective inquiry to essences and their relations reduces the region of possible error, but it does not eliminate error entirely.

The assumption of a nonparticipating observer has been made in pure phenomenology in order to make reports on the structure of experience in a detached way. Actually, there is no such thing as a nonparticipating observer, and there are always strands of connection to and from the social order. There is seen to be more than one dimension of participation, when one considers the human knower as a whole in his interrelationships with the natural-social world. If one maintains a natural attitude toward the objects of experience, living in the experience and reacting to the world, there can be no talk of nonparticipation. With the natural attitude, one may even try to revise or remake the world in part. All conduct is therewith conditioned by a world which is independent of any single human being, and largely independent of all human beings. Reactions to the environment are selective, and one's conduct is largely influenced by one's interests, or by what one is persuaded to regard as his interests.

If this is a fair account of the natural man, what can be said about the reflecting man, with or without the performance of an *epoché* and retirement to reflective consciousness? Nothing enters the realm of reflection without the prior accumulation of a process of experience, which is influenced by natural and social conditions. The nature of social classes and of economic relations remains unchanged for reflection. For one who accepts the practices of the social order in his natural experience, there is not likely to be any change when a suspension of beliefs has been instituted. A person who enjoys a preferred and secure place in society is not likely to seriously place it in question in a suspension of beliefs, which in effect leaves all actual existence unchallenged and unchanged. Too much has been claimed for the suspension of beliefs; no device of that kind has much to say for it if it merely tries to be a kind of impartial witness, seeing necessary ("eidetic") structures, and doing nothing about their real counterparts. First of all, the claim to nonparticipation is unwarranted; it is not borne out by the facts. Secondly, that observer is a kind of pure nonentity, incapable of doing anything practical to change the world.

Like the conception of a life-world in phenomenology, the non-participating observer is a fiction. It may be a useful fiction when utilized critically, recognizing that all observers participate in one way or another in the real world, and that nonparticipation may be regarded as being merely an ideal warning to take due note of all such avenues of participation.

6. The Question of the Way from "Here" to "There"

The so-called problem of proving or showing the way to the existence of an external world is either methodogenic or a pseudo-problem, toyed with needlessly. Even naturalistic philosophers have thought it necessary to grapple with that problem. One who does not begin with subjectivistic premises and their restricted realm for inquiry does not have an artificially induced problem of the existence of the world. What is there to be done philosophically in that case? The question is not to justify acceptance of a world, for those who have not suspended the thesis of an independently existing world. Nor should it be the aim to undertake to do what scientific inquiry is equipped to accomplish in showing what is involved in experiencing the world, physically, organically, psychologically, and culturally. The integration and interpretation of scientific knowledge, and its consequences for philosophical issues – methodogenic, traditional, or current cultural issues – is, however, a proper theme for philosophy. But that is not to be confused with the assumptive question of showing philosophically how one gets from "here" (the knower) to "there" (the world), if no artificial separation has been instituted.

In general, it is the independent physical world which is referred to. It seems relatively easy to push that world into any desired framework, with even more drastic consequences than would be possible with nuclear weapons. Such freedom of the imagination is not likely to affect the social world, however, for even the purest philosopher could not afford to interfere with such things as institutions of higher learning, the publication of books and articles, and, above all, salary schedules, with all that they involve. The social world is usually accepted with its inequalities and vested privileges; it is rarely held to be in need of justification philosophically, or of any philosophical account of getting from "here" (the individual worker, or the procurer of business, etc.) to "there" (in the social world, meaning the place of work, or of prospects for the procurer of business, etc.). After all, there are centers of information for bus lines, trains, and planes, and there is sufficient guidance for procurers of all kinds – all nonphilosophical. Most philosophers have nothing to say on this question, and they are inclined to leave unchallenged the relationships of individuals and social classes, with all their conflicts. On the other hand, a materialistic reinterpretation of the general suspension of beliefs is in a position to show how one can get from questioning everything to challenging all settled arrangements and privileges, as a necessary element in social change. One thinks of possible changes on the basis of the actual world, which is to undergo transformation. It will be in place to add some comments in clarification of the concept of possibility.

7. On Possibility and Potentiality

The concept of possibility is epistemic. In accordance with the Kantian doctrine of the categories, it is a form of experience and knowledge, which is supposed to be also a condition of the objects of experience and knowledge. Like probability, it is not ontological, and it is used because we do not have the positive knowledge of existence which is referred to in assertoric judgments of reality. To say that possibility underlies reality, and that the real world is only one case out of an indefinitely large number of possible worlds, is to apply formal-epistemic terms ontologically. Possibility is broader in its scope than probability, which is a quantification of a possibility. This conceptual tool does not condition reality; that would be to place the cart before the horse. The various concepts of possibility range all the way from empty possibility to what can be allowed as possible in a restricted system or context.

It is desirable to distinguish potentiality from the general concept of possibility. Anything that happens or develops is said to be an actualization of a potentiality. That is true analytically of any individual situation or event, as well as of reality as a whole. Not much is said thereby, for the present is indeed actualized out of the past, which must have potentially involved the present. No matter what happens in the near future – even the destruction of life on this planet – that eventuality would have been potentially engendered by the antecedent conditions.

Considered quite generally, possibility should not be misplaced, as an idealistic dogma for which the mind conditions reality by the imposition of pure forms, with possibility one of them. Potentiality is either analytically instated as true although trivial, or it yields to positive determinations which are effective in concrete individual cases. Thus, one person may contract tuberculosis and another person avoid it, although living under similar conditions. The knowledge of various determining factors, in accordance with scientific findings, will help to explain what potentiality means in each case.

Both terms, possibility and potentiality, are useful in their ways, and they can also be misleading when too much is claimed for them. It is easy to be deceived by words, which can be used assumptively in so many ways.

8. The Question of Epistemological Transcendence

If one thinks of possible social changes on the basis of the actual world, does that require some kind of epistemological transcendence of the present? This question appears to raise a serious difficulty on the basis of tacit subjectivist premises. In other words, the talk of an epistemological breakthrough suggests that an artificial frame delimiting the field of experience has been transcended by a larger frame. Hence, if an attempt at the epistemological containment of ontology has been penetrated, that amounts to a breakthrough in an artificial frame. The epistemological limitation brings on what seems to be a dramatic exodus, so that after the transgression the redemption follows. But there is no such problem when one understandingly resorts to a plurality of procedures.

Would there be any point to speaking of an existential breakthrough? Only if there were built-in restrictions, including subjectivistic premises. In the latter case, one must pass beyond the subjectively limited sphere of existence to the larger independent domain of existence, which is all-comprehensive.

The talk of a breakthrough may be assumptive in its way – as though the field of experience were really something *sui generis*, and as though existence must be correlated with the experience and knowledge of existence, which would be an unwarranted dogma. The point to be noted is evident: procedures are always partial and selective; and there is talk of a breakthrough if a unitary procedure is used solely. Intermethodological judgments, or judgments from different methodological perspectives, do not involve breakthroughs in that sense. Thus it is possible to examine the subjective mode of inquiry from a historical or evolutionary perspective, and the historical perspective from the subjective or purely reflective point of view. Whether such intermethodological judgments are worth making must be determined for each case.

On the other hand, it may be said that there is a kind of breakthrough when a thinker in a historical form of society seeks to introduce fundamental changes which would lead to a new social system. No artificial frame need be involved, and no epistemological restrictions or ontological assumptions. The desired breakthrough is in that case within the natural world, and it merely signifies a transformation of the existing social system, with a supplanting and modification of existing social relations and the introduction of new arrangements. The far-reaching cultural changes affect institutions and ideas, with consequences for political, social, educational, religious, scientific, and philosophic thought.

9. *The Sociohistorical World and the Materialistic "Epoché"*

From the subjectivist reduction to pure experience nothing results for the real world, which continues to exist with all its conflicts, dislocations, and limited happiness. There is no superior vantage point for examining the problems of the social system. The nonparticipating observer places himself at the nullpoint of human activity, which is the negation of all that is real. If the transcendental point of view is not to serve as a support for the existing social order, it must be treated as a specialized type of procedure, and hopefully as an aid in the treatment of human problems, which can only be in a narrow, selective manner.

Prejudices of various kinds provide revealing examples. The methodological suspension of all beliefs is supposed to be a precondition for the weighing of evidence, and for the achievement of objectively valid knowledge. There are prior questions to be answered before prejudices can be clarified and defined. The events of natural and cultural experience must be considered. There are historical, national, class, and individual factors, in stating or preserving prejudices. Prejudgments of Norwegians vs. Swedes and vice versa, and a host of others concerning Scotsmen, Jews, Italians, Negroes, etc., would not be affected by a universal suspension of beliefs, for they are deeply rooted in social and economic circumstances. The only effective way to approach the problem of prejudice is by considering the actual historical causes. This is conspicuously illustrated by such complex phenomena as racial and national prejudices. Anti-Semitism is causally connected with the Christian tradition, along with other factors. A relatively simpler illustration would be the depreciation of manual labor in the slave economy of ancient Athens. The attempts, consciously or unconsciously motivated, to justify slavery, helped to preserve a group of prejudices. Modern attempts are historical continuators of classical Greek reasons adduced in support of vested prejudices representing the interests of a slaveholding class. It is fair to ask how closely the ideal of objective knowledge would be approached in such cases, even if the attitude of radical reflection of subjectivism were adopted.[4] In general, it is pertinent to ascertain whether the subjectivist ideal of rigorous, absolute knowledge would draw attention away from sordid facts, by a one-sided treatment of prejudice. The all-sided factual account of prejudice, making use of reflective analysis along with historical and scientific data, is intended to deal with concrete cases of prejudice, and to correct as well as understand them – not only structurally, but as real events affecting our lives.

Human beings should be considered at all stages of social devel-

---

[4] V. I. Lenin denied that there can be "an 'impartial' social science in a society based on class struggle." He maintained that "in one way or another, all official and liberal science defends wage-slavery ... To expect science to be impartial in a wage-slave society is as silly and naive as to expect impartiality from manufacturers on the question whether workers' wages should be increased by decreasing the profits of capital." Cf. V. I. Lenin, *Selected Works*, Vol. XI, *The Theoretical Principles of Marxism* (New York: International Publishers, 1935–1938), p. 3.

opment, from obscure and conjectural beginnings to more complex forms leading to the societies which are known historically. The ego or self, whether empirical or transcendental, is always a function of an organic body, is always an organization of physical matter and energy, and is always a result of historical development. If a factory worker, an investment procurer, or a fundamentalist preacher is taken as an example, one sees how little can be contributed by subjective analysis, whether pure or mixed existentially, and how thin the findings must be in any case. If the example is an expression of grief, or an experience of anxiety, the most important thing is the real event itself, and the whole complex of circumstances producing that event. The philosophic change to a subjective view, usually involving eternalistic elements, amounts to an avoidance of the real cases of grief and anxiety, which may be due to misfortunes resulting from alienation, economic insecurity, or the threat and consequences of war.

The vacuous subjective dimension of descriptive analysis must follow the course of the real world and actual experience, so that it always operates with borrowed contents. By its very nature it thus becomes a means of evading the pressing problems of mankind. In general, it can be viewed as one more way to search for and to find an alternative to changing the social order, as a learned way to allow the *status quo* to stand in its basic relations. That is done while pronouncing noble-sounding but still vacuous ideals of freedom, happiness, harmony, etc., at a time when there is still so much lack of freedom, so much unhappiness, and so much conflict. At a time when the profit motive has developed to such a point that the continued existence of mankind is threatened by a possible terminal war, it is worse than impotent to pronounce categorical imperatives in the traditional style; it is a travesty, and a relic of philosophic thought which once had its restricted historical significance. Above all, it is necessary to make concrete reference to existing social relations: does one propose to be a nonparticipant, or to change those relations; does one propose to continue the profit system, wage labor, and the competitive conflicts leading to wars, or to change them, with the greatest possible satisfaction of the needs of all human beings the goal to be achieved? The abolition of the private ownership of the means of production and distribution was advocated by socialists and also by Lewis H. Morgan,[5] who asserted that "a mere property career is not the final destiny of mankind," and that "the dissolution of society bids fair to become the termination of a career of which property is the end and aim."

Such radicalism of thought was never achieved by pure philosophers, and was rarely approached by any philosophers in the tradition. It is only a materialistic type of suspension and critical examination of beliefs that could become a methodological stage in a process leading to a real transformation of social relations. Impotent in itself, it must be informed by the factual knowledge disclosing the nature of the economic system and the nature of actual human problems; and it must be understood and given sufficient political as well as industrial expression if it is to be effective. For the materialistic reflective procedure there is no flight to subjective processes and essences. The structures discerned in human relations and in experience are always disclosed by means of the facts themselves, on the basis of a world in which human knowers – and philosophic thought – are recent and passing events in a beginningless and endless cosmic process. The specialized *epoché* of pure subjectivism leads nowhere socially or historically. The materialistic reflective analysis under which the pure *epoché* may be ordered, with appropriate reinterpretation and elimination of dogmas and rigid elements, leaves nothing out. Nothing human is foreign to it; everything in real existence is proper to it; and all phases of experience and thought, including philosophy, are in its domain, which makes it truly universal. The presumed universality claimed for the subjective *epoché* is really an unfounded claim, for it operates on the surface of the world with vacuous fictions in a nonexistent, artificial realm.

Viewed factually, every knowing being is conditioned by a social system and by a cultural tradition. That is just as true as the location of man and all his activities in the natural world. These are general truths. In particular, there are special conditions and circumstances constituting the setting for an individual or a social class, and these circumstances determine the starting point for their thought and action. The social setting differs in

[5] Cf. Lewis H. Morgan, *Ancient Society*, published in 1877 (Cleveland: World Book Co., 1963), p. 561.

medieval Europe, in England in the seventeenth century, in France in the eighteenth century, and in England and America in the nineteenth and twentieth century. The point is to see the various ways in which an individual inherits from and reacts to traditions of culture and to existing social institutions and practices.

From the physical and organic perspective, an individual is an organization of matter described by a group of sciences. From the sociohistorical perspective, he is an organization of matter conditioned by social realities: he is a member of a social class, with or without religious beliefs; he is indebted to an intellectual tradition; and he has his individual peculiarities, which may lead him to oppose the social class to which he belonged. In the usual case there is not a total immersion in a tradition, and all its offerings are rarely absorbed. The diverse ways in which people select ideas for their purposes add to the complexity of their sociohistorical relationships. A person may derive ideas and thought patterns from extinct social orders; and he may inventively imagine conditions which probably never have existed. Although it is possible to formulate dominant cultural traits for a given period, allowance must always be made for individual and group differences.

To view the matter concretely, it can be revealing to consider what a given philosopher says or implies about property relations and social classes, and to ascertain whether there is any relationship between those views and his general philosophy. Are there any effects on his ontology, epistemology, and philosophy of values? The same line of inquiry could be directed to others – to social scientists, mathematicians, etc. The relevance, if any, of such views to their problems, methods, solutions, and doctrines would have to be determined. Some philosophers were explicitly concerned with such questions and took a definite stand on them – in the recent past, for example, Comte, Spencer, Huxley, Marx and Engels, Lenin – and at the opposite extreme are those who renounced the existing world *in toto*.

The domain of philosophy and its problems varies historically. The important question to be answered is, how ideas and problems are related to the social order, and that requires historical inquiry. The so-called perennial problems of the philosophical tradition, including what have been called "the great problems of thought and being," have been regarded as being above the "accidents" of history. A closer examination of those problems from a more complete historical perspective is accordingly called for. By means of assumptive reasoning and linguistic usage, philosophy has been lifted definitionally to a transcendent realm. Sociohistorical criticism and a clarification of meanings are necessary in order to return the subject matter of philosophy to its natural habitat. It is seen therewith that philosophy occurs as one item among many others in a cultural context. It may therefore be advantageous to formulate the question about relationships to the social order in a more general way, considering ideas and the social reality in general.

Not all ideas are vital and real in their reference. Especially in philosophy there is a large amount of traditional material, carried on even where innovations and new motives occur. No one begins his thinking with a clean slate; there is always indebtedness to the past, including the most recent past and present social motivations. This applies also to the most radical of pure subjectivists. The very apparatus for his procedure, and the entire content of the "inner" realm which he delineates, are themselves products or by-products of a natural and cultural process of development, with indebtedness to society and the historical past. Nothing could be more false in fact than to suppose that one could make a completely fresh start, placing all existence in abeyance, and making no use of the knowledge derived through natural experience. What such an attempt shows is not a new foundation for philosophy, but rather what can or cannot be accomplished by means of a specialized, contrary-to-fact procedure. As a part of nature and the result of a long process of development, man is both causal and caused in his activity. The sons of men can never get away from their lineage, even if they confuse abstraction with existence by means of the seductive cloak of an "ontology." That tenuous term has been used to shield illicit thought processes, applying the term "being" where "existence" would hardly be condoned. This observation also applies to the expression "formal ontology," which is readily extended to apply to all ideal meanings, with the result that the domain of existence becomes greatly overpopulated.

10. The "Cooperation of Methods" and Methodological Pluralism

Throughout the present essay a place was provided for the rigorous methodological use of subjectivism as a specialized procedure which can be employed along with other procedures for appropriate problems. That the subjectivist procedure can be reinterpreted critically and embraced to other scientific methods has been pointed out; for it is indeed an addition to scientific methods in its rigorous form. It is more properly called "radically reflective epistemic analysis" in its de-transcendentalized, non-idealistic, and critically revised form. The class of scientific methods is never closed and all rational methods which are logically acceptable, including philosophical procedures, can be regarded as scientific. When the present writer spoke of the "cooperation of methods" in his *Foundation of Phenomenology* and later writings (cf. *Naturalism and Subjectivism*, for example, where it is discussed in connection with the idea of methodological pluralism), he had this thought in mind. There was no intention to effect a "compromise" in using the phrase "cooperation of methods." Originally, it was a warning to pure phenomenologists against overextension of their method, and it meant no more than the recognition of a plurality of procedures to solve diverse problems, including methodogenic problems. It is a characteristic philosophic practice to embrace one type of procedure to a standpoint, and to oppose that procedure to all others, while making tacit use of their findings.

The spectacle of a philosopher seeing only deduction as a method, in opposition to any or all inductive procedures, would be quaint. The principle of a plurality of logically acceptable methods is now well instated. Quite different, of course, is the more complex question of total philosophies which are at war with one another. To suggest that lions and lambs lie down together peacefully, that they "cooperate," would be worse than foolish, and no such thing was ever intended. Similarly, a total subjectivistic philosophy, or any one of its opponents, including a thoroughgoing materialism, would not "cooperate" as opposing philosophies, and that was never suggested by the present writer. That could only appear possible to those who have failed to understand the meaning of subjectivism and materialism as total philosophies. Taken as a universal philosophy, idealistic subjectivism simply fails, just as so many other attempts fail because of dogmas and inadequacies. But the same is not to be said for any type of procedure which has a specialized function and has been rendered acceptable logically. Such types of procedure, including a restatement of all rigorous methods in naturalistic or materialistic terms, may be assimilated to a larger, science-oriented philosophy employing an open-ended methodology. The pluralism in this case is methodological, whereas the basic ontology is monistic in at least one sense of that term. But this conception of monism does not preclude diversity.[6]

When the *Foundation of Phenomenology* was first published (1943), it was especially important for serious phenomenologists to avoid insulation and to come to terms with science-oriented philosophers giving full recognition to the importance of their methods of inquiry; and also, on the other hand, that all descriptive findings be accepted in the total corpus of scientific knowledge, which includes philosophically achieved knowledge worthy of being designated scientific. At the present time (1970), the present writer would not be inclined to speak of "cooperation" because of the enormous post-Husserlian literature, ranging from "right" to "left"; it is sufficient for all purposes to place the emphasis upon pluralism, or methodological pluralism. But it may be possible that pluralism in turn could lead to misunderstanding, for historical reasons. In short, one must use such terms as cooperation and pluralism with critical caution, and not arbitrarily attach the thought of compromise to cooperation, or perhaps scattered diversity to pluralism. That would be as superficial as it would be mistaken.

The very nature of phenomenology itself has become problematical in the larger literature of that philosophical tendency. The early and middle periods of Husserl, which were largely impelled by his logical interests, have been contrasted to the later development of Husserl, with interest turning to the problems of a constitutive phenomenology, the conception of a life-world, and the critique of science. The writings of the later period have been regarded by some scholars as opening up a new way to philos-

[6] Cf. M. Farber, *Basic Issues of Philosophy* (New York: Harper & Row, 1968), pp. 153ff.

ophic thought. There is some degree of resemblance to the contrast between the early and the older Marx, resulting in the distinction between the humanistic and the economic-revolutionary images, which have been opposed. In both cases the overdrawn contrasts have been misconstrued and misused. Thus a materialistic realism has been declared to be indicated in Husserl's late period, on the basis of passages in his treatment of "Passive Synthesis." However, such an interpretation neglects the overriding subjectivism of his total philosophy.

The term phenomenology is not intended to be restricted to Husserl's version of it. Anyone is free to use the term in any way he pleases, and a whole spectrum of possible usages has already appeared. Husserl's conception of a pure phenomenology is the most important version appearing in the subjectivistic literature, in that it represents a strict methodological discipline which seeks to determine a special science, despite the serious objections which have been raised at numerous points. It is also important historically as representing, in the universalized form of a supposedly complete philosophy, a distinctive and perhaps final form of idealism.

To order the phenomenological procedure among the methods of inquiry under the heading of general methodology is not to subordinate or compromise the whole notion of methodological pluralism in an unwarranted manner, as suggested by L. Rossi,[7] on the ground that it is not really a pluralism if the phenomenological method winds up with a subordinate role. With the qualifications already indicated, there is sufficient reason to regard it as worthy of being recognized as a member of the group of acceptable methods, and it is not at all necessary that all procedures be equally fruitful or important to be associated as methods of inquiry and knowledge. China and Chile are both appropriate candidates for membership in the future "pluralistic" organization of the nations and peoples of the world, and membership in the class of methods of knowledge should be open to the many kinds of procedures proving useful or promising for the solution of the great variety of problems. The subsequent assimilation of the phenomenological procedure to a materialistic, science-oriented philosophy undertakes at the same time to preserve its merits

[7] Cf. Il Verri, Nr. 32, Bologna, March 1970.

and findings. Originally achieved in an idealistic and subjectivistic setting, they can now be seen not to require that setting. An equivalent formulation can be provided by the endless science-oriented conception of methodology, on the ground of a natural and cultural world which is not only being interpreted, but also, in part, progressively changed by the contributive activities of human beings.

ARON GURWITSCH

PERCEPTUAL COHERENCE AS THE FOUNDATION OF THE JUDGMENT OF PREDICATION

In three books, which belong to the last period of his life, Husserl laid down the program for a phenomenological theory of logic (understood in a very broad sense) and the sciences, especially physics, and took decisive steps towards its implementation.[1] According to this program, the disciplines in question have to be referred, and their phenomenological origin or genesis of sense (*Sinnesgenese*) has to be traced back to perceptual consciousness.[2] The guiding idea is that perceptual consciousness contains the germs or roots of whatever entities are the subject matter of study in the disciplines in question, and that those entities are brought to full development and given their definitive shape by means of specific mental operations.

Here we propose to reexamine a problem already dealt with by Husserl in *Erfahrung und Urteil*, namely the problem of the phenomenological origin of the judgment of predication – that is to say, the judgment of the form "this S is p" as exemplified by "this table is brown." However, we shall be led to modify Husserl's account in a certain respect because we shall avail ourselves of results which we have established in the phenomenological theory of perception. It is therefore necessary to begin by discussing some problems related to perception and to dwell upon those problems at some length.

---

[1] The books are *Formale und transzendentale Logik* (Halle, 1929; English translation by D. Cairns, *Formal and Transcendental Logic*, The Hague, 1969 – henceforth referred to as *F.T.L.*); *Erfahrung und Urteil* (Prague, 1939, reprinted Hamburg, 1948; henceforth referred to as *E.U.*); *Die Krisis der europäischen Wissenschaften und die transzendentale Phänomenologie*, Husserliana VI (The Hague, 1954; English translation by D. Carr, *The Crisis of European Sciences and Transcendental Phenomenology*, Evanston, 1970; henceforth referred to as *Crisis*).

[2] For the formulation of that program with respect to the phenomenological foundations of logic, cf. especially Husserl, *F.T.L.*, § 86.

1. General Outline of the Adumbrational Theory of Perception

All phenomenological discussion of matters pertaining to perception must take its departure from the adumbrational theory of perception which Husserl has developed in several of his writings.[3] According to this theory every particular perception is a one-sided apprehension of the thing perceived. The latter appears from a certain side, under a certain aspect, in a certain orientation (as far or near, as centrally or peripherally located, and the like); it displays some of its properties and qualities, and its behavior under the given conditions. At the same time the thing presents itself as capable of appearing under different aspects, of exhibiting other qualities than those it exhibits at present, of displaying a different behavior under conditions more or less well specified. Furthermore, the thing perceived through a particular one-sided perception is encountered [4] as identically the same over and against the mentioned possible variations concerning its manner of appearance.

Two implications of the adumbrational theory of perception have to be brought out.

In the first place, perceptual consciousness yields an immediate and direct access to, and contact with, the thing perceived. In perceptual encounter we are at the thing itself without there being any need of, or room for, any intermediary to mediate between the act of perception and the thing perceived through that act. Because it is essentially characterized as intentional, consciousness must not be conceived of as an isolated and secluded domain severed by an unbridgeable gulf from whatever is

[3] Husserl, *Ideen zu einer reinen Phänomenologie und phänomenologischen Philosophie* (Halle, 1922, and *Husserliana* III, The Hague, 1950; henceforth referred to as *Ideen*, I), §§ 41ff. and 149ff.; *Cartesianische Meditationen* (*Husserliana* I, The Hague, 1963; English translation by D. Cairns, *Cartesian Meditations*, The Hague, 1960), §§ 17ff.; *E.U.*, § 8; *Crisis*, §§ 45ff.; *Phänomenologische Psychologie* (Husserliana IX, The Hague, 1962), § 36, App. XVI and XVII.

[4] Following the suggestion of R. Sokolowski, *The Formation of Husserl's Concept of Constitution* (*Phaenomenologica* 18, The Hague, 1964), pp. 4f., we use "encounter" as the English equivalent of "Erfahrung" and "experience" as that of "Erlebnis." We encounter whatever is "transcendent to subjectivity," that is to say things and objects in the widest possible sense so as to include not only material things but also ideal entities of every description such as propositions and concatenations of propositions, numbers and relations between them, geometrical systems as well as historical events, social situations, political and legal institutions, and so forth. What we experience are our own mental states, among them those through which we encounter objects. To express it briefly, we encounter objects and experience our encounters.

exterior to that domain. In experiencing acts of consciousness we do not, so to speak, move within a self-contained domain of interiority; on the contrary, we are in contact with the objects encountered.[5] To be sure, not every encounter takes place in the distinguishing mode of originarity, which is the privilege of perceptual consciousness, though not of that consciousness exclusively. In the present context it suffices to note that perceptual encounter is an originary apprehension of the thing perceived offering itself in bodily presence, in flesh and blood, so to speak, and we do not have to enter into a discussion of the relations of derivative modes, such as memory, expectation, mere representation and the like, to the originary mode of perception. At any event, we wish to stress again what we have repeatedly emphasized elsewhere: [6] the insight that in our perceptual life we are directly and immediately at the things and at the world, far from being due to the subsequent emergence of existentialist philosophy, must be seen as a consequence following from Husserl's theory of the intentionality of consciousness, especially perceptual consciousness.

In the second place, because of its one-sidedness every particular perception, though a direct and immediate apprehension of the thing perceived, proves to be incomplete and insufficient, that is to say, in need of complementation. Its insufficiency and limitation are not ascertained from a point of view beyond or outside the particular perception in question, as though, so to speak, to find it incomplete the experiencing subject had to step out of his perception, as though rather than living it he had to look back at it in retrospective reflection, in one word, had to thematize and objectivate it. Here as everywhere reflection consists in nothing other than rendering explicit and disengaging what had pertained to the act reflected upon, albeit in an undisclosed fashion, previously to and independently of its being reflected upon. Incompleteness and insufficiency denote a phenomenal feature inherent and immanent in every particular per-

---

[5] Husserl, *Ideen* I, § 43; *F.T.L.*, pp. 141, 206, 248 (the pages of the German edition are indicated in the margin of the English translation); *Phänomenologische Psychologie* App. VII; *Crisis* pp. 236 and 238 (English translation, pp. 233 and 235).

[6] A. Gurwitsch, "Husserl's Theory of the Intentionality of Consciousness in Historical Perspective," II, b, in *Phenomenology and Existentialism* (ed. by E. N. Lee and M. Mandelbaum, Baltimore, 1967), and "Towards a Theory of Intentionality," *Philosophy and Phenomenological Research*, XXX (1970), pp. 366f.

ception, a feature which manifests itself in that perception pointing and referring to further perceptions through which the thing
perceived will appear under different aspects and from other
sides, will present properties and qualities which it does not display at present, will exhibit its behavior as varying along with
the changes of the concomitant circumstances. Noetically speaking, every particular perception is pervaded and permeated by
anticipations and expectancies to be fulfilled by further perceptions.

These expectancies may be, and are, affected by indeterminacy
to a higher or lesser degree depending on the comparative familiarity or unfamiliarity of the thing perceived as well as upon the
conditions (e.g., of illumination) under which it is perceived.
What is seen in the dusk of the evening at some considerable
distance appears to be a quadruped, but not until we come nearer
will we be able to tell what kind of animal that quadruped is.
Similarly, the house in front of which we are standing presents
itself as a residential building whose interior architectural arrangement and organization remains more or less indeterminate;
in the case of a building we have never entered before they even
remain highly indeterminate as far as the present perception goes.
Still by whatever indeterminacy the anticipated yieldings of
further perceptions, to which the present one points, might be
affected, those yieldings are nevertheless subject to the condition
of being in agreement and conformity with both one another and
what the present perception yields. Differently expressed, every
thing perceived is encountered in the light of a certain typicality,
it presents itself as a thing of a certain kind or type which, however, is delineated and determined in a more or less schematic
way, more correctly along more or less generic lines. What is
indeterminate is the special and concrete manner in which the
type is realized. However indeterminate the yieldings of anticipated further perceptions might be, the condition imposed upon
them is their fitting into the generic pattern and framework which
defines the typicality in whose light the thing appears through
the present perception.[7]

This is borne out when, instead of abiding by it, we change the

[7] We refer to the detailed account we have given in *The Field of Consciousness*
(Pittsburgh, 1964; henceforth referred to as *Field*), Part IV, Chapter II, 3.

standpoint from which we observe the thing either by having it move with regard to us or by moving ourselves or both. In so doing we make the thing appear under varying aspects and from different sides. Anticipations which had accompanied the initial perception find fulfillment; indeterminacies are brought to determination; properties and qualities which the thing had not exhibited thus far now present themselves, among them also the unexpected ones which likewise fit into the generically delineated framework of the type in question. For the sake of simplicity we deliberately exclude the case of a later perception being at variance with and nullifying a former one, such as when upon entering the house which had appeared as a residential building we discover that it is a medical one, as a result of which the initial perception turns out to have been deceptive.

It follows that an individual perceivable thing is related to a multiplicity of perceptions, not a single one. That multiplicity is not merely a succession of disconnected perceptions isolated from each other. On the contrary, every further perception making what had only been anticipated appear in the mode of originarity, yielding a determination of what thus far had been comparatively indeterminate, and so on, the particular perceptions come to be united with one another.[8] They coalesce into one sustained and coherent process of which the particular perceptions are experienced as phases. The unity of this process depends upon its intrinsic coherence, that is to say, upon its phases harmoniously enlarging, continuing and confirming one another. The unity and identity of the thing perceived depends upon the harmony and agreement between the phases of the perceptual process to which the thing in question is related; its existence depends, more specifically, upon the successive phases of the process mutually corroborating each other.[9] As the incompleteness of every particular perception and its need of complementation manifests itself in the anticipatory references to further perceptions, so the actual complementation takes place in the course of the perceptual process evolving in a smooth and harmonious fashion. Still that complementation is never fully consummated. However far the

[8] In this respect Husserl speaks of a "synthesis of unification" (*Einigung*) in preference to the phrase (used in earlier writings) "synthesis of identification," *Crisis*, p. 161 (English translation, p. 158).

[9] A. Gurwitsch, *Field*, Part IV, Chapter I, 3, and Chapter III, 3.

perceptual process may have developed, it always remains susceptible of further continuation. That is to say, the perceptual
process to which an individual perceivable thing is related proves
to be infinite.[10] For this reason the idea of a complete and adequate perceptual apprehension of a perceivable thing is termed
by Husserl an "Idea in the sense of Kant," i.e., the idea of an
infinite process exhibiting intrinsic coherence – in the sense just
mentioned – between all of its phases, the past ones as well as
those which are to come.[11] Since the existence of the thing
depends upon the future phases of the perceptual process agreeing
with and confirming both one another and the past phases, the
existence of the thing has the sense of presumptiveness.[12] In
other words, no perceivable thing may be posited as truly existing
and as being in reality such as it has thus far appeared to be
except with the provision that the further course of the perceptual process related to the thing in question will not necessitate
revisions, corrections or nullifications. This must not be construed to mean that the existence of perceivable things rather
than being certain is only more or less likely or probable. Rather
it must be understood as the clarification of the very sense of the
existence of those things and of the contingency by which their
existence is affected in principle.

2. Noematic Organization and Internoematic Unity

According to the theory of the intentionality of consciousness,
corresponding to every act there is an intentional correlate or
noema, that is to say, the object intended (object being understood in the widest possible sense), however taken exactly as,
and only as it is actually intended through the act in question.[13]
For example, if we think of Shakespeare as the director of the
Globe Theater, the corresponding noema is not the real historical
person who was born in 1563, died in 1616, wrote the Sonnets,
"Hamlet," "King Lear," and other plays, was director of the

---

[10] Husserl, *Ideen* I, pp. 8of., and 311ff. (The reference is to the page numbers of
the original edition given in the margin of *Husserliana* III.)
[11] *Ibid.*, § 133.
[12] *Ibid.*, pp. 86f.; *Cartesianische Meditationen*, § 28.
[13] As to the general meaning of the term "noema," cf. Husserl, *ibid.*, Abschnitt III,
Chapter III.

Globe Theater, and so on. The noema is instead that historical person under the aspect of his role and function with respect to the Globe Theater. Correspondingly, the perceptual noema is not the thing encountered *per se* with all the properties, qualities, modes of behavior under specified conditions (causal properties) which belong to it regardless of whether or not they are actually perceived, regardless also of whether they are known or still to be discovered. Rather the perceptual noema is the thing as it presents itself through the given particular perception, that is to say, the thing as appearing under a certain aspect, from a certain side, in a certain orientation, briefly in a certain manner of one-sided adumbrational presentation.[14] Among the constituents of the perceptual noema must also be counted aspects under which the thing does not appear at present, properties which it does not exhibit through the given perception, but to which the latter contains anticipatory references – however only so far as and to the extent to which those aspects and properties are actually referred to and play a role for the perception in question. In one word, the analysis of the perceptual noema as, for that matter, of any noema, must follow a strictly descriptive direction.[15]

A plurality of perceptual noemata severally correspond to the successive phases of the perceptual process in the course of which the identical thing presents itself under varying aspects. To preclude possible misunderstandings, a distinction between two cases must be made. In one case we repeatedly perceive a thing appearing in the same manner of adumbrational presentation, such as when while abiding by the same point of observation we alternately open and close our eyes, or when after an absence from a certain point of observation we return to it, such that the same noema corresponds to a multiplicity of acts. Here we are not interested in this case of which in several of our writings we have availed ourselves as a point of departure for defining intentionality as noetico-noematic correlation.[16] We are concerned

---

[14] For the notion of perceptual noema or, as he also calls it, perceptual sense (*Wahrnehmungssinn*), cf. Husserl, *ibid.*, §§ 88f. and 97f.; *Phänomenologische Psychologie*, §§ 34 and 36.

[15] A. Gurwitsch, *Field*, Part IV, Chapter II, 2.

[16] A. Gurwitsch, "On the Intentionality of Consciousness," *Philosophical Essays in Memory of Edmund Husserl* (ed. by M. Farber, Cambridge, Mass., 1940), and *Studies in Phenomenology and Psychology* (Evanston, 1966; henceforth referred to as *Studies*); "Husserl's Theory of Intentionality in Historical Perspective," II, *loc. cit.*; and "Towards a Theory of Intentionality," *loc. cit.*

instead with the second case in which an identical thing appears in the course of the perceptual process in varying manners of adumbrational presentation such that a plurality not only of acts but of noemata is involved as well.

At once the problem arises as to the noematic counterpart of the unity of the perceptual process. *What kind of noematic organization and internoematic unity corresponds to the successive acts of perception coalescing into one sustained process of which, because of the intrinsic coherence prevailing among them, they become phases?* Obviously, the multiple noemata belong together by virtue of their common relatedness to the same thing. We are then confronted by the questions: What is the identical thing in contradistinction to the multiple noemata which all differ from one another? How is their relatedness to the identical thing and also to one another to be understood? To formulate our problem in a still more precise way: *What makes each one of the noemata in question to be one particular adumbrational appearance of a thing which as identically the same is susceptible of presenting itself under different aspects and from different sides? What founds the consciousness of the identity of the thing in the face of the multiple perceptual noemata?* The same question may, and must, be raised with regard to the properties: What makes the different qualities and properties, visual, tactile, causal, etc. properties and qualities of one and the same thing?

Husserl has dealt with this problem by means of analyzing the noema in general. At the first stage of his analysis he makes a distinction between what he calls the "noematic sense" or – as we might also say – the noematic What and noematic characters, especially those concerning the mode of givenness such as given in perception, in memory, in clear intuition (*klar anschaulich*), in thought (*denkmässig*), etc.[17] Disregarding the characters which indicate the mode in which we are conscious of something, we retain the noematic sense, that is to say, that of which we are conscious, taken in a strictly descriptive orientation exactly such

[17] Husserl, *Ideen*, I, § 130. As to the noematic characters in question, cf. also § 99. In the terminology of the *Logische Untersuchungen* (Halle, 1913; English translation by J. N. Findlay, New York, 1970; henceforth referred to as *L.U.*), II, V, § 20, the distinction is expressed as that between the matter (*Materie*) and the quality of the act. We may also mention the doxic characters or, noematically speaking, existential characters (*Seinscharaktere*) such as real, likely, presumable, questionable, doubtful (*Ideen*, I, § 103), although Husserl does not refer to them in *Ideen*, I, § 130.

as it presents itself.[18] The expressions to be used for the description of the noematic sense or noematic nucleus may be formal-
ontological in character such as "object," "property," "state of
affairs," material-ontological such as "thing," "figure," "cause";
they may, furthermore, have material content (*sachhaltig*) [19] such
as "rough," "hard," "colored," and finally they may include
indeterminacies as when in describing a thing as it presents itself
in perceptual encounter we accurately say that its back, not seen
at present, will have some color – though it remains indeterminate which particular color.[20] This justifies the designation of the
noematic sense as noematic What.

At the second stage of his analysis Husserl discerns within the
noematic sense a central core or, more correctly, a central point
of unity or of connection, a "carrier of predicates," a "carrier of
sense," a carrier which is but a pure X devoid in itself of all
determinations, yet capable and even in need of being determined; the "determinable subject of its possible predicates, the
pure X apart from all predicates" is to be distinguished from the
very predicates.[21] The terms "subject" and "predicate" must not
be construed as logical categories, rather they are to be understood to express perceptual structures – all logical categories
deriving from underlying structures of perceptual encounter. For
this reason we prefer Husserl's terminology in *Phänomenologische
Psychologie* [22] and, in the further exposition and discussion of his
theory as developed in the text of *Ideen* I referred to, we shall
replace "subject" by "substratum" or "substratum pole" (Husserl's phrase) and "predicate" by "property," "quality," or "attribute" (*Merkmal*). Though they have to be distinguished, substratum and attributes can neither be severed nor separated from
one another. Because of its being devoid of all determinations,

---

[18] Sometimes Husserl also calls the noematic sense the "noematic nucleus," a term
we have used in *Field*, pp. 179f. However, Husserl also gives to the term "nucleus"
a somewhat different meaning (*Ideen*, I, § 132).

[19] We are indebted to D. Cairns for rendering "*sachhaltig*" by "having material
content."

[20] Cf. Husserl, *E.U.*, pp. 31f., §21, c, and p. 370 concerning "open possibilities"
in contradistinction to "problematic possibilities"; see also A. Schutz, "Choosing
Among Projects of Action," VII, *Philosophy and Phenomenological Research*, XII
(1951) and *Collected Papers* (*Phaenomenologica*, XI, The Hague, 1962), Vol. I; and
A. Gurwitsch, *Field*, Part IV, Chapter II, 4.

[21] Husserl, *Ideen*, I, § 131.

[22] Husserl, *Phänomenologische Psychologie*, § 35.

the substratum as a pure X calls for attributes by which it is determined. Conversely, the attributes as attributes of "something" require a substratum pole in which they inhere. Every noematic sense as a one-sided adumbrational presentation of a thing susceptible, i.e., encountered as susceptible, of appearing in different manners of adumbrational presentation must contain the pure X, the substratum pole which alone makes possible the distinction between the "noematic object" *simpliciter* (*schlecht-hin*) and that object as determined in a particular manner of presentation (*Gegenstand im Wie seiner Bestimmtheiten*). On the other hand, since no thing can be encountered except in a certain manner of adumbrational presentation, there can be no substratum pole without attributes inhering in it, no carrier of sense without a noematic sense which it carries.

By pointing out a special noematic element, Husserl seems to provide an answer to the questions raised before. If multiple properties and qualities are encountered as attributes of the same thing it is because the several noemata, of which the properties in question are constituents, have, all of them, the same central noematic element in common. Quite in general, noemata which differ from one another as to their noematic sense and also as to their mode of givenness (some corresponding to perceptions, others to memories) are related to the same thing and, hence, also to one another by virtue of the same pure X being contained in every one of them. The noematic counterpart of successive perceptions coalescing into the unity of one sustained process is the internoematic unity which is based upon the presence and the unifying function of an identical element in all the noematic senses concerned. Upon the presence of that element depends the consciousness of the thing perceptually encountered as identically the same, of which the multiple noemata are various adumbrational presentations. In the course of the perceptual process the noemata involved prove to agree as to their central element or, as Husserl puts it, their determinable X's come to coincidence (*Deckung*) with one another.

With regard to the central noematic element the question may, and must, be raised as to whether it actually corresponds to ascertained and ascertainable phenomenal findings or whether it is not rather posited as a theoretical construct. Examining a noema we find indeed the difference between the noematic What or sense and the noematic characters. However, we do not discern within the noematic sense a central element, a pure X, a mere carrier of sense. To be sure, there is the consciousness of the identical thing which, in the course of the perceptual process, appears under varying aspects and from different sides, and to which various noemata are related. But it does not follow that the consciousness of the thing's identity must be based upon an identical element common to all noemata related to that thing. The consciousness in question may depend upon the form in which the pertinent noemata are organized with respect to one another, upon the specific form of unity prevailing in the group or system which they compose and to which they belong – a form of organization which, in the final analysis, is rooted in the specific organization of each particular noema. Although in *Ideen* I, he has introduced and emphasized the notion of the noema and has devoted extensive analyses to it, Husserl has not explicitly dealt with problems concerning noematic and internoematic organization.[23] In the context under discussion he finds himself confronted with an organizational problem. The descriptive analysis of the noematic sense yields a set (*Inbegriff*) of formal-ontological and material-ontological terms (*Prädikate*) and, finally, such terms as have material content to a higher or lesser degree of determinateness. Within this set and among its terms there prevails unity which, however, Husserl points out, is not "unity in the sense in which any complex, any combination (*Verbindung*) ... would be called unity."[24] We take that to mean that the set in question is not a mere sum, a mere aggregate of terms. Rather than entering into an analysis of the structural organization of the set, Husserl resorts to positing a special noematic element, namely the pure X or pure carrier of sense which has no other function than that of bestowing unity upon the set by

---

[23] With the possible exception of *Ideen* I, Husserl's analyses move, for the most part, along the noetic rather than noematic lines. This, of course, is not to say that the noematic aspect of consciousness is disregarded or neglected. But it does mean that it is almost always approached from the noetic side and with closest reference to the latter, hence not sufficiently in its own right. This holds for Husserl's writings subsequent to *Ideen* I, both those published in his life-time and those posthumously published. Obviously, it holds for *L.U.* in which the notion of the noema is not yet explicitly formulated, though amply prepared.

[24] Husserl, *Ideen* I, p. 270.

serving as a substratum or pole of inherence for its terms. In this respect Husserl's theory is somewhat reminiscent of Locke's notion of substance which is assumed by us because the qualities, which cannot be conceived as capable of subsisting by themselves, require a substratum in which they inhere; but the latter has no further function nor serves any further purpose since the perceived thing is to be accounted for exclusively in terms of its qualities.[25] With respect to Husserl's theory, the question must be raised as to what distinguishes the pure X as central element of all the noemata related to a house from the central element common to all the noemata related to a tree, all determinations being yielded, and all anticipations being motivated, by constituents of the noematic sense or perceptual sense (*Wahrnehmungssinn*) other than the pure X.[26] The conclusion that the pure X as a mere carrier of noematic sense is the same for all perceivable things appears to be as unavoidable as it is unacceptable.

Gestalt theory provides the theoretical means for dealing with the problems of both noematic organization and internoematic unity. Elsewhere[27] we have introduced the notions of functional significance and Gestalt-coherence for the descriptive characterization and analysis of a Gestalt-contexture (one of the simplest examples being a melody) whose constituents mutually determine and qualify one another. A constituent of a Gestalt-contexture is phenomenally defined and made to be what it is by the role which it plays for, and the function which it has within, the Gestalt-contexture as a whole, that is to say, with respect to its other constituents. The constituents of a Gestalt-contexture may be said to be present or to be contained within one another, if "being contained" is understood in the sense of their mutual qualification and determination such that a constituent loses its phenomenal identity and ceases to be what it was by being removed from its Gestalt-contexture either by being taken isolatedly or by being inserted into another Gestalt-contexture in

---

[25] Locke, *An Essay Concerning Human Understanding*, Book II, Chapter XXIII, 1ff.

[26] Our criticism is borne out by Husserl's own discussion (*Phänomenologische Psychologie*, pp. 181f.) of the empty horizon of anticipated properties – partly highly indeterminate, partly even unknown – of the thing perceived as a character pertaining to the substratum pole.

[27] A. Gurwitsch, *Field*, Part II, 6, 8, 10.

which it would have a different functional significance – both cases at times amounting to a most radical phenomenal transformation. Another way of expressing the same state of affairs is to say that the Gestalt-contexture as a whole is present in each of its constituents so far as each constituent realizes the whole contexture at the specific place which it holds within it. We thus come to be confronted with a kind of unity – unity by Gestalt-coherence – which is not due to a supervenient special factor bestowing unity upon materials which, because they are lacking unity by themselves, are in need of being unified from without. *Unity by Gestalt-coherence* denotes, on the contrary, *an internal unity* which consists in nothing other than *the constituents of a Gestalt-contexture deriving from, and assigning to, one another their functional significances in thoroughgoing reciprocity*. It is needless to stress that unity by Gestalt-coherence is totally different from categorial unity established merely by thought, namely by taking together and colligating any unrelated elements which are just juxtaposed, and which from their being taken together derive no phenomenal feature whatever.[28] Categorial unity is mentioned here merely for the sake of completeness.

The notions of functional significance and Gestalt-coherence may be employed for the analysis of the structure of the perceptual noema.[29] Within the perceptual noema the distinction has to be made between constituents which are, and those which are not, given in direct and originary sense-encounter, the latter constituents being the noematic correlates of the anticipations and expectancies which pervade and permeate the present perception. All the constituents mutually determine and qualify one another. Suppose we perceive a building presenting itself from the front. That perceptual encounter could not be what it is were it not for references to other sides of the building, not seen at the moment, which contribute towards determining the noematic sense of the present perception as one-sided adumbrational appearance of the building from its front side. Moreover, the front appears as an architectural form requiring a specific total architectural configuration into which it fits. On the one hand, the

[28] Husserl, *Philosophie der Arithmetik* (Halle, 1891), pp. 77ff.; *L.U.*, II, III, § 23, and II, VI, § 61.
[29] For the following, cf. A. Gurwitsch, *Field*, Part IV, Chapter II, 1 and 7.

perceptual appearance in question arouses or rather motivates [30] certain expectancies concerning the total architectural configuration or, noematically expressed, it predelineates and pre-traces the total architectural configuration along more or less indeterminate but specific generic and typical lines. On the other hand, the total configuration determines the front of the building as an architectural detail occupying a specific place within the total architectural configuration. In this sense the latter may be said to be present in each and every detail; conversely, each and every detail makes its specific contribution towards the architectural configuration as a whole. The phenomenon under discussion is by no means confined to perceptual encounters which pertain to the same realm of sensibility. At night we hear a noise as emanating from a passing automobile which we do not see. The noise is experienced as an auditory encounter of an automobile.[31] Again that which is given in genuine sense-encounter is determined as to its sense, significance, or "meaning" by what is accessible in the mode of originarity through perceptions other than auditory ones.

It is now possible to answer the questions raised before in a different way than Husserl has done it. All perceptual noemata related to the same thing mutually qualify and determine, even demand and support, one another. That is to say, the noemata in question form a system which has unity by Gestalt-coherence. As to the *perceived thing*, it is – we submit – *nothing other than the internoematic system itself, i.e., the system of the multiple adumbrational presentations and of the properties and qualities exhibited in those presentations.*[32] Since the unity in question is unity by Gestalt-coherence, no special unifying factor or agency is required

[30] "Motivation" is meant in the strict phenomenological sense as defined by Husserl, *Ideen*, I, pp. 89f. and 292.

[31] Cf. M. Merleau Ponty, *Phénoménologie de la Perception* (Paris, 1945), pp. 265f. (English translation by C. Smith, *Phenomenology of Perception*, New York, 1962, pp. 229f.)

[32] According to Merleau Ponty, *ibid.*, p. 48: "Un objet est un organisme de couleurs, d'odeurs, de sons, d'apparences tactiles qui se symbolisent et se modifient l'un l'autre et s'accordent l'un avec l'autre selon une logique réelle ..." (English translation, p. 38.) Cf. also J. P. Sartre, *L'Etre et le Néant* (Paris, 1943), p. 236: "La fluidité, la tiédeur, la couleur bleuâtre, la mobilité onduleuse de l'eau d'une piscine sont données d'un coup au travers les unes des autres et c'est cette interpénétration totale que se nomme le *ceci*." (English translation by H. E. Barnes, *Being and Nothingness*, New York, 1956, p. 186.)

any longer, and the pure X or mere carrier of sense, which is a theoretical construct rather than being phenomenally ascertainable, proves dispensable. In other words, *Husserl's account of perceptual encounter in terms of inherence is replaced by an account*, derived from results due to Gestalt theory, *in terms of coherence*. The consciousness of the thing perceived as identically the same throughout the perceptual process and in the face of the various noemata concerned is not founded upon a special element common to those noemata. Rather it is the consciousness of the very identity of the internoematic system itself. The difference between a particular perceptual noema and the thing to which that noema is related proves to be that between a member of a system and the *system itself* which *as a whole is present in each of its members*, in every one-sided adumbrational presentation, in every property exhibited. The term "substratum" is either to be eliminated altogether from the phenomenological account of perceptual encounter or, if retained, it is to be given a different meaning so as no longer to denote the relationship of inherence but instead that of the pertaining of a "part" to a "whole" – the "whole" being the very system of its "parts," each one of which is made to be what it is by virtue of the functional significance it has with respect to the other "parts" of the system.[33] Herein we see the noematic counterpart of the organizational structure of the perceptual process whose phases mutually continue and confirm one another.[34] What in the structure of a particular noema is given in an enveloped form, namely its constituents reciprocally determining and qualifying each other, comes to be disenveloped, unfolded, and unravelled in the course of the perceptual process.[35] We claim for our account faithfully to render the phenomenal state of affairs: *the thing itself* appearing under different aspects and from different sides, being manifest in its various properties and qualities or, as we may say, the *internoematic system as a whole presenting itself from the varying vantage points of its several members*. Finally, the indeterminateness by which every perceptual encounter is affected may also be accounted for in terms of

[33] As to the Gestalt theoretical conception of "parts" and "wholes," cf. A. Gurwitsch, *Field*, Part II, 10.

[34] For a Gestalt theoretical account of the perceptual process, cf. *ibid.*, Part IV, Chapter I, 5.

[35] *Ibid.*, pp. 294f.

Gestalt theory. If a Gestalt-contexture is not yet completed, but still sufficiently established as to its generic style and type, its continuation and, perhaps, completion is subject to the condition of agreeing with, and fitting into, the generic and typical framework as established thus far. We may refer to the "law of good continuation" or "law of Prägnanz" as formulated by Wertheimer.[36] Elsewhere [37] we have proposed the expression "Principle of conformity to sense" (*Prinzip der Sinneskonformität*), a principle of which the law of good continuation is a special case.

3. The Phenomenological Origin of the Judgment of Predication

Passing from perceptual encounter to predication, we shall follow Husserl's treatment of this transition as presented in *Erfahrung und Urteil*. Some of Husserl's analyses will be modified, others will be reinterpreted in the light of the results achieved in the preceding part.

In accordance with his general program, Husserl takes his departure from perceptual encounter of which he distinguishes two kinds. One is "simple apprehension" (*schlichte Erfassung*), the other is "explicating contemplation" (*explizierende Betrachtung*).

In simple apprehension the thing is merely surveyed; it is perceived in a rather global way with little or no discernment of details.[38] Husserl refers to the case of a vague perception as when a visual object appears at the periphery of the field of vision such that hardly any of its properties are given with any distinctions. Repeatedly he calls the thing as given in simple apprehension an indeterminate substratum susceptible of undergoing perceptual determinations by explicating contemplation.[39] The notion of an indeterminate substratum is reminiscent of the previously discussed conception of the pure X or mere carrier of sense. While the latter terms do not occur in *Erfahrung und Urteil*, the notion

---

[36] M. Wertheimer, "Untersuchungen zur Lehre von der Gestalt" II, *Psychologische Forschung*, IV (1923), p. 324. (The relevant passage is translated in W. D. Ellis, *A Source Book of Gestalt Psychology*, New York, 1967, p. 83.) Cf. also K. Koffka, *Principles of Gestalt Psychology* (New York, 1935), pp. 110, 171, 174f.

[37] A. Gurwitsch, "Beitrag zur phänomenologischen Theorie der Wahrnehmung," *Zeitschrift für philosophische Forschung*, XIII (1959), p. 436; also in *Studies*, p. 348.

[38] Husserl, *E.U.*, pp. 112ff.

[39] *Ibid.*, pp. 126, 130, 242, 249.

of a substratum, understood as pole of inherence, plays a pre-
dominant role. Apart from the criticism which we have formulated with respect to the notion of an indeterminate substratum,
this notion is at variance with Husserl's emphatic insistence upon
every perceived thing presenting itself in the light of a certain
typicality or under the horizon of some pre-acquaintanceship.[40]
In fact, however indistinct the perception of a thing might be, it
appears at least as a spatial object, no matter how vaguely
localized. On the level of perceptual encounter, the notion of an
indeterminate substratum cannot even be admitted as a legitimate idealization since the actualization of the ideal limit-case
is in principle precluded by the essential nature of perceptual
consciousness.

More adequate – we submit – is Husserl's description of simple
apprehension in terms of the interest of the perceiving subject
who aims at surveying the perceived thing in a global way rather
than entering into, penetrating and studying its details.[41] In
elaborating somewhat this hint of Husserl, we first note that the
comparative familiarity or unfamiliarity of the thing perceived
as well as the comparative distinctness or indistinctness of the
perception of it are hardly of importance in the present respect.
For a thing to be perceptually accessible, it must exhibit some
property or quality. Even when it is observed under the most
unfavorable circumstances, the thing appears as having some
spatial shape and being somehow colored, no matter how vague
its shape and how unobtrusive its color. Regardless of the degree
of distinctness or indistinctness of the perception, *in simple apprehension the perceiving glance does not stop at, still less focus upon,
the property or quality*, which yields an entry into the thing
perceived. Rather the *perceiving glance passes through that property* which, in a certain sense, is transparent; *the glance is directed
to the thing perceived in its globality*. Noematically expressed, *the
thing appears as an undifferentiated unity*,[42] none of the constituents of the perceptual noema having any prominence.

Explicating contemplation presupposes simple apprehension
and is accounted for by Husserl in terms of thematizing activ-

[40] *Ibid.*, § 8; see also pp. 125 and 143.
[41] *Ibid.*, p. 113.
[42] In *E.U.*, p. 243, Husserl himself speaks in this connection of "ungeschiedene
Einheit."

ities.[43] In passing from simple apprehension to explicating contemplation, the thing as given in the former mode, the substratum
S, understood in the sense of pole of inherence, remains "maintained in grasp." [44] At the same time, another thematizing glance
comes to be directed to some property p of S, which has aroused
perceptual interest. Both thematizing activities, however, do not
occur merely simultaneously, side by side, so to speak. Between
them an overlapping (*Überschiebung*) or a coincidence (*Deckung*)
takes place, such that while S is throughout maintained in grasp
as the primary or principal theme, p is grasped as a subservient
theme subordinate to S. That is to say, p is not grasped as a
theme in its own right, but as a theme relative to the theme S,
as something concerning S and, in this sense, dependent upon
S.[45] In other words, p is grasped as a determination or an attribute of S. Following Husserl, the notions of substratum as such
(*"Substratgegenstand als solcher"*) and attributes or determinations (*"Bestimmungen"*), as these notions are to be understood
on the perceptual level, have their phenomenological origin in
explicating contemplation [46] – S as given in simple apprehension
now becoming a substratum ready for, and requiring, determination by attributes. Such a determination takes place by means
of a *synthesis*, the attribute p by virtue of the mentioned coincidence being incorporated into S which, in turn, undergoes a
modification, namely an enrichment of sense and content. Still
more to clarify the point in question, let us consider Husserl's
account of a continuing explicating contemplation which passes
from the property p to another property q. At the second step,
S is still maintained in grasp as the principal theme. However,
it is no longer maintained as it was at the first step, as a "pure"
S, so to speak, but as a S(p) – that is to say, as having undergone
a first perceptual determination. The primary thematizing activity is directed to S(p) as resulting from the first determination;
the secondary thematizing activity is directed to q as a further

---

[43] For the following, see *ibid.*, § 24, c.

[44] Concerning "grasping," "holding in grasp," and modalities thereof, see Husserl,
Ideen, I, § 122, and *E.U.*, § 23, b.

[45] Though this statement holds for "independent" and "non-independent part"
alike, we here confine ourselves, for the sake of simplicity, to "non-independent
parts." For this distinction, cf. *L.U.*, II, III, §§ 2ff. (The rendering of "unselbständig"
by "non-independent" is Findlay's.)

[46] Husserl, *E.U.*, p. 127.

perceptual determination. No thematizing activity is directed to p any longer. Still, p does not vanish from consciousness; it is still retained in grasp. But it is thus retained as incorporated into S, as sedimented upon S, and not as a theme, not even a subordinate one.

For the sake of continuity of presentation we now proceed to summarize Husserl's account of the phenomenological origin of the judgment of predication. According to Husserl,[47] predication is an activity which in some respects bears similarity, in other respects dissimilarity, to practical activity. All activity is motivated by, and arises out of, a decision of the will. Whereas in the case of practical activity the volitional decision aims at the possession of some object, its modification, or the bringing about of a certain state of affairs, the goal of the specific cognitive will, which motivates predication and, quite generally, all logical activity, is the generation and production of knowledge about an object. More precisely, it is knowledge as an abiding possession, available at any time and for everybody.[48]

Perceptual encounter yields acquaintance with the thing perceived, but that acquaintance lasts no longer than the encounter itself. To be sure, circumstances permitting, the encounter may be repeated, the thing may be perceived again or it may be remembered. Such reactivation, however, is contingent upon circumstances and, furthermore, the acquaintance in question remains in principle a matter of the perceiving and remembering subject who cannot communicate it to others. The transformation of perceptual acquaintance into abiding knowledge, that is knowledge in the proper sense, requires the generating production of specific entities, "categorial objects" (*Verstandesgegenständlichkeiten*). In the first place, that means predicative judgments through which perceptual acquaintance is made a permanent acquisition which may be communicated by means of linguistic expressions and, hence, may become the possession of everybody and which, finally, may motivate the reinstatement or the reactivation of perceptual encounter on the basis of which a certain predicative judgment arises and by which it is validated.

Predication requires a specific attitude induced by the will to

---

[47] Cf. for the following, *ibid.*, §§ 147f.
[48] Cf. *F.T.L.*, §§ 42f., and 73.

cognition. In this specifically cognitive attitude, the process of explicating contemplation is in a way recapitulated.[49] Having performed the explicating contemplation, we again return to S, not as the principal theme still maintained in grasp, but as a theme *simpliciter* more or less as it was grasped in simple apprehension which underlies the explicating contemplation. The latter still being retained as having just been performed, it is at the same time protended as repeatable. In other words, there is a tendency to pass to p again. Under the impact of the will to cognition, the transition from S to p is now effectuated actively. Whereas in explicating contemplation p is incorporated into S by means of "passive coincidence" (*passive Deckung*), there is now the intention to refer p to S in an active way, by an active synthesis.[50] If this intention is fulfilled, both p and S undergo a transformation of sense: p which had been a property found to inhere in the substratum S acquiring the logical sense of a predicate to be explicitly asserted about S which, in turn, acquires the logical sense of the subject about which assertions can be made – while previously it had simply appeared as a carrier of attributes and properties. What in perceptual encounter is merely ascertained is, on the basis of an active transition from the subject S as *terminus a quo* to the predicate p as *terminus ad quem*, explicitly asserted in a judgment of predication.

Predication undoubtedly rests on perceptual encounter, more particularly on what Husserl calls explicating contemplation whose distinction from simple apprehension is here not challenged either. But whereas, according to Husserl, explicating contemplation arises out of simple apprehension by virtue of a thematizing activity, we account for the difference under discussion in terms of noematic organization. In simple apprehension, as mentioned before, the perceptual noema is undifferentiated. On the contrary, in the case of explicating contemplation the perceived thing, as it actually presents itself, appears as centered with regard to a certain property. One of the constituents of the per-

[49] Husserl, *E.U.*, pp. 242ff.

[50] The difference between the thematizing activity which, according to Husserl, is involved in explicating contemplation and the activity here in play seems to depend upon the cognitive will being absent from the former case, while intervening in the latter. In this sense we interpret Husserl's distinction (*E.U.*, p. 244) between "synthetic activity in general" (*überhaupt*) and "activity of synthesis itself" (*Aktivität der Synthesis selbst*).

tinent noematic sense predominates over the others or – as it may
likewise be expressed – has special phenomenal weightiness.[51]
Because the organizational structure of the perceptual noema is
that of Gestalt-coherence, the internoematic system as a whole
is "contained" and present in each of its members from whose
vantage point it appears through a given perception. In explicating contemplation the perceptual noema may be characterized
as a *differentiated unity*, the differentiation being between the
system of properties pertaining to the thing perceived to the
extent to which those properties actually play a role in the
perception under consideration and taken in the very role they
play, on the one hand, and, on the other hand, a particular property with regard to which the thing appears centered in its perceptual presentation. Husserl describes the phenomenal state of
affairs in question to the effect that in and through encountering
the properties we become acquainted with the thing perceived as
manifesting itself in its properties,[52] and that every partial apprehension, namely of a property, is at the same time a total apprehension of the thing as a whole.[53] While we fully endorse these
descriptive formulations, our account differs in two respects from
that of Husserl who resorts to thematizing activity by means of
which the property p is incorporated into S as substratum in the
sense of inherence. In the first place, it is – we submit – S, understood as an internoematic system or the system of properties,
which is incorporated in the particular property p, rather than
conversely. In the second place, *what Husserl presents as the result
of an operating activity is with us a matter of noematic structure and
organization*. Differently expressed, *while Husserl conceives of explicating contemplation as a synthesis, we see in it a kind of analysis*. In fact, through successive acts of explicating contemplation the thing perceived successively displays its various properties, being present in each one of them. Continuing explicating
contemplation proves a progressive analysis of the total system
into its several members.

While absent from explicating contemplation, thematizing
activity does play a role in predication, and even a preeminent

[51] Cf. A. Gurwitsch, "Phänomenologie der Thematik und des reinen Ich," Chapter
I, § 5, *Psychologische Forschung*, XII (1929). (Also in *Studies*.)
[52] Husserl, *E.U.*, pp. 126f. and 148f.
[53] *Ibid.*, p. 131.

role. Granting that the will to cognition motivates that activity and sets it in motion, no more is established hereby than a condition, perhaps a necessary one, under which alone that activity may operate. Consequently, the very nature of the activity involved in predication requires definition and analysis. After the preceding discussion, the activity of predication can no longer be conceived of as recapitulation of explicating contemplation in the specifically cognitive attitude.

In explicating contemplation, the perceptual noema presents the structure of differentiated unity, containing two terms in unity. That is to say, the constituents of the noema may be considered as pertaining to one or the other of two terms; one term being the system of properties other than the one with regard to which the system is centered, while the latter property is the second term. This differentiated unity or duality in unity is rendered explicit, thematized, or to express it more properly, articulated. *Articulating thematization consists in dissociating the mentioned terms from, and opposing them to, one another.* By virtue of being thematized, the system of properties making up the first term acquires the logical sense of the *subject* about which assertions are made when the system is explicitly and actively articulated into its members. Correspondingly, the second term, by being opposed to the system of which it is a member, acquires the logical sense of an asserted *predicate*. It must be remembered that all constituents of a perceptual noema qualify each other in thoroughgoing reciprocity and mutuality. In the present context, the property p, which becomes the predicate p in the way just described, is seen as to its contribution to qualifying the other constituents; its being qualified by the latter will presently be taken into consideration. Because of the mentioned dissociation, the act of predicative judging which arises on the grounds of, or which may even be equated with, articulating thematization, is polythetic in contradistinction to perceptual encounter which is essentially monothetic.[54] By articulating thematization the differentiated unity of explicating contemplation is nonetheless modified, though not broken. In its place there is now a different kind of unity which may be called *articulated unity*. As the terms themselves, so must the connection between them be thematized.

[54] *Ibid.*, p. 245.

This thematization is expressed by the copula "is" which denotes the specific unity of subject and predicate.[55] To state it in a more detailed fashion, the copula expresses the relation of articulated unity which results when a property, hereby becoming a predicate, is at the same time both dissociated from, and explicitly referred to, the system which comprises it. Whereas in monothetic perceptual encounter the table presents itself *as* brown, it is in the polythetic judgment of predication asserted to *be* brown. Moneta[56] has very aptly formulated it: "the 'as' of perception ... becomes the 'is' of predication." The circumstance that some languages do, while others do not, have a special word for denoting the copula is immaterial in the present context. Undeniable and obvious though the importance of linguistic formulations is for purposes of communication, the first concern, even with regard to a theory of language, must be the phenomenological clarification of that which is expressed in linguistic formulations, namely the noematic correlate of the act of judging.

Articulating thematization proves to be a special mental operation performed upon a given perceptual situation which hereby undergoes categorial formation. To that specific operation corresponds a specific noematic correlate, namely the state of affairs (*Sachverhalt*) which is the *judgmental noema* [57] founded upon, but different from, the perceptual noema. Husserl has formulated the difference in question as that between what is judged, the "What is judged" (*das Geurteilte*) and that on which the judgment bears or to which it refers (*das Beurteilte*).[58] The latter denotes the thing perceived, the former the state of affairs which results from, and is constituted by, the categorial formation of the thing perceived by means of articulating thematization. As it is to be expected in the case of an inquiry into the phenomenological origin of the judgment of predication, our discussion has brought us before the state of affairs apprehended in the mode of orig-

[55] *Ibid.*, pp. 246 and 254.

[56] G. Ch. Moneta, "The Identity of the Logical Proposition" (Unpublished doctoral dissertation, Graduate Faculty of Political and Social Science, The New School for Social Research, N.Y., 1969), p. 156.

[57] Husserl, *Ideen*, I, p. 194; and *F.T.L.*, § 45; cf. also *L.U.*, II, 1, pp. 402 and 445 (English translation, pp. 579 and 611) – though the term "noema" is not yet used in this earlier work.

[58] Husserl, *Ideen*, I, p. 194; W. James, *Principles of Psychology*, I, pp. 275f., makes a similar distinction between "object" and "topic" of thought; the "topic" corresponds to Husserl's "Beurteiltem" and the "object" to Husserl's "Geurteiltem."

inarity or, equivalently stated, the judgment understood in the noematic sense in the mode of not only distinctness but also clarity [59] – that is to say, the judgment as fulfilled. Originarity here refers to both the bodily presence of the thing in perceptual encounter and the manner in which the operation of articulating thematization is performed.[60]

As repeatedly emphasized, every constituent of a perceptual noema contributes to the qualification of the other constituents and is at the same time qualified by them. This is of consequence for the sense of perceptual properties as well as the corresponding predicates. Logicians have pointed out that when a piece of cloth is judged to be blue, the intention is not to assert that it is a member of a class which also comprises certain kinds of ink, the eyes of certain persons, the sky as it appears on a cloudless day, the Mediterranean, and the like.[61] "Blue" does not in this connection have a general and conceptual sense, but rather a generic, typical, even physiognomical one denoting the specifically typical way which cloths have of being blue. Because of the presence of the properties of a perceived thing, the ones within the others, these properties prove to be thing-tied.[62] Katz has noted that primitive people, though not they alone, have the tendency to designate colors after the things whose properties or attributes they are,[63] and such a tendency strikingly manifests itself under pathological conditions.[64] In an orientation totally different from the phenomenological one, namely from a phylogenetic point of view, Pradines has emphasized that colors as well as sounds are primarily and fundamentally thing-tied, that is to say, belong to things as their attributes and do not have the status of "pure qualities," a status given to them in the arts (painting and music)

[59] Husserl, *F.T.L.*, § 16, b and c.
[60] *Ibid.*, p. 150 and especially App. II, § 2, a.
[61] Ch. Serrus, *Traité de Logique* (Paris, 1945), p. 213.
[62] Merleau Ponty, *Phénoménologie de la Perception*, p. 361: "Une couleur n'est jamais simplement couleur, mais couleur d'un certain objet, et le bleu d'un tapis ne serait pas le même bleu s'il n'était pas un bleu laineux." (English translation, p. 313.)
[63] D. Katz, *Der Aufbau der Farbwelt* (Leipzig, 1930), pp. 4f.
[64] A. Gelb and K. Goldstein, "Über Farbennamenamnesie," *Psychologische Forschung*, VI (1924), pp. 133f.; and K. Goldstein, "L'Analyse de l'aphasie," *Psychologie du Langage* (Paris, 1933), p. 480. See also the detailed discussion by E. Cassirer, *Philosophie der Symbolischen Formen* (Berlin, 1929), III, pp. 258ff. (English translation by R. Manheim, *The Philosophy of Symbolic Forms*, New Haven, 1957, Vol. III, pp. 223ff.)

and in the sciences (physical optics and acoustics).[65] Pradines goes so far as to raise the question as to whether those "pure qualities" which, according to him, are certainly not primary data, are *data at all* and not rather products of a special mental operation.[66] From the point of view of constitutive phenomenology the operation in question proves to be that of ideation. We cannot go along with Husserl when he maintains that in the judgment of predication at least the predicate contains an implicit, not yet thematized reference to a general essence, e.g., redness.[67] The term "implicit" is here somewhat ambiguous. Husserl has explicitly rejected the view that the essence redness may, by an appropriate direction of attention, be "extracted" from the red color of a perceptually given object, to be referred to in a predicative judgment, like "this rose is red," in a way more or less similar to that in which a thing appearing at the periphery of the field of vision may be made a theme by appropriately directing the perceiving glance.[68] On the other hand, the term "implicit" may be understood to refer to the perceptual basis underlying the apprehension of essences. For this apprehension, however, a special mental operation, namely ideation, is required, the study of which cannot be undertaken within the present context. Husserl writes: "... if I judge *This paper is white*, then ... the predicate acquires, over and above its own material content, a relation to the subject, *paper*, and engages significationally with the relatedness of the subject to subject-matter." [69] According to the account here proposed, the predicate has its relation and relatedness to subject and subject-matter to begin with or, as we have expressed it, is tied to it. The problem then is rather how the predicate comes to be dis-

---

[65] M. Pradines, *Philosophie de la Sensation* (Paris, 1928), Vol. I, Book I, Chapter V and Chapters VI, II; cf. also the distinction which Merleau Ponty makes between "couleur-fonction" and "couleur-qualité" (*Phénoménologie de la Perception*, p. 352; English translation, p. 305).

[66] Pradines, *op. cit.*, Vol. I, p. 40: "... la question est de savoir si ces états sensoriels sont primitifs ou seconds, et même dans la seconde hypothèse, s'ils sont *donnés*, ou s'ils ne sont pas *produits* par quelque opération mentale qui pourrait dépasser l'ordre de la sensation."

[67] Husserl, *E.U.*, pp. 240f.; cf. also § 80.

[68] Husserl, *L.U.*, II, II, Chapter 3.

[69] Husserl, *F.T.L.*, p. 263; the translation is by D. Cairns. The original reads: "... wenn es heißt, *dieses Papier ist weiß*, so gewinnt ... das Prädikat über seinen eigenen Sachgehalt hinaus Beziehung auf das Subjekt *Papier*, in dessen Sachbezüglichkeit bedeutungsmässig eingreifend."

engaged from its relation and relatedness so as to acquire a general and conceptual meaning.

4. Conclusion

Our discussion has been confined within certain limits. Because of our concern with the phenomenological origin of the judgment of predication we have in studying it kept as close as possible to its perceptual foundation. We have not, in that connection, considered the modifications it undergoes and the status it assumes when it is severed from that foundation and is taken in itself as, so to speak, a self-contained independent entity. Our purpose being to lay bare the structure of predication in its essential purity, we have deliberately excluded from consideration all problems related to conceptualization and ideation in order to avoid additional complications. For this very reason it is not before the end of our discussion that we raise the question as to whether or not in a systematic study of the phenomenological origin of the forms of judgment, in a systematic "genealogy of logic" (the subtitle of *Erfahrung und Urteil*), precedence should be given to the judgment of subsumption, that is to say, the judgment of the form, "This is a S" (e.g., "this is a rose"), over the judgment of predication. Judgments of subsumption – we submit – stand to simple perceptual apprehension in a relation analogous to that of judgments of predication to explicating contemplation. Obviously, an account of the judgment of subsumption requires a theory of conceptualization as does likewise the account of the transition from predicates expressing thing-tied properties to predicates which have general and conceptual meaning.

Those limitations notwithstanding, we claim for our results symptomatic significance. Quite in general, the transition from the perceptual to the logical realm ("logical" understood in the most inclusive sense) rests upon, and is motivated by,[70] predelineated and pre-traced perceptual structures. *Mutatis mutandis* the same holds for the transition from a lower to a higher level within the logical or conceptual realm. Again the transition involves thematization of what is pre-given. However, thematiza-

[70] Concerning "motivation," cf. the reference in note 30.

tion need not always be articulating thematization, which is but one kind or variety among others. At any event, because of the intervention of thematization as a special mental activity in every such transition a jump or leap occurs, as it most strikingly appears in the transition from the perceptual to the logical realm. Articulating thematization, e.g., though founded upon, and taking its departure from, explicating contemplation, is as such not of the order of perceptual encounter. Moreover, to the intervening mental activity there corresponds a specific noematic correlate which, though founded upon, is different from, that which pertains to the underlying level – be it a perceptual or other level. This new noematic correlate lends itself, in turn, to further mental activities operating upon it.

In fact, our analysis has traced the phenomenological origin of the state of affairs, the noematic correlate of the judgment of predication, as arising by means of articulating thematization of a perceptual situation encountered in explicating contemplation. However, it is the perceptual situation that is thematized, not the resulting state of affairs which is constituted, but not thematized itself. For its thematization further mental operations are required.[71] Among the latter is the one called "nominalization" by means of which a categorical judgment is made a member of a disjunctive, hypothetical, etc. one, or a judgment such as "the weather has been clement" is made part of a more complex judgment such as "the fact that the weather has been clement has been most welcome to the vacationers." [72] Nominalization is likewise involved when the predicate of a judgment ("this rose is red") appears in a subsequent judgment as an attribute of its subject, or when it is sedimented upon the latter – for instance, "this red rose is fragrant." [73] Within the logical realm the notion of sedimentation has its legitimate place while, as we have argued elsewhere,[74] perceptual modifications and alterations have to be accounted for in terms of reorganization and restructuration. In conformity herewith we have presented the difference between

---

[71] Husserl, *L.U.*, II, VI, § 49; *F.T.L.*, §§ 42, b and 48f.; *E.U.*, § 58.

[72] *L.U.*, II, V, §§ 26 and 38; *Ideen*, I, § 119; *F.T.L.*, pp. 69f. and App. I, §§ 1 and 8f.

[73] *L.U.*, II, 1, pp. 324f. (English translation, pp. 515f.), and II, V, § 35; *F.T.L.*, § 13, b, and pp. 148 and 275.

[74] A. Gurwitsch, "The Phenomenology of Perception," 3, *An Invitation to Phenomenology* (ed. by J. M. Edie, Chicago, 1965); cf. also *Field*, Part II, 3b.

simple perceptual apprehension and explicating contemplation
as a difference in noematic structure and organization rather than
resorting to a synthetizing activity, as does Husserl. Finally, a
special case of thematization, entirely different from nominalization, is formalization or algebraization.[75] Applied to judgments
of predication, this operation leads from a concrete judgment or
proposition such as "This table is brown" to the mere form of
that judgment or, as it is called in contemporary logic, the propo-
sitional function, "This S is p." [76] All these operations and kin-
dred ones as well as conceptualization and ideation are here
mentioned as posing problems which arise on the horizon of the
present inquiry. Their discussion and treatment, however, do not
fall within the purview of this inquiry.

---

[75] The notion of "formalization" in contradistinction to "generalization" has from
the very beginning been central to Husserl's theory of logic and mathematics; see
especially *Philosophie der Arithmetik*, Chapter IV; *L.U.*, I, §§ 67 and 70, II, 1, pp. 284f.
(English translation, p. 482); *Ideen*, I, §§ 10f.; *F.T.L.*, §§ 24, 27ff., 87; *Crisis*, §§ 9f.
[76] *F.T.L.*, § 12.

CHARLES HARTSHORNE

HUSSERL AND WHITEHEAD ON
THE CONCRETE

My personal relation to Husserl is perhaps a bit unusual. I was
in Freiburg for more than a year beginning in November, 1923.
I read a lot of Husserl, participated in his seminar, heard him
give some lectures, and had a few discussions with him. He
interested but did not satisfy me. I did not share his confidence
that he could divest himself of theories and read off the exact
traits of the given; particularly since, as I told him, I was fairly
confident of some truths about the given which he seemed to
have badly missed. Then too I was learning about a number of
things at that time from Richard Kroner, Jonas Cohn, Oscar
Becker, Julius Ebbinghaus, and the young Heidegger starting his
extraordinary career. It was indeed a brilliant department, and
I presume much of the credit for this should go to Husserl himself.

After Freiburg came Marburg, whither Heidegger had gone,
and where Natorp and N. Hartmann lectured. I also managed to
get a good idea of the philosophy of H. Rickert at Heidelberg.
Then, at Harvard, in the Fall of 1925 came the task (in addition
to some teaching) of editing Peirce, and, in the same semester,
of grading papers in the metaphysics class of Whitehead. Husserl
almost dropped out of my mind for years. Peirce and Whitehead
spoke to me intellectually more than any of my teachers, those
I had while technically a "student" (predoctoral or postdoctoral)
had done. These two thinkers saw much of what I thought I saw
phenomenologically, and had vast stores of knowledge which I
lacked.

It should be understood at the outset that my discussion in
what follows is based, not on Husserl's work in its entirety, but
in *Ideen* I, some parts of which I have recently reread (referencse

will be to this work), plus my recollections of some lectures and discussions, and the masterly essays of Cairns, with whom I began discussing Husserl in Freiburg, in 1924. How far deeper research into Husserl's writings might show that Husserl moved beyond the views I attribute to him I do not undertake to say. My aim is more to state issues than to resolve them.

Husserl's defense of essences and eidetic ontology and his critique of empiricism and positivism are in some respects not very different from Whitehead's defense of metaphysics, and also of Pierce's phenomenological theory of categories. Whitehead thought of his "categories" as illustrated in the directly given or intuited, and so did Peirce of his. Moreover, one of the difficulties I have with Whitehead's system also troubles me in Husserl, namely the dichotomy of concrete singularities (Whitehead, "actual entities") and timeless essences or "eternal objects." I incline to the view that only the most abstract or general essences are strictly eternal, and that between these and the concrete there are essences of intermediate generality which have emerged into being in the course of creation's history. Thus I do not think any definite hue of color is timeless, or even "color" as terrestrial animals can experience it, but only sensory quality in some extremely general sense. Peirce hints strongly, though somewhat obscurely, at such a view.

Both Whitehead and Husserl talk as though almost the entire *what* of a concrete entity, all but its *that*, can be completely abstracted from becoming. Whitehead does qualify this, for to him the relations of an entity to its predecessors (not to its contemporaries or successors) are included in its own internal quality. But still he allows so much of this quality to consist of eternal objects, to the complexity of which no limit is set, that one wonders what can be left. Husserl seems, if anything, to go still further, since I do not find that for him relations even to predecessors are allowed to be immanent in a concrete actuality, say in an experience. What I try to do is rather to hold that nothing is strictly eternal save what Whitehead calls creativity, or the process of experiencing as creative synthesis, which is the essence of becoming itself. There can be creativity without magenta red, say, but not without quality, without feeling, or without some form of subject-object relation ("prehension"). If there is an eternal aspect of deity, it must be an aspect of becoming as such.

I shall not pursue the question of Whitehead's or Husserl's rather extreme "Platonism" further in this essay. Yet it did seem worth noting that, as Professor Schrader of Yale once suggested to me, the two thinkers face similar problems on this head. Just how much of the quality of reality can be assigned an eternal status? Richard Zaner confirms my guess that the split among Whiteheadians between those who do and those who do not accept the "eternal objects" doctrine is duplicated among phenomenologists.

What I wish to discuss in some detail is rather some differences between Whitehead and Husserl concerning the concrete. Here the two thinkers diverge very sharply, and in several basic respects. (1) Husserl accepts a form of radical dualism between experiences, *Erlebnisse*, and physical or spatiotemporal "realities," while Whitehead holds that a sufficiently generalized and adequate view of *Erlebnisse* gets rid of the dualism. (Husserl could be said to do this also, but in a very different sense). Husserl has been quoted as having said that perhaps Leibniz was right in his monadological conception of matter. But in published works it is Descartes and Berkeley, or Kant, not Leibniz, who seem to haunt Husserl when he considers the question of physical nature. *Erlebnisse* are nonspatial, physical realities are spatial (§ 41). In particular, physical objects have appearances, partial or one-sided aspects revealed from diverse perspectives, and the object itself is the unity of the possible perspectives. Experiences, by contrast, are intuited not perspectivally but integrally.

(2) For any who take Leibniz seriously, the first question must be, what are the singulars and what the aggregates among physical realities? Husserl seems to regard this as scarcely a relevant question. He dismisses scientific doctrines of atoms (or cells) as beside the phenomenological point. A single thing for phenomenology is what we ordinarily take as such, e.g., a desk. Yet the query is as old as Greek atomism, how does one know that what appears as "one" is anything more or less than a "many" whose constituent units are too small for our powers of discrimination? For Greek atomists, and for Leibniz too, all the objects of unaided perception are lacking in genuine singularity, except – and here Leibniz is sharper than the atomists – ourselves. Correspond-

ing to the animal body there is a sequence of experiences each of which, whether or not the sequence, is genuinely unitary and indeed a paradigm of unity. But apart from such animal "souls" or "monads" the perceptible world consists entirely of singulars which are perceptible not distinctly and as such but only "confusedly," in aggregates appearing as singulars.

I have argued in many places that direct experience cannot possibly refute this doctrine. If a perceived object moves, we know that its constituents alter their loci, but if a perceived object remains for perception in one place, nothing follows as to motions of imperceptible constituents, save that these motions (with perhaps negligible exceptions) remain within the area occupied by the object as a whole. Thus the seeming "inertness" of inanimate matter is no evidence that activity is absent from some parts of nature. The kinetic theory of heat, and many other scientific conclusions, supports the atomic or molecular hypothesis which direct experience cannot refute – unless on the assumption that direct experience means absolutely distinct experience, a view that attributes a form of intuition to man that some of us think defines deity. (And now and then I seem to sense Husserl almost taking himself to enjoy divine privileges.) And if the kinetic theory of heat is false, scientists ought to review their theories. I think it is the phenomenology that is false. It makes claims for direct experience that fail to fit what I at least find that experience to be. I do not find the type of distinctness that is in question, but rather every evidence of indistinctness. I propose the principle: positive data of direct experience can be trusted, but negative deliverances, such as inertness and lack of internal differentiation into individual constituents, must be argued for. We do not distinctly see the manyness of the table, yet it may be there.

Very well, the diverse perspectives are, then, not appearances of one and the same singulars, but of now this, now that, group of singulars. But with singulars, one by one, in what sense would there be *Abschattungen?* At least the idea becomes a bit problematic.

(3) This is far from all. *Erlebnisse* are not things but events. (Note § 42.) There is a category difference here, not between one kind of enduring thing and another, but between thing and event.

One should either compare *Erlebnisse* with physical events, or compare the enduring self with enduring physical objects. But if the latter, then for a Whiteheadian both are abstractions, identified by what the various possible events making up the continued existence of the thing or self have in common. Only states or events are fully concrete. And the diverse perspectives, in Husserl's favorite examples, are not primarily or clearly of one and the same event, but of diverse events. And it is no small matter to decide what time lapse would correspond to a single state in an atom or particle, or for that matter in a table. Time has different meanings on different levels of magnitude and organization. Human time is very slow, so to speak, compared with atomic time.

(4) Husserl argues also from modes of givenness. He says that diverse experiences can be united in one stream of consciousness, but neither any physical reality nor any experience belonging to another stream can enter integrally into a given stream. However, though it is tautological that there must be a difference between how "my" experiences are united in "my "stream of consciousness and how things not my experiences are connected with that stream, it does not follow that some of these cannot be somehow integral to my stream of experiences. I hold that bodily feelings, and this in a sense includes all sensations, are directly given to us, not as simply our feelings but as subhuman feelings (perhaps cellular, molecular, or something in between) in which we directly but indistinctly participate. And I hold that this experience is the primary contact with physical reality. Husserl seems to think of the physical world first of all as something seen or touched, and then also and secondarily felt as furnishing us with feeling qualities. I argued with Husserl forty-eight years ago that feeling qualities are *given* as qualities of physical realities. The realities may be inside our skins, but physical nonetheless. They qualify us only by being given to us; they do not first qualify us and then by reflection become data. One should note also that bodily feelings are spatial, spatially separated in more or less definite degrees and directions. The toothache is not where the legache is. And they are, in objective fact, spatially located, for so are the invisible bodily members, perhaps nerve cells, whose feelings they in the first instance are.

Other human beings' experiences are less directly given than our own, but not simply because their feelings are theirs rather than ours, but for the more special reason that, like ours, they are human, and human beings need and enjoy a certain protection from each other. (Imagine a high degree of telepathy and the confusion this would introduce into our chains of reasoning and emotional lives). But our cells are not to the same degree protected from us or we from them. Precisely this is the mind-body relation. It is that of experience of one kind to experiences of very different kinds, not of experience to mere physical things. It is a special form of social relation, with the human experience being the "presiding" spirit in a society of extremely humble forms of experiencing.

If phenomenology conflicts with this view, which is to give way? What we positively experience must be somehow there, but I find only his negations between my view and Husserl's. I grant that there are the appearances, and that they have the unities of meaning he speaks of. But I say that these unities are somewhat abstract, and that on the concrete level of singular events the richness of the world in experiences is vastly greater than our human form of experiencing can distinctly and directly reveal. With Democritus, Leibniz, and Whitehead, I refuse to allow the poverty of our power of discriminating dynamic singulars to determine my beliefs. The discriminated exists, but the undiscriminated often exists also. Science magnifies our powers of discrimination. That is its great gift. Microscopic experience is also experience, and that in two obvious senses. Here there is a subtle but important difference between: a) For all I can know from inspecting my direct experience, that experience, just as it is, would be logically possible even in the absence of such things as atoms, molecules, or cells; and b) I can know by inspecting my direct experience that it would be logically possible even in the absence ... The basis of the distinction between (a) and (b) is the indistinctness or (Leibniz) the "confused" character of our perceptions. Had we divine clarity of intuition the distinction would be invalid. If I am not mistaken – I may well be – Husserl's claims for the *epoché* rest, at least in part, upon an identification of (a) and (b).

In Whiteheadian terms, we cannot read off the independence

of experience from the world it inclines us to believe in because so many of our prehensions are "negative," that is, eliminative, rendering their data inaccessible to introspection, yet not without influence upon the experience. At this point Leibniz, Bergson, Peirce, and Whitehead have somewhat similar views. All believe that human consciousness is rather pervasively and incurably opaque to itself. If I am not, here also, mistaken, Sartre and Heidegger recognize this opaqueness in their own way.

(5) Consciously Husserl (pp. 85–87) repeats the doctrine of Descartes: the self and its experiences of the moment are indubitable, but it is always logically possible that the world of physical realities does not exist. Thus he is an epistemological solipsist. What this means is that an experience, or at least a stream of experiences, is logically self-sufficient, requires nothing but itself to exist. It is a "substance" in the most extreme sense. Relations of experience to anything spatial, or to the experiences of other subjects, are extrinsic. I disbelieved this when I read Descartes, I disbelieved it when I read or listened to Husserl. And I hold the following view, which is essentially Whitehead's, but is also close to that of Peirce.

a. Any verbal report, whether it refers to one's own experiences, or to physical things, or to other persons, is either minimal in logical content (to take the extreme case, "I experienced *something* not just that experience itself and independent of it") or it is corrigible, might be somehow mistaken. Physical realities and experiences are alike in that neither kind of entity comes furnished with its own verbal description. And verbalization is a fallible procedure.

b. One's own experiences are indeed the only concrete *singulars* given both integrally ("bodily," to use Husserl's phrase), and also distinctly. Other singulars are less distinctly given, and any specific judgment about one of them, or a definite set of them, logically could be mistaken. This is an additional uncertainty besides that referred to in (a) above.

c. Indistinctly, but yet integrally, many other singulars are given, and it is logically impossible that an experience such as mine could occur *solus*. (Cf. § 44.) In this sense perception is as certain as what Husserl calls reflection or self-awareness. It gives us a world, with *certainty* as to its existence and *some* of its features, but with pervasive indistinctness as to its singular constituents. (Cf. § 46.) The greatest distinctness here is with respect to other animals, whose experiences are true singularities, at least as at a given moment.

In (a) the existence of something independent of the experience is taken as a certainty. This means that I hold it to be of the essence of experience as such that it reveals an independent reality. No experience is merely "of" that very experience, nor even merely of an earlier moment in the same stream of experiences, nor can merely "intending" an object which may not exist constitute the "of" relation in "experience of." Experience is in principle relative, not absolute; it is logically dependent upon given concrete entities whose existence is necessary to, and independent of, the given experience.

The relativity of an experience, simply as such, has two main forms, memory and perception. The former makes the experience logically dependent upon previous phases of the same "stream" or personal sequence; the latter makes it dependent upon previous phases of other processes. I say previous, for with Whitehead, and Peirce in some passages, I take perception to be always and necessarily of the past of the world, not its contemporary state. This has more than scientific grounds. It inheres in the very idea of experience as *of* something. The past alone is already settled, determined; it alone can be given as definite. The present is nascent, in process of being settled. The future is partly unsettled, it can only be intended with a certain margin of indefiniteness. Contemporaries, if close in space, are given as virtually determinate; for they follow approximately from the past common to them and the experience in question. The past is, for an experience, its dimension of dependence or relativity, the future, its dimension of independence or absoluteness. No matter what may come, this is what we are or do now; but "no matter what has happened ..." will not pass; for we sum up our histories and antecedents, and given what we are, they could not have been otherwise.

Differently put, earlier events are immanent in later, but not vice versa. This Bergsonian doctrine was also Whitehead's and is mine. It is not, I gather, Husserl's. On his side may seem the fact that we make mistakes about the past, both as perceived and as remembered. But here I appeal not only to the fallibility of verbalizing, which we are constantly doing and always with some risk, but also to the indistinctness of direct intuition, which to me is a phenomenological truth. (There are the speckled hen case and many others).

I miss in Husserl a *clear doctrine of givenness as the dependence of an experience upon a reality which it presupposes but which did not presuppose it*. I miss also the clear recognition that self-awareness is really memory, especially short-run memory, used for the purpose of knowing, not what things I formerly experienced, but what experiences I formerly had of them. (However, note § 45.) ("Formerly" may here mean a fraction of a second earlier.) Introspection is retrospection with a special aim. If this is erroneous, how is it known to be so? Does Husserl argue the matter, or merely take for granted that self-awareness is not mnemonic? "Memory," ordinarily so-called, is mostly recollection, long, rather than short-run (minutes, days, or years, rather than seconds and fractions thereof). If memory is intuition of the past, then perception, on my view, may be called "impersonal memory," intuition of the past of the rest of the world, including especially one's own body.

Descartes confused the uniqueness of self-awareness, as the sole *distinct* and certain experience of singular concrete realities, with a supposed but baseless uniqueness of being the sole certain experience of concrete realities, collective or singular. When I feel pain, it is certain that something concrete is going on, not just in "my mind" but in something else, and that what is going on is in some sense bad, not good. There is trouble, and it is not just my trouble. I once had psychosomatic pain around my eyes, but the pain was a physical fact, not just a mental one. The mental strain had produced muscular strain and this had produced slight cellular damage. There are, I hold, no *merely* illusory feelings or sensory states. Look for some time at a very bright filament and then turn out the light: in total darkness one then seems to experience brilliant changing colored lights. The intense activity thus enjoyed or suffered is by no means merely mental, it is in the retina and nervous system, it is physiological.

There is no such thing as mere imagination, or mere dreaming, in the sense which Descartes and, I suspect, Husserl take for granted. And I do not admit that it is even logically possible. An experience cannot generate its own data; to say that it can is to empty words of their meanings. Taking the body into account, all experience exhibits the physical world as at some point it really is. But many philosophers stubbornly refuse to take the body into account. Merleau Ponty, I gather, is an exception; but I wonder how much he adds to what James, Peirce, Dewey, and Whitehead, and Bergson too, could have taught us.

What is a physical reality? Husserl, like Kant, turns it into a pattern exhibited in experiences such as ours, especially our visual experiences. But first of all the concrete reality of patterns is in events. My experience as an event, for me and for Husserl, is no mere pattern. It is not a rule governing its appearances to others. Is this not true of every animal's experiences? What about microorganisms? And where do you stop? The whole physical world as a system of events may similarly have internal qualities everywhere not to be reduced to any pattern of appearances to such as we are. True, I do not know what this could mean if not that physical singulars are experiences, however subhuman and even subanimal they may be in some cases. This is the Leibnizian vision, modified by the substitution of momentary experiences for the ultimate singulars. Is there some good reason in Husserl for rejecting this conception? If so I have missed it.

Things can appear to others because they are actual in themselves, strings of events actually occurring. What is occurring is not first of all that others experience these events; rather these events are themselves experiences, there in the animal, there in the protozoan, there in the atom, there in the particle. What we experience is actual past occurrences of "experient occasions." Nothing can ever undo the fact that they have occurred. The past of the world is real, no matter how chaotic subsequent experiences may be.

Husserl, if I understand him, allows as given concrete entities only experiences as reflexively given to themselves. But then memory, perception, and reflexive experience constitute three irreducible forms of awareness, only the last of which does what all three seem to common sense to do, furnish us with experienced concrete realities. The remembered and perceived are, it seems, only intended, but the reflexively prehended is actually given;

it alone is guaranteed to exist. Now my view is that reflexive experience is just a special functioning of memory, including extremely short-run or immediate memory, employed to answer questions like, what or how am I thinking, feeling, or perceiving? By remembering what I thought, felt, or perceived a second ago or less, I know for practical purposes what I am now thinking, feeling, perceiving. For the past implicates rather definite outlines of its very near future. Reflexive awareness is not one more basic function in addition to memory, perception, and intending, but a high-level form of these, especially the first and the last, working together. The other animals largely lack such explicit awareness of awareness because they lack linguistic and other high-level forms of sign-usage.

Cairns holds, with Husserl, that the objects of experience could not be what some forms of realism require them to be, things in themselves, whose existence would not presuppose that of consciousness. In my view he is at least partly right in this. Basic philosophical questions are modal, a priori, eidetic, or, as I would say, metaphysical, not empirical or merely factual. However, although I am a metaphysical idealist, I think the eidetic necessities favor a more realistic epistemology than Husserl's seems to be. Experiences are given (most clearly in short-run memory) and thinkable only as *essentially* relative to antecedent actualities, not as logically absolute entities meaning or intending what may or may not be actual. Yet what all experience must depend upon is simply other, antecedent, often very differently qualified (e.g., radically subhuman), experiences. And any experience implicates the subsequent occurrence of experiences able to relate themselves to that experience as their predecessor.

It is quite true, as Cairns says, that things are meant by a subject as capable of being given to other subjects as well. They are not and cannot be intended as merely intendable by me. But I add that they are *given* as givable to others as well as to me. For past events cannot depend upon *my* later experiencing them. *Whatever* is later can, and indeed on some level of awareness *must* experience them, for this is what constitutes "later."

It is clear, I suppose, that the whole theory of time, space, and causality is drastically affected by the issues I am discussing. The "process" theory makes one relation, givenness, explain temporal, spatial, and causal relations. Other theories must have at least two principles to do the same work. Since without givenness there is no barrier to complete skepticism, if this necessary relation will also furnish what Hume sought in vain, experience of real connections, this is all to the good. Not only Whitehead, but Bergson and Peirce, taken broadly, support this reduction. Concrete singular entities are momentary experiences, each of which has as its data, and therefore is causally influenced by, its predecessors. The subject side of the subject-object relation (where the object is the given, not the merely intended) is the effect; the object side is the cause or set of causes. Whether the givenness is in the form of memory, perception, or self-awareness, the causal structure is basically the same. My past experiences, and the bodily and environmental states I perceive, cause my present experience. If my subjective states are also causes, and indeed they are, this is because future subjects (including some constituents of my own body) will enjoy or suffer them as their objects. This is the simplest, neatest, of all comprehensive theories of experiencing and causation. It gives real spatial processes and real causal connections, accounts for both space and time, as well as all forms of experiencing, by a single conception of cumulative experiencing of experiencing. It is one of the most powerful generalizations ever accomplished. And I believe it is good phenomenology as well. But it does imply that valid phenomenological insights are even more difficult to achieve and in some respects farther from traditional views than Husserl supposed.

Perhaps Husserl has somewhere reflected upon the question, What would the very first experience of a human individual be like? (I assume that he did not believe in reincarnation.) As the "first," the experience could not be memory in the usual sense. Does this mean that there would be no intuition of the past, the *Vorhin?* I think that this is to be rejected. But then the intuition of the past would have to be what I call "impersonal memory." This is the other of the two possible forms of what Whitehead calls "prehension," i.e., memory in a sense neutral to the difference between self and other. If I am not mistaken, it is only memory in the personal sense which Husserl, like Leibniz, takes as logically essential to all experience. This is illogical if one admits that a "stream of experience" can have a first member.

And it is in any case sensible to admit that events are definite entities, ready to be experienced, only when they have already occurred. So perception is temporally akin to memory. The absolutely essential relation of an experience as such is to preceding experiences, which may not in all cases be members of the same personal series. For many reasons, including ethical and religious ones, we western philosophers need to learn from the Buddhists (though Whitehead may not have learned it in this way) to be severely critical of the pluralistic notion of soul-substances which has haunted nearly all philosophy outside of Buddhist circles. Self-identity is only one prominent strand of the basic unity or continuity of becoming. It has no absolute priority.

According to Cairns, and no doubt Husserl also, intentionality is an ultimate function or relation, inexplicable by anything else. Whitehead says the same of his creativity or creative synthesis, of which the becoming of a single human experience (*Erlebnis*) is an instance. Whitehead distinguishes, as the most basic aspects of an experience, its prehensions of various antecedent objects, including abstract objects which, at least so far as eternal in God, are always antecedent to any given experience. Corresponding to intentionality is Whitehead's "symbolic reference," which involves the interplay of diverse modes of prehension, not all of them sensory, and some awareness of the future. Since for Whitehead every experience is *essentially* a contribution to whatever future experiences there may be, to prehend any experience is in some fashion to be aware of the future as implied by that experience. The double sense of "intends" – as both "means" and "wills to do" – is not arbitrary. It is the temporal (and teleological) structure of experiencing that makes its various aspects intelligible, as Kant rightly held.

The phrase "symbolic reference" brings out the intimate connection between intentionality and sign-usage. We take something given (in the sense which entails the existence of the something) as for some purpose a substitute for, or representative of, something else which may or may not exist. Thus intentionality presupposes givenness, not merely for the confirmation of intentions but for their very occurrence. In my opinion, Peirce and Whitehead are clearer about this than Husserl. They are also clearer about the intimate relations of meaning to valuation and future-regarding purpose.

Is intentionality unique to mind, leaving large portions of nature that can be intended but cannot themselves intend? The Whiteheadian view is that the truly singular constituents of nature are all "subjects" which at least prehend or feel their predecessors. They are also all "mental" in having some sense, however minimal, of the future or the possible. This seems to mean that they have intentions. Whitehead does deny that they all have conscious intentions. All singulars feel the past and the possible or probable future, but not all *know* that they do this. Consciousness or knowledge, in the sharp or distinctive sense, is a rare thing in nature. But the dualism of experiences (*Erlebnisse*) and wholly insentient ("vacuous") merely material things or events seems unnecessary, if not meaningless. Experience is pervasively social, and given singulars are other experiences or sequences of such.

One final point. Husserl rightly stresses the role of imagination in enabling us to explore possibilities as well as actualities. But what is imagination? There is an idea that it is a purely immanent affair, the mind exploring or utilizing its own states. On the contrary, generalizing Bergson's forcible explication of the role of actual bodily states in dreams, we should regard imagination as a form of sign usage, where the signs physically exist, at least as events in the nervous system. It follows that to study a universal in an imagined instance is not really to study it in a merely possible instance. It is to take an actual instance, say a visual image (really a neurological process as we intuit or feel it) to stand for possible instances that might exist in some other form. An experience never generates its own particular data; the possible is to be studied only in the actual; the universal only in the particular, and the particular actuality of a single experience is not one which *that* experience can study. Always there is the givenness of other and antecedent experiences, without which nothing could be either intended or given.

I admire Husserl's writing. He used to say that he owed his success to a great deal of "honest work." And indeed only immense labor, as well as great talent, could have produced *Ideen*. If anything like Descartes' doctrine of extended matter and inextended mind could be made persuasive, Husserl, I should think, would have made it so. And as counter-balance to positivism and materialism, his work is eminently wholesome. I believe as firmly as Husserl: there are nonempirical truths, and they are philosophy's prime business. And they are truths about experience, phenomenological truths. To have put so much power into these contentions is a great service.

ROBERT WELSH JORDAN

BEING AND TIME: SOME ASPECTS OF THE
EGO'S INVOLVEMENT IN HIS MENTAL LIFE [1]

The most obvious cases of ego-involvement in conscious life are
those which Husserl calls conscious *acts* or *cogitationes*.[2] They are
the most obvious cases because they are the ones in which the
ego explicitly involves himself in some way; they exhibit the
character of being engaged in by the ego or having been engaged
in by him. This ego-quality or character belongs demonstrably
to every conscious process in which the ego engages or lives. In
the ego's conscious life, the life to which his, her, or its acts belong, there also occur mental or intentive processes in which the
ego does not or did not engage, and these Husserl calls passive
or non-actional processes as contrasted with the active or actional
processes characterized by ego-engagement.

The ego does not engage in all the mental processes occurring
in his life, but it is only insofar as the ego does engage that we
may speak of any particular process as having only *one* object or
a *definite* set of objects. It is characteristic of *acts* that they
objectivate.[3] This is not simply to say that the ego engages in all
those and only those mental processes having definite objects,
nor is it to say that the objects of conscious processes in which

[1] This paper is a somewhat enlarged and revised version of that read by the author
under the title "The Involvement of the Ego in his Mental Life" in the symposium
"The Phenomenology of the Ego" held under the auspices of the Society for Phenomenology and Existential Philosophy at Evanston, Illinois on October 23, 1969.

[2] In the terminology developed by Edmund Husserl in his *Ideen zu einer reinen
Phänomenologie und phänomenologischen Philosophie. I. Buch, Allgemeine Einführung
in die Phänomenologie* (Halle a. d. S.: Max Niemeyer, 1913), § 35. This work is more
generally available as Volume III of *Husserliana: Edmund Husserl, Gesammelte Werke*
(The Hague: Martinus Nijhoff, 1950), a much changed and enlarged edition by Walter
Biemel, whose "Textkritischer Anhang" nevertheless permits reconstruction of the
text of the 1913 edition. Hereafter, this work will be cited simply as *Ideen* I; the
page numbers given will be those of the 1913 edition which are printed in the margins
of the Husserliana edition.

[3] *Ideen* I, p. 244.

the ego does not engage are a confused, undifferentiated manifold. Rather, it is only by virtue of ego-engagement that "something" is the object of an intentive process. To the extent that
the ego is engaged in a conscious process, the process *becomes* an
act, and there belongs then to the objective sense of this act a
"this" which is *the* object or one of *the* objects of the act.[4]

Engaging in a mental process, the ego busies himself with something intended to in that process. Objectivating may also be
understood as *thematizing*.[5] More precisely, objectivating is only
one specific kind or way of thematizing. But it is the basic way
of thematizing in the sense that it is so to speak the *sine qua non*
of thematizings on which all others are founded, without which
no other kind of thematization occurs. Like all other "doxic"
thematizings, objectivatings always have to do with the object
in some modality of *being*.[6] Let us say the ego engages in a perceiving, a seeing perhaps of the flyswatter with which he means
to kill a fly: doing so involves his thematically grasping and
positing the objective sense of his seeing; it is a "this" and more;
it is in fact just the thing he was looking for, namely, the flyswatter. The seeing involved here will, in the normal case, have
the quality of a simple believing. This believing is a character of
the act of perceiving, i.e., of the noesis, and is what Husserl calls
a doxic thetic character or positional character. The object of an
act having the thetic character "believing" may be said to have
the positional character "something that is." The object of a
disbelieving would have the character "something that is not."
Believing in and disbelieving in and, indeed, all modalities of
believingness are *doxic* thetic characters of acts, and all *acts* having such characters will be what we have called objectivatings.

The ego, having engaged in a mental process and thus posited
objectivatingly an intentional objective sense belonging to that
process, may go on to objectivate the thetic character of the act
or noesis. The objective or noematic correlate of this further
objectivating would be the believedness of "something that is,"

---

[4] *Ideen* I, pp. 270–273. See also Edmund Husserl, *Phänomenologische Psychologie*,
ed. Walter Biemel, *Husserliana*, Vol. IX (1962), p. 481; cited hereafter as *PP*.

[5] *Ideen* I, p. 253. For a consideration of the complexity of thematization, see *ibid.*,
§ 117 and *PP.*, Appendix XXIV.

[6] *Ideen* I, § 103.

the disbelievedness of "something that is not," the uncertainty of "something that may be or may not be," and so forth.

It would be a serious error to go on from here to assert that the being-sense of a noema is simply its believedness and is exhausted by its simple believedness. For, even if it could be shown that "believingness" is a thetic quality universal to all acts that are positings, i.e., that the thetic character "believedness" is objectivatable in principle for each "something that is"; still, the believing which is an act's thetic character is inherently characterized as believing in the intentional object of that act with just that objective sense which it has for the consciousness of it. The object with its objective sense is the *theme* of the act. The manner in which the ego is directed toward the theme – believingly, disbelievingly, liking it, disliking it, loving it, hating it, shaping it, using it, etc. – is the *thesis*. The theme and the thesis do not arise separately in order then to be linked externally, not even in those cases in which the ego is passively affected.[7] The object, its objective sense, and its noematic thetic character or characters would, therefore, all have to be included in anything which could legitimately be called the "being-sense" of the noema of the specific act in question. This is precisely the composition of what Husserl calls the *act-thesis* or positum.

The act-thesis may be a very complex affair. It is fairly complex even in the case of our seen flyswatter. To see a flyswatter is to see something having many qualities and determinations that belong certainly to the act-thesis but are not themselves seen; and at least some of these are, strictly speaking, not seeable at all. The flyswatter's tactile properties, the feel of its handle, its heft and balance, its suitability for killing flies, even its having been manufactured may all belong to the act-thesis of a flyswatter seeing along with those qualities that are genuinely seen. That this is so and is possible at all is an outcome of what Husserl calls "internal tradition" in the *Analyses of Passive Synthesis* and what he later calls "internal historicality" in "The Origin of Geometry."[8]

---

[7] *PP*. pp. 479–480, and Edmund Husserl, *Erfahrung und Urteil*, ed. Ludwig Landgrebe, 2nd ed. (Hamburg: Classen, 1954), § 17.

[8] *Analysen zur passiven Synthesis*, ed. Margot Fleischer, *Husserliana*, Vol. XI (1966), pp. 10f.; cited hereafter as *PS*. "Der Ursprung der Geometrie," published as "Appendix III" to *Die Krisis der europäischen Wissenschaften und die transzendentale*

With the phrases "not themselves seen," "not seeable," "genuinely seen," and "strictly given," we have been referring to a further moment in the full noema of any act, one that is of crucial importance for anything that is to be called the being-sense of the noema. This moment is the manner or way in which the "something" is there for the ego, and Husserl calls it the "mode of givenness," the "mode of appearing," and occasionally "the How of the object's mode of givenness." [9] Heidegger appears to refer to the same thing when he speaks of the "uncoveredness of what is" or "what is in the How of its uncoveredness." [10]

In the act of flyswatter seeing of which we have been speaking, the seen determinations are genuinely or originarily given: they are given directly and "in person" to the ego; they are there in person for him. Now, the determinations we mentioned that are not genuinely given are no less there for the ego than are the originarily given ones; they belong, as we said, *equally* to the thesis of the act in question. Indeed, when he sees a flyswatter with which he means to kill a fly, the sense which what he sees has of being a suitable means to this end will be far more relevant to the ego's prime interest than the seen and therefore originarily given color of the thing.

Non-genuine, non-originary manners of givenness are still ways of being there for the ego, and each determination *not* genuinely given has nevertheless its "mode of appearing," its specific way of being there for the ego. If the object in question be a *familiar* one and if and *only* if it be *individually* familiar, then some of its non-originarily intended determinations will be there memorially for the ego. There will be at least a passive or automatic retrotentive consciousness of them. But – as seems obvious and as we have been maintaining – these selfsame determinations may very well belong to the thesis of an act in which the ego is not at all engaged in remembering but rather in perceiving, an act in which he is busied with something seen rather than remembered. The thesis or positum of such an act is not just "something that

Philosophie, ed. Walter Biemel, *Husserliana*, Vol. VI (1954), pp. 365–386; see pp. 380f. See also Robert Welsh Jordan, "Husserl's Phenomenology as an 'Historical' Science," *Social Research*, 35 (1968), pp. 245–259.

[9] *PP*. p. 207.

[10] Martin Heidegger, *Sein und Zeit*, 8th ed. (Tübingen: Max Niemeyer, 1957), p. 218.

was" and is also not just "something that has been." Nor, in any normal case, are the moments of objective sense divided up into some that were and some that are. The thesis of a perceiving may involve, and normally does involve, the object's having been, being now, and continuing to be and its having, in all of these temporal modalities, non-originarily as well as originarily intended determinations. Moreover, all this may be so even if the object in question is not individually familiar so long as it is an object of a familiar *kind*.

Nevertheless, it is quite inconceivable that – or, as might be more aptly said, *how* – there could belong to the theme of any act, the objective sense of any noema, any *non-originarily* intended determination which is not in *some way* there already for the ego. This character of being there already for the ego indicates involvements of the ego with his mental life which, although having to do with engagement and the formation of act-theses, seem – at least at first glance – to involve far more than merely being interested in and paying attention to something. Husserl himself, however, seems inclined to regard these further involvements as less obvious intricacies of ego-engagement. His view entails a much broadened and extended conception of interest.

In the *broadest* sense in which Husserl uses the word "interest," it is another expression for intentionality. In this sense, that the ego is interested in something means the same as "the ego is intentionally directed toward something." This is the "fundamental essence of all acts." What the ego is interested in is what we have called the *theme* of the act. Interest, in the broadest sense, means that the ego, by virtue of the act in question, is continuously and consciously with [bei] his theme *and with whatever pertains to his theme in the course of its determination*. Husserl even refers to the theme as the ego's aim [Ziel] and as his *telos* though he clearly does not mean to imply here that the ego purposefully creates his theme *ex nihilo* as it were.[11]

On the contrary, the ego, in his acts, is busied with, is interested in, something having to do either noetically or noematically with the mental process in which he is said to engage. The ego, in his acts, is interested in, turns to, and busies himself with something that calls to, stimulates, or appeals in some way to

[11] *PP.*, p. 412.

him. What he turns to and grasps has appealed to or stimulated his interests. That this is so means that the ego's interest – in the broadest sense – comes into play only through the mediation of the conscious process in which he engages. Fundamentally, interest is only his being intentionally with something intended to in his mental life. Not that the ego is interested only in his mental life but the only things there to stimulate his interest and the only things there for him to grasp and objectivate are things that are there in some way for consciousness. The ego is involved in some way with whatever stimulates or appeals to him. Appealing to or stimulating ego interest is a character of the noematic mode of appearing and is a character which must, in each case, be conceived to precede actual engagement, actual thematization by the ego of what stimulates him, since the appeal to the ego is precisely an appeal for his interest and advertence.

Analysis of the noema of any act or *cogito* shows that, in every case, the manner of givenness belonging to this noema includes the theme's having been given in some modality, having been there in some manner, not just for "consciousness" but for the ego as well prior to the ego's specific turning to and objectivating of it. Having stood out within a field and called for attention belongs to what Husserl calls the subjectively relative mode of appearing just as much as does the object's being grasped, used, judged, enjoyed, etc. In this way, the *cogitatum* itself evinces an involvement of the ego in conscious processes that are not yet *acts* in which the ego spontaneously does something. That is to say, the *cogitatum* itself evinces an involvement of the ego in conscious processes that are not yet *cogitationes*.[12]

The ego's being intentionally directed toward his theme or themes, his being intentionally with or among them, involves also his being with whatever pertains to a theme in the course of its further determination. This refers us to an explicitly temporal dimension of ego "interest." Here, *inter esse*, being between, refers in effect to the way in which the ego *lasts*, to internal tradition, and is intimately involved in the reciprocal relation of originary and non-originary manners of givenness:

[12] Edmund Husserl, *Ideen zu einer reinen Phänomenologie und phänomenologischen Philosophie. II. Buch, Phänomenologische Untersuchungen zur Konstitution*, ed. Marly Biemel, *Husserliana* Vol. IV (1952), pp. 99f., and *PP*. pp. 479f.

The ego's being intentionally with the object is ambiguous, depending upon whether the being-with is an anticipation or an actuality. The latter is genuine being-with. An *actus* is anticipative so long as it lacks any fulfilment, if it brings actualizing intentional actuality with it intrinsically, then it is anticipative insofar as it does not yet actualize.[13]

What this and the "reciprocal relation of originary and non-originary manners of givenness" mean will take some explaining.

Originary givenness is *intuitive* givenness. It is also *adequate* givenness with respect to *some* moment or moments of the noematic objective sense.[14] Non-originary givenness is, in every instance, a modification of originary. This being so, non-originary givenness of any object or of any moment of objective sense necessarily points back to that originary mode of which the non-originary is a modification.[15] Indeed, the adjective "originary" is meant to convey that givenness of this sort originates or at least makes possible a range of *other* ways of being conscious of the same thing and of other things of the same kind.

Its pointing back to originary givenness means that non-originary givenness carries with it an implicit rule for bringing what is not itself given to self-givenness. Non-originary givenness thus involves the projecting of *potential* originary givenness. That moments of sense which are not genuinely given nevertheless are there for the ego and belong to the noema means that non-originary givenness points *forward* to an originary givenness which would be the same in kind as that to which it points *back*.

In the objective sense of the noema of an act, whatever is there for the ego without being given originarily nevertheless has its mode of originary or genuine givenness even though it is not yet actually given in the manner characteristic for objective senses of its kind. The self-givenness of what belongs to the act-thesis without being given originarily is a *projected* futurition. Here, self-givenness is *pending;* it is anticipated or protended self-givenness of something posited as being now. This means that, by virtue of the ego's historicality, the being-thesis of his acts in-

[13] *PP.* p. 412, fn 1.
[14] Edmund Husserl, *Logische Untersuchungen. II. Band, Elemente einer phänomenologischer Aufklärung der Erkenntnis*, Part 2, 3rd ed. (Halle a. d. S.: Max Niemeyer, 1922), pp. 118f.; cited hereafter as *LU II, 2*.
[15] Edmund Husserl, *Formale und transzendentale Logik* (Halle a. d. S.: Max Niemeyer, 1929), p. 277; cited hereafter as *FTL*.

cludes a dimension that is pending, that is yet to be verified and established.[16]

Analysis of the full, concrete noema thus reveals the ego to have a *transcendental* status. For, without the ego and his historicality, no intentional object, no synthetic unity of originarily and non-originarily presented determinations is conceivable. And this means that, without the ego in this pre-objective and pre-mundane sense, no intramundane ego, no ego within the world, is given since every such intentional unity is there for the ego only by virtue of his own internal historicality.

This, at least in part, is what Husserl means when he asserts that every kind of intentional unity can serve as "transcendental clue" for constitutive analyses. Constitutive analysis does not stop with what actually is present at hand in the thesis of the act being analysed. It is rather an unveiling of intentional implications of what is present at hand. It may proceed, for example, "forward" from the single experience in question to the system of experiences predelineated in and through it as potentialities of the ego or "backward" toward the experiences of which the potentialities are projected modifications. Constitutive analysis of the "transcendental clue" shows that intentionality involves a coherence of functionings that are comprised, as a sedimented history, within the intentional unity currently constituted and its current mode of givenness.[17]

Constitutive analysis of modes of givenness shows the constitutive function of the ego. More particularly, this noematic trace of the ego's transcendental status is the reference of projected, anticipated, or protended self-givenness to the ego's internal historicality. The transcendentality of the ego – his having a status and a function by virtue of which an objective world is there for him – should not be allowed to obfuscate the basic and insurmountable conditionality of his constitutive functioning. The ego's having this or that object or object determination there for him in the world and, indeed, the being there for him of that world itself are subject to continual *verification*.

Non-originarily intended portions in the act-thesis of our fly-swatter seeing are posited along with the originarily intended

---

[16] *PP.* p. 356, and *LU* II, 2, §§ 36–39, referred to by Heidegger, *loc. cit.*
[17] *FTL* p. 217.

portions. They may even be posited with the same simple certainty; but, to the extent that this is so, certainty harbors and conceals a radical conditionality. Every perceiving of "something" posits a "being" which refers beyond that perceiving to new and further new potential perceivings of the same object and may also refer to further cognitive, affective, and conative acts potentially built up upon these perceivings and having the same object. Moreover, the current perceiving refers to these predelineated potentialities as harmonizing, as agreeing synthetically in the selfsame object. If and when such a potentiality is actualized, the *actualized* originary givenness contributes a verification of being to the object; and it does so by virtue of the new synthetic unity.

Synthetic unity of this kind is again inconceivable apart from the historicality of the ego. Moreover, non-originary modes of givenness carry with them – by virtue of the same historicality – rules for bringing the non-originarily intended to genuine givenness, and these rules are rules for verifying or nullifying anticipations and for verifying or nullifying along with them the projected being sense anticipated. Yet, verification and nullification, establishment and disestablishment of what is there for the ego is accomplished not by fiat of the ego but by the self-givenness, the self-presentedness of what is there for him.

Whether a given anticipation will be verified or quashed is not decided in advance: "In the sphere of experience, the two possibilities remain open so long as no verifying has occurred." [18] The fulfilment or the nullification of which we have been speaking is no matter of fate or destiny – not, at least, if fate and destiny are always decided before the fact. But fulfilment and nullification are also not determined in advance by the ego – neither by his fiat nor by anything that the ego obscurely is "in himself." If phenomenology knows an ego, he, she, or it is never an absolute spirit having the force to actualize of itself whatever it potentially is. [19]

---

[18] *PS.* p. 104.
[19] Georg Wilhelm Friedrich Hegel's *Werke*, 3rd ed. by Marheineke *et al.*, Vol. 9, *Vorlesungen über die Philosophie der Geschichte*, ed. Eduard Gans (Berlin: Duncker und Humblot, 1848); see "Introduction," pp. 13, 25, 45, 91, 98.

FREDERICK KERSTEN

HUSSERL'S DOCTRINE OF NOESIS-NOEMA

Ever since he first fully formulated the doctrine of noesis and noema in the first volume of *Ideas* in 1913, Husserl consistently and conscientiously made it the central theme of his philosophical analysis. And even though in later writings the terms "noesis" and "noema" become more and more infrequent, even though the doctrine of which they are part was never again subject to full-scale critical appraisal, the importance of the doctrine remains unaltered. Nonetheless the course of Husserl's work was such that it implicitly changed the content of his doctrine in substantial ways. The main purpose of this essay is to state the doctrine of noesis and noema and then reformulate it first as regards those changes implicitly made by Husserl, and second as regards changes suggested by Aron Gurwitsch and Dorion Cairns. For the most part the changes implicitly made by Husserl concern the dimension of "passivity" peculiar to intentionality; the changes suggested by Gurwitsch and Cairns, taken together, concern the relationship of noesis and noema and the concept of "hyletic data."

§ 1. *Intentional Analysis*

In the *Cartesian Meditations* Husserl says that an intentional analysis of any actual or possible full constitutional concretion must be carried out both *noetically and* noematically.[1] In the language of *Ideas*, volume 1, what is discovered as a consequence of the transcendental phenomenological epoché is seen as having "an entirely fundamental distinction in respect of intentionality,

---

[1] Edmund Husserl, *Cartesian Meditations* (The Hague: Martinus Nijhoff, 1960), translated by Dorion Cairns, § 59.

namely the distinction between *components proper* of intentive processes and their intentive correlates, or of their components." [2] On the one hand this signifies that we have to discriminate that which we find by an "analysis of the really inherent [*reelle Analyse*]" belonging to mental processes, that is, an analysis of those moments composing the processes in question (perceivings, believings, thinkings, willings, likings, etc.). On the other hand, it signifies that which we find by an analysis of those moments which are not really inherent to the intentive process itself: a mental process always intends *to* something, and the something to which it intends forms an essential part of the analysis of the mental process.[3] A mental process is called by Husserl a "noetic" process:

> that signifies that it is of its essence to include in itself something such as "sense" and potentially manifold sense, and to effectuate on the basis of and concretely with these sense-bestowings further productions which thereby become "sense-ful." [4]

In the context of *Ideas*, volume I, such noetic moments of intentionality are, for instance, directings of the gaze of the ego to the objects meant and intended to by the mental process in which it lives, graspings of the object in question, holding it in grip while the ego's gaze is directed perchance to other objects meant and intended to, explicatings, relatings, and the like. And just as the manifold of mental processes points back to what is really inherent in them, intendings are always "self-intendings," so they likewise point to components which are not really inherent in them: the "noematic content" or, in short, the "noema." [5] In the language of the *Cartesian Meditations*, intentional analysis always and of essence deals with the dual topic of "*cogito-cogitatum (qua cogitatum)*." [6] In the earlier language of the *Ideas*, and without the explicit Cartesian nuance, the mental process is called the "noesis"; correlatively, the intended to and meant as such is called the "noematic sense of the noesis," or simply the noema. The noema is that which is intended to and meant purely and

[2] Edmund Husserl, *Ideen zu einer reinen Phänomenologie und phänomenologischen Philosophie* (Halle: Max Niemeyer, 1928), I, § 88, p. 181. (Hereinafter referred to as *Ideen* I.)
[3] *Ibid.*
[4] *Ibid.*
[5] *Ibid.*, pp. 181f.
[6] *Cartesian Meditations*, § 8, §§ 14f.

precisely as it is intended to and meant in the noesis. For example, every perceiving is a perceiving of something, the perceived. Perception has its noema, its "perceptual sense," or the "perceived as such." [7] The noema is analyzed under the general heading of *sense*.[8]

§ 2. The Phenomenological Signification of Sense. Objective Sense and Intentional Object

In any noesis, in any intentive mental process such as the seeing of this ashtray, the ego can be busied with something as having certain determinations, qualities and relations. We also say that this *active* meaning and intending to the ashtray has its "objective sense." Husserl also calls the objective sense the "what" of the intending to the object. But the term "what" does not signify the species of the object; instead it signifies the determinations, qualities, relations the object is meant as having. The object meant is sometimes called the "intentional object." Since the terms "objective sense" and "intentional object" are sometimes employed as equivalents by Husserl, the distinction requires clarification.

Relative to a given act of consciousness, i.e., a mental process in which the ego is now living and busied with the object of the mental process, the object meant and intended to is said to have this or that "objective sense." The limiting case would be the meaning and intending to something as having the objective sense, "something, no matter what." However, it is usually the case that the object in question has a more or less determinate sense relative to the mental process in which it is given. For example: in one act of consciousness I mean and intend to Napoleon as the victor at Jena and in another act I mean and intend to Napoleon as the vanquished at Waterloo.[9] A Husserlian way of expressing this is that throughout variation in several dimensions of intentionality "Napoleon," the object meant and intended to, remains identical. But the objective sense is different in each case. This raises the question as to when something is self-same throughout variations in dimensions of intentionality, and

---

[7] *Ideen*, I, § 88, p. 182; § 98, p. 206; § 128, p. 268.
[8] *Ibid.*, § 88.
[9] See Edmund Husserl, *Logische Untersuchungen* (Halle: Max Niemeyer, 1928)[4], II, 1, § 12, p. 47.

when something is the objective sense.[10] To take another example: I remember X as "a great man," and also the unique greatness of the man. In the former case, I remember X with the sense, "a man"; in the latter case, I remember X with the sense, "greatness." In remembering Napoleon, I am busied with him as having the sense, "great man"; then I am busied with the sense, "greatness," then with the military aspects of the greatness of the man, and so forth. That is to say, in the one case I am busied with an "ultimate" or fundamental substratum X as having a particular determination, "this – great man." Whereas in the second case the determination "greatness" has become my object: "this – greatness of someone." And I mean this second sense as greatness, military capacity of someone. Military capacity is now my object: "this – the military capacity peculiar to the greatness of someone."

Within the framework of the first volume of *Ideas*, these examples suggest that the distinction between the object intended to and the objective sense, depends on the function of the "ego-quality," of the busiedness of the ego in the intending in question – the remembering of Napoleon, the moral and military approving of him. This function is expressed by Husserl with his concept of "objectivation" (*Vorstellung, Objektivierung*). I am busied with, engaged or living in the intending to X_1 as having such and such objective sense. When now I turn to X_2, which may have been part of the sense of X_1, X_2 is said to be *objectivated* by virtue of my being busied with it – I am not now busied with the object of the first act. The "objectivity" of something objectivated is more than simply being intended to; it is also being intended to by an ego.[11]

Terminologically we shall designate X_1, that which is meant and intended to as the substratum of a particular determination, as the *intentional object;* and the particular determination relative to an ego-dimension of consciousness as the *objective sense* of the intentional object.

So far we have confined ourselves to stating the explicit doctrine of the first volume of *Ideas*. But in later writings, such as

[10] Cf. *Ideen* I, § 94.
[11] Cf. Aron Gurwitsch, *The Field of Consciousness* (Pittsburgh: Duquesne University Press, 1964), pp. 185f.

the *Cartesian Meditations* and *Experience and Judgment*, Husserl more and more makes explicit that dimension of intentionality which he called "inactuality" in *Ideas*, and which he calls "passivity" in later writings. In line with that explicitation, Dorion Cairns has noted that the concept of intentional object must be correspondingly broadened. Thus anything meant and intended to in a mental process is an intentional object, be the mental process an act in the pregnant sense or be it "inactual," "passive." In this light, we can further distinguish from this broadest sense of the term "intentional object" the narrowest sense of the term, which seems characteristic of *Ideas:* only that which is meant and intended to by a mental process in which the ego is *doxically* engaged is an intentional object. A possible *narrower* sense of the term, characteristic of the *Cartesian Meditations*, is that which is meant and intended to by mental processes in which the ego is engaged – be they doxic or non-doxic mental processes.

In line with the broad extension later given to the concept expressed by the term "intentional object," Cairns has also noted that another and broader concept of "objective sense" must be introduced. This is the concept which includes not only an *explicit* objective sense, but also an *implicit* objective sense. If we follow Cairns here, then we may formulate the situation in the following way: in the broadest sense of the term, the intentional object can be anything meant and intended to by a mental process, "actual or inactual," "active or passive." When "inactual" or "passive," the mental process in question has an *implicit* objective sense; the "what" of the "inactual" or "passive" intending is not (perchance, not yet) an object for the ego potentially living in the intending in question. When the mental process is an act, lived in by the ego, then it has an *explicit* objective sense.

§ 3. The Phenomenological Signification of Sense. Continued

It is well-known that the concept of sense which we have been discussing was first developed by Husserl as regards perception and the "content" of perception. In this connection, though not simply in this connection, Dorion Cairns has pointed to

the tendency to think still of the "relationship" of transcendental consciousness to the world as analogous to the objective relationship of phenomenal consciousness to other real processes in the world – to think, let us say, of the relationship between, on the one hand, a transcendental process of perceiving a material thing and, on the other hand, the material thing itself, as analogous to the objective relationship between the "same" process, as an event in the world, and the material thing. The difficulty has its roots in the fact that, in the world, perceiving and perceived are not only related *as* perceiving and perceived but also as realities in time, with objective temporal relations. There is some sense in asking how soon after a change takes place in the thing a change in the perceiving (as an event in the world) takes place. The question would, however, be absurd if asked concerning the perceiving as transcendental and the object as phenomenal. The "relationship" of consciousness *purely* as intending and objects *purely* as intended is utterly *sui generis;* it has no objective analogue.[12]

In these terms the term "content" is clearly inadequate since not only is the "relationship" of consciousness as intending and objects purely as intended to *sui generis*, but the term "content of a perception," as Aron Gurwitsch points out, can only refer to an entity *sui generis* – designated by the term "sense" – e.g., "perceptual sense" or "perceptual noema." [13] Generalized beyond the domain of perception, the concept of sense in Husserl can be accounted for in terms of the completely universal characteristics of intentional object and objective sense spelled out in the previous section. Intentional objects, taken in the broadest as well as narrower and narrowest ways, turn out to be "identical and identifiable ideal entities, devoid of both spatiality and temporality, and, of course, also of causality ..." [14] Thus not only must the doctrine of noesis-noema be reformulated to include the broadened concepts of intentional object and objective sense as regards "active" and "passive" intentionality, but the very *sui generis* "relationship" must be reformulated as the

---

[12] Dorion Cairns, "An Approach to Phenomenology," in *Essays in Memory of Edmund Husserl*, edited by Marvin Farber (Cambridge, Mass.: Harvard University Press, 1940), p. 17. Cf. below, p. 237.

[13] Aron Gurwitsch, "Towards a Theory of Intentionality," *Philosophy and Phenomenological Research*, XXX (1970), p. 363: "By virtue of its 'content' a perception is not only a perception of a certain thing, e.g., a house rather than a tree, but also that determinate and well specified perception which it actually is, that is to say, a perception through which the house presents itself under *this* aspect, from *this* side, and not in a different (though equally possible) manner of adumbrational appearance. For that reason, Husserl calls the object as perceived – to be taken exactly as it appears through a given perception – the "perceptual sense" (*Wahrnehmungssinn*) or *perceptual noema*, a term which henceforth replaces that of "content."

[14] *Ibid.*

conception of consciousness as a correlation between items pertaining to two entirely different planes: on the one hand, the plane of temporal psychological events; on the other hand, that of ideal, i.e., atemporal meanings in the wider sense.[15]

These formulations, however, carry us far beyond our present stage of discussion of the doctrine of noesis-noema. It is to that stage that we now return.

§ 4. The Phenomenological Signification of Sense. Concluded

Earlier we noted that the terms "intentional object" and "objective sense" are sometimes used ambiguously by Husserl.[16] At times it would seem to be more consistent with Husserl's later usage to designate that moment of the noema which is called in the *Ideas* the "substratum X" of determinations, the "central noematic moment," as the intentional object *qua* intentional object, or the intentional object as such.[17] This appears to be in line with the following passage of the *Cartesian Meditations* where Husserl says that

descriptions of the intentional object as such, with regard to the determinations attributed to it in the modes of consciousness concerned, attributed furthermore with corresponding modalities, which stand out when attention is directed to them.[18]

But then Husserl goes on to speak as though the intentional object were an objective sense when, as an identity throughout a multiplicity of intendings and throughout a multiplicity of perspectival appearances, it is taken as continuously immanent in the noesis, though not as a really inherent component part: it is immanent as a "being-in-it 'ideally' as something *intentional*, something appearing – or, equivalently stated, a being-in-it as its immanent 'objective sense.' "[19] Here the term "objective sense" is what we have called the "intentional object" in § 2.[20] The passage itself may be *interpreted*, I believe, in the following way:

What Husserl is describing is the object of the intending taken precisely and purely as intended to, the object intended to as

[15] *Ibid.*, p. 364.
[16] See, e.g., *Ideen*, I, § 37, pp. 66f.; § 90, pp. 185f.
[17] *Ibid.*, § 131, p. 271.
[18] *Cartesian Meditations*, § 15, p. 36.
[19] *Ibid.*, p. 42.
[20] Cf. *ibid.*, § 20.

such in the sense which it has for consciousness of it. As a consequence, the intentional object is contrasted with the objective sense of that object for consciousness of it and, on the other hand, the term "objective sense" is so broadened in that it now signifies the intentional object *with respect to the objective sense it has for consciousness.* The virtue of this formulation for Husserl's doctrine of noesis-noema is that not only does it point to the fact that intentionality consists in having a sense, but also to the fact that no intentional object is presented as such without having a more or less determinate sense.

In this connection it is necessary to observe something else. In the first volume of *Ideas* Husserl also speaks of the intentional object under the heading of the "determinate X in the noematic sense." [21] A distinct Kantian nuance is apparent at first sight in Husserl's speaking of the *"pure X in abstraction from all predicates* – and it is distinguished *from* these predicates or, more precisely, from predicative noemata [*Prädikatnoemen*]." A brief consideration of this Kantian nuance will help clarify what it signifies to say that the intentional object and the objective sense are moments of the full noema.

In the *Critique of Pure Reason*, Kant speaks of a "something = X":

All our representations are, it is true, referred by the understanding to some object; and since appearances are nothing but representations, the understanding refers them to a *something*, as the object of sensible intuition. But this something, thus conceived, is only the transcendental object; and by that is meant a something = X, of which we know, and with the present constitution of our understanding can know, nothing whatsoever, but which, as a correlate of the unity of apperception, can serve only for the unity of the manifold in sensible intuition.[22]

The profound difference between Husserl and Kant is clear without further commentary: The *X* of which Husserl speaks is determined and further determinable, hence known and further knowable. In § 131 of *Ideas* Husserl is saying that in the noema of any particular mental process we can distinguish phenomenologically between the determined and determinable object X, the intentional object, and the determinations imputed to it in the mental

---

[21] *Ideen* I, § 131, p. 270. See also *ibid.*, § 88, p. 181, where the term "sense" also has this broad extension.

[22] I. Kant, *Critique of Pure Reason* (London: Macmillan, 1953), translated by Norman Kemp Smith, p. 268 (A250).

process in question. Obviously then the Kantian notion of a "transcendental X" and the Husserlian notion of a "pure X" are completely distinct.

§ 5. *The Concept of Objectivation*

Defined in a word, objectivating acts of consciousness are those in which the ego makes something "objective" for himself. This is the *explicit*, as contrasted to the implicit, objective sense of the act. Living in mental processes, the ego can be busied with intentional objects in various ways: doxically (e.g., believingly, doubtingly, supposingly), non-doxically (emotionally, likingly, valuationally), and willingly, strivingly.[23] However, active valuing or active willing, for instance, still do not make the valued or the willed an object for the ego living in the intending in question; equivalently stated, if the intending is non-doxic or conative, nothing is objectivated for the ego even if he is living in the intending in question. Reformulated in a positive way, only a *doxic* intending in which the ego lives can be an act wherein something is made objective for the ego.[24] For example, a hammer is constituted as such in the hammering; yet the hammer is not grasped, let alone objectivated, in the hammering. Nonetheless, such an act is said by Husserl to be a "potential objectivating act" so far as it is subject to a new and further act, namely a doxic objectivating.[25]

Here as before we can see the "relativity" of the objective sense to those mental processes in which the ego is engaged. Precisely this phenomenological situation requires further clarification in order to further develop and critically revise the concept of objective sense, the "noematic What."

In this connection perhaps the first thing to note is that not only are all non-doxic intendings non-objectivating, but that *some* doxic intendings are also non-objectivating. For example, I judge step by step that all men are mortal, that Socrates is a man, that therefore Socrates is mortal. Another and further doxic act is required to objectivate the syntactically formed state of

[23] *Ideen* I, § 117, p. 244.
[24] *Ibid.;* also § 121, p. 251.
[25] *Ibid.*

affairs constituted in the judging. Or, suppose that I am living in the act of collecting things – this, that and the other thing; living in the act I am busied with the collection, forming it for myself. But, again, this is still not an objectivating of the collectivum as such for me; another doxic act is required to invoke the collection as a "theme," to make the collection as such thematic, "objective." [26] We shall return to these examples again in a later section.

§ 6. Continuation. Objectivation and Attention

The two examples of doxic acts which do not objectivate can be contrasted with two examples of doxic acts which do objectivate. In developing these examples it is necessary to invoke the concept of attention as employed by Husserl in the first volume of *Ideas*. Let us take the case of a sensuous perceiving, such as a seeing, in which the ego is engaged and busied with something. In this case of busiedness, though as we shall suggest later (§ 9) not in all cases, I am paying attention to something, and what I am paying attention to is objectivated for me (even though not all that which is intended to in that act is or need be objectivated). Suppose that I am living in the seeing of the ashtray; I turn my attention to the ashtray which I had been seeing all along, but "inactually." Something is now objectivated for me: "This – X." But X is not merely intended to as X; this is not a mere seeing of X. Instead it is actively intended to as X, as "This – blue, elongated rectangular ashtray." When I first turn to the seeing of the ashtray, X is posited by me in the mode of simple certainty. Until I turn my attention to the seeing of a quality or part whereof there continuously was a seeing, and grasp it, the quality or part in question are not objectivated for me.

In other words, if I am paying attention to the ashtray, it is objectivated for me; or if I am paying attention to its color or shape, then they are objectivated for me, made thematic. As it

---

[26] See Edmund Husserl, *Formale und transzendentale Logik* (Halle: Max Niemeyer, 1928), § 39, p. 95. See also Aron Gurwitsch, "Phenomenology of Thematics and of the Pure Ego: Studies of the Relation between Gestalt Theory and Phenomenology," *Studies in Phenomenology and Psychology* (Evanston: Northwestern University Press, 1966), pp. 247ff.

were, objectivation orients and centers the perceptual field, gives to the field a center of attention. As a rule anything that is the center of attention as regards perception becomes spatially central to the visual field, for instance. But this need not be the case; for example, suppose that I do not want someone to know that I am watching him; in this case the spatial center of the visual field and the center of attention are not the same. But if we are interested in something which we wish to see with maximum clarity we make the center of attention the spatial center of the perceptual field.

Still another example of an objectivating doxic act is that of recollection. I no longer see the ashtray, but now recollect it as having been seen before. Living in the recollecting, I make "objective" for me what was perhaps only implicitly imputed to the ashtray in the seeing of it: the bottom of the ashtray which had been previously apperceived.

All of these examples point to a distinction important for the understanding of the concept of objectivation, namely the distinction between objectivating and grasping.

§ 7. Continuation. Objectivating and Grasping

Let us return to our earlier examples of a step-by-step judging. I am presently looking at a table and now proceed to judge that it is dark oak in color. First I pay attention to the table, then to its color, then turn my attention back to the table, step by step judging that this table has that color. In this case there is constituted a complex mental act at each stage of which something is objectivated for me. It makes sense, to be sure, to say that I am living in acts and busied with the table, but in the further course of the act I am busied with the table not only in paying attention to it but also in judging about the table as a "substrate object." Indeed, I am living primarily in judging about the table rather than in the seeing of it. But even though I am busied doxically with the seen table, the seen color of the table, and the judgment I produce about the colored table, I am busied with the seen table and color "receptively," so to speak. In contrast, I am busied with the judgment productively. And the productive busiedness does not objectivate; rather it takes still another doxic act to objectivate the judgment produced. In each of the examples we have considered, but especially in this last one Husserl holds that all objectivatings are *ipso facto graspings* of the things or states of affairs objectivated.

In this last example, in virtue of grasping and objectivating the seen oak-colored table, I proceed to produce the judgment that this table is colored. In virtue of grasping and objectivating the judgment about the table I can proceed to grasp and objectivate its judgmental form, and so forth. The constituting of the objective sense in each case points back to mental processes not only in which I am living, but also to ones, specifically, which grasp and objectivate. Thus not only is the objective sense "relative" to the ego-dimensionality of consciousness, but only to those acts which grasp and objectivate. This, however, need not be the case. Indeed, were this the case, then it would mean that to objectivate, e.g., the predicative form of the judgment, "This table is oak-colored," not only would that form have to be grasped, but also there would have to be a grasping of the seen table, the seen color, etc. Clearly this is not necessary. Or, in the case of recollecting having seen the ashtray, to objectivate the unseen but apperceived bottom of the ashtray it not only would be necessary to grasp it but also to have grasped (and perchance objectivated) the bottom on the basis of an original seeing of it. Or, consider still another example: objectivating the Pythagorean Theorem. To grasp the Theorem, according to Husserl, it would be necessary to rehearse its demonstration step by step – just as in the case of the judgment, "This table is oak-colored." Then on this basis, namely of rehearsing the demonstration, I would proceed to grasp and objectivate the Theorem. But clearly I can turn to the Theorem, advert to it, for instance, as a general topic of discussion, without having to demonstrate it; moreover, I can do so without necessarily having to recollect what it is about – just as I can objectivate the apperceived bottom of the ashtray without actually having had to see it. (Of course, I might want to see it, or I might want to demonstrate the Theorem to prove my prowess at geometry – but this is an entirely different matter.)

Even in terms of the first volume of *Ideas*, all of this suggests 1) that grasping is not the same as objectivating, making thematic, and 2) that grasping is not a sufficient, let alone necessary, condition for objectivating.[27]

These conclusions allow for significant revision of the concept of objective sense, of the "noematic What," and provide for, among other things, the distinction between explicit *and implicit* objective sense.

§ 8. Conclusion. Objectivating, Paying Attention to and Grasping

So far as the first volume of *Ideas* is concerned, doxic acts which are graspings of that to which attention is turned are *eo ipso* objectivating acts. But this seems to be a limitation, and definitely not a necessary one. The chief reason for this is two-fold. In the first place, what Husserl in effect has done is to take a special case of intentionality as actuality, namely *attention*, and make it go bail for all other cases of actuality, all other cases where the ego lives in mental processes. As a consequence, Husserl uses the special case to explain objectivating.[28] Because of this the concept of the objective sense, indeed of the noema as a whole, is defined with respect to the ego-dimensionality of the noesis.[29] All grasping turns out to be the paying attention to something, and all paying attention to something is objectivating.[30] But if this is not necessarily the case, then the noema cannot be defined relative to *acts* of consciousness alone. We shall return to this point at the beginning of § 9.

In the second place, Husserl also defines the "belief quality" of the noesis with respect to ego-engagement in mental life. Thus in our earlier example of perceiving the ashtray, that perceiving was a believing in the ashtray as existing. According to Husserl, just as I may actually posit a part or quality of an intentional object, so I may likewise turn my attention to its existence, grasp it, make it "existence for me." As in the case of the objective

---

[27] This view has been systematically developed by Dorion Cairns in his lectures on "Husserl's Theory of Intentionality" at the Graduate Faculty of Political and Social Science, The New School for Social Research. Also cf. Edmund Husserl, *Ideen zu einer reinen Phänomenologie und phänomenologischen Philosophie* (The Hague: Martinus Nijhoff, 1952), Vol. II, edited by Marly Biemel, § 10, p. 23, lines 28–38.

[28] See *Ideen* I, § 113; also *Ideen* I (The Hague: Martinus Nijhoff, 1950), edited by Walter Biemel, Beilage XX (1914), pp. 406f.; and Edmund Husserl, *Analysen zur Passiven Synthesis (1918–1926)* (The Hague: Martinus Nijhoff, 1966), edited by Margot Fleischer, p. 322; and *Logische Untersuchungen*, II, 1, pp. 409ff.

[29] Cf., e.g., *Ideen*, I, § 103, pp. 214ff.

[30] See especially *ibid.*, § 37, pp. 66f.; also § 35, p. 63 and § 92.

sense, the "characterization" of the noema, its "thetic character,"
is relative to the ego-dimension of consciousness. But more than
with the case of attention, this is inconsistent with the later
results of Husserl's work. Husserl himself realized this perhaps
as early as 1916,[31] and certainly no later than 1918.[32] By that
time he had begun to fully develop his insight into "passive Doxa"
and hence had begun to break away, in the actual course of his
analyses, from the idea that non-attention was simply a special
case of attention, that it must be defined solely in terms of attention and attentional modifications, and from the idea that attention, as a special case of act, could explain all cases of acts. Both
the noema at large and the objective sense in particular must be
reformulated to take account of these developments in Husserl's
thought. In the next section we can briefly indicate the extent of
this reformulation suggested earlier in the distinction between
explicit and implicit objective sense.

§ *9. Revision of the Concepts of Objective Sense and Objectivating*

   a. *Husserl's Concept of "Passive Doxa."* The title of § 4 of
Formal and Transcendental Logic reads: "The Problem of Ascer-
taining the Essential Limits of the 'Thinking' Capable of the
Significational Function." [33] Under this heading Husserl defines
"thinkings" as mental processes whose objective senses are expressed or expressible by locutions, or which can be the significations of mental processes. Such mental processes are said to be
"sinngebend," to bestow signification on locutions. Taking §§ 3
and 4 together, examples of mental processes having this capacity are judgings, wishings, askings, commandings, and doubtings.
Husserl then goes on to distinguish those mental processes which
do not have the capacity to bestow signification, that is, whose
objective senses cannot be significations of expressions or expressed by locutions. An obvious case would be the objective
sense of a sensuous perceiving; for instance, the touched as touch-

[31] Cf. *Ideen* I (Biemel), pp. 406f. See also Theodor Celms, *Der phänomenologische Idealismus Husserls* (Riga: Lettland, 1928), pp. 331f.
[32] See especially the manuscripts published in *Analysen zur Passiven Synthesis*, pp. 342ff., in particular, p. 345.
[33] *Formale und transzendentale Logik*, p. 22. The translation is by Dorion Cairns, *Formal and Transcendental Logic* (The Hague: Martinus Nijhoff, 1969), p. 25.

ed cannot itself be expressed by a word or sentence. § 4, however, also offers a somewhat different contrast.

From judgings, wishings, askings, etc., Husserl distinguishes those mental processes characterized by "original passivity," by "passivity" which would include "passive Doxa." Examples are associating mental processes, retentions, protentions and the like.[34] That is to say, he suggests a classification which cuts across the difference between mental processes capable and incapable of bestowing signification, across the difference ultimately between mental processes in which the ego is or can be engaged and those in which he is not and cannot be engaged. Thus not only must the objective sense be defined with respect to those mental processes in which the ego is or can be engaged, but it must also be defined with respect to those in which the ego cannot in principle be engaged. These latter mental processes likewise not only intend to but also mean their objects as this or that. To be sure, according to Husserl's later view [35] originally passive mental processes are never full objectivatings if by "to objectivate" we not only mean to invoke the objective sense as theme but also to "seize upon" and "have" it as it itself. For this reason it is necessary to introduce the distinction between explicit and implicit objective sense. We cannot develop this distinction further here, however.

b. Husserl's Concept of Attention. Once the distinction between explicit and implicit objective sense is drawn, and once it is seen that grasping is not *ipso facto* a necessary and sufficient condition for objectivating, that even in original passivity there is a partial objectivating, it is possible to set the concept of attention within a different framework, namely one in which it no longer serves as the special case of act of consciousness explaining all acts of consciousness in the pregnant sense.

[34] *Ibid.*, p. 22: "Denn nicht alle haben diese Fähigkeit. Erlebnisse ursprünglicher Passivität, fungierende Assoziationen, die Bewußtseinserlebnisse, in denen sich das ursprüngliche Zeitbewußtsein, die Konstitution der immanenten Zeitlichkeit abspielt und dgl., sind dazu unfähig." See also *ibid.*, Beilage II, for concrete examples.
[35] See, e.g., *ibid.*, §§ 58f., and *Cartesian Meditations*, § 20, p. 48: "... that is to say: not only the actual but also the *potential* subjective processes, which, as such, are 'implicit' and 'predelineated' in the sense-producing intentionality of the actual ones and which, when discovered, have the evident character of processes that explicate the implicit sense."

As with the case of passive Doxa, we can only indicate the nature of the reformulation which has been carried out on several occasions by Aron Gurwitsch, but most notably in his essay, "Phenomenology of Thematics and of the Pure Ego" (1929).[36] The theory of theme and thematization developed by Gurwitsch in this essay purports to be an adequate account of the "noematic What." [37] The concrete phenomenological analyses he reports show what we have already suggested in the previous section, namely that Husserl's account of the objective sense is incorrect because it is finally explained by the theory of attention. But Gurwitsch does not stop here; he goes on to show that the theory of attention is itself incorrect since it falsely holds that attention and attentional modifications do not affect the material content of what is given.[38] This is shown on the basis of the analysis of three kinds of attentional modifications, the results of which

contradict precisely the thesis that attentional modifications are without import for the noematic material What. We have shown that the noema is affected just as to its material content and that, furthermore, the sense and the direction of its alteration varies from case to case. Attentional modifications must, therefore, not be considered as changes in illumination; nor is the comparison with the moving beam of light appropriate at all. On the contrary, attentional modifications affect the material content of the noema to such an extent that a radically different noema results.[39]

This leads Gurwitsch to the formulation of the "general transformation law" pertaining to the objective sense:

To every datum correspond other data, to every theme in its thematic field other themes in their fields, in such a way that any given experience motivates certain transitions as possible. ... Thus, we are confronted with a system of different noemata interconnected in such a way that each one of them contains motivations for possible transitions to any one of the others.[40]

---

[36] *Op. cit., loc. cit.,* pp. 175ff.

[37] *Ibid.,* pp. 184f., 249, 265.

[38] *Ibid.,* pp. 213ff., 248f., 265f.

[39] *Ibid.,* p. 265. The three kinds or series of modifications examined by Gurwitsch are 1) the identical theme over against variations in thematic surroundings, 2) the situation where the theme ceases to be the theme, even though it nevertheless remains the same as to its material content, and 3) where there is a change or alteration in the material content of the theme.

[40] *Ibid.,* pp. 266f. See *ibid.,* pp. 248f., and Aron Gurwitsch, "Contribution to the Phenomenological Theory of Perception," *Studies in Phenomenology and Psychology,* pp. 346ff. It remains to be seen whether or not certain cases of possible transitions involve objectivating ("thematizing") which always and of necessity presupposes a grasping simpliciter of the objective sense.

Ultimately this revision demands a formulation of noesis-noema which goes beyond Husserl and which concerns Gurwitsch's theory of the organization of the field of consciousness. It is outside the scope of the present essay to consider that theory. It is rather necessary to deal with several other aspects of Husserl's noesis-noema doctrine.

§ 10. Other Noetic-Noematic Components

In addition to the objective sense, the "noematic What," Husserl distinguishes several other components of the noema: chiefly the "noematic How" or manners of presentation, "givenness," and the existential characterization of the noema, "positionality." [41] In addition, and in what is perhaps the only full commentary published on Husserl's noesis-noema doctrine, Theodor Celms further distinguishes the noematic sense "in the mode of fulness" [42] – a concept which Husserl had first developed in the Sixth Logical Investigation.[43] Finally, on the noetic side there is hyletic data. As in the case of the objective sense, these "analytic" distinctions present difficulties and ambiguities whose full clarification and reformulation lie outside our present inquiry. As with our discussion of the concept of objective sense, so here we shall be primarily interested in suggesting the extent to which the initial formulation of the doctrine of noesis-noema must be changed to allow for Husserl's later views.

§ 11. Manners of Presentation

An intentional object can be meant and intended to as having the same or different objective senses in intendings which themselves differ in such a way that the manners of presentation or

[41] See below, § 12. Cf. Gurwitsch, "Phenomenology of Thematics ...," pp. 184f.

[42] Celms, op. cit., pp. 335f. See also the commentary of Paul Ricoeur to Ideen, I, § 88: Idées directrices pour une phénoménologie (Paris: Gallimard, 1950), translated by Paul Ricoeur, p. 305, note 2.

[43] Celms summarizes Husserl's view as follows: "Das jeweils sinnlich Anschauliche ist also dem Akte selbst immanent, d.h. nicht ein Moment der Transzendenz, sondern der Immanenz. Der 'Sinn im Modus seiner Fülle' bedeutet dann auch nicht den Sinn als abstrakte Form, sondern den anschauungsmässig erfüllten Sinn und nur sofern diese Erfüllung jeweils wirklich vorhanden ist, d.h. das konkrete Ganze aus der Sinnesform und hyletischem Inhalt. Es leuchtet auch ohne weiteres ein, dass derselbe absolut identische Sinn verschiedene Füllen haben kann." P. 330.

"givenness" of the intentional object differ accordingly.[44] This
suggests a dimension of description different from the one we
have been pursuing up to now. So far we have been concerned
with a line of description in which we would apply such formal
ontological expressions as "object," "syntactically formed state
of affairs"; or we would apply such material ontological expressions as "thing," "shape," "cause"; or, again, we would apply
such expressions of material determinations as "rough," "colored," and the like.[45] But the dimension or line of description with
which we are now concerned deals rather with that in which we
would employ such expressions as "perceptual," "memorial,"
"clearly intuitive," "conceptual," "presented," and the like. That
is to say, it deals with the manners in which there is consciousness
of something.[46] This line of description is completed if we further
speak of that in which we also employ such expressions as
"original," "less original," "non-original" – the "modes of fullness." [47]

The gist of Husserl's view may be stated as follows: an apple,
for example, can be presented in a sensuous perceiving or in a
remembering, or in an "empty" or "blind" intending as having
the sense, "This – red, hard." The term "presentation" (or
"givenness") is to be taken in a very broad sense to express not
only what is strictly presented, but also to express what is not
strictly presented. And within the sphere of strict presentation –
for example, perceptual or memorial presentation – the difference
between, say, tactual and visual presentations, is said to be a
difference in the manner of presentation of the "what" of the
intending. For instance, the perceived or remembered sense "red"
is presented visually; the perceived or remembered sense "hard"
is presented tactually. Also within the sphere of one such manner
of presentation we find, for example, that the visual objective
sense remains identical throughout variations in clarity or obscurity of presentation.

Basically for Husserl we may speak of two kinds of presentation: 1) presentation which is intuitive and clear; 2) presentation
which is non-intuitive (e.g., symbolic presentation, obscure pres-

---

[44] *Ideen* I, § 99, pp. 209f.; § 132, p. 273.
[45] *Ibid.*, § 91, p. 189; *Logische Untersuchungen*, II, 1, § 20, pp. 415f.
[46] *Ideen* I, § 99, p. 209; § 130, pp. 267ff.
[47] *Ibid.*, § 132, p. 273; § 136, p. 284; § 138, p. 287.

entation). As regards the first kind, intuitive presentation can be either original or non-original, either a "giving" of the affair as it itself, "in person," or not. For the most part this distinction holds in Husserl's later writings, although it must be extended to the domain of "passivity," of "passive 'pregivenness.'" Thus intentional analysis of manners of presentation is an analysis of the How or the way in which there is active and/or "passive" meaning and intending to something as it itself, or as symbolized, or depicted by something else. It should be noted here that in writings after the first volume of *Ideas* manners of presentation are dealt with more and more under the heading of "evidence." [48]

§ 12. Positionality and Noematic "Characterization"

Objects appear to us through our consciousness of them in various manners of presentation not only meant and intended to as having this or that implicit or explicit sense, but also as "characterized," as being thus and so. The "characterization" involves the "positional character" of the noesis, the positional modality of consciousness.[49] Within the framework of the first volume of *Ideas*, a main class of positionality is that of doxic positionality which includes all acts which are believing in, or disbelieving in their intentional objects either with simple certainty or with some degree of uncertainty.[50] Disbelievings, doubtings, neutrality and the like are said to be modifications or modalities of believing with simple certainty. In this connection Husserl also speaks of "potential" or "inactual" positionality,[51] the concept of which must be extended to include purely "passive" positing and its modes as well as, ultimately, the primal, yet unmodalized, "passive Doxa" at the basis of all experiencing of the world.[52]

More particularly, Husserl distinguishes the "act thesis" or "noetic thesis" of intendings from the "thetic character" as their noematic correlate.[53] For example, in perceiving the ashtray I

[48] See, for example, *Cartesian Meditations*, § 24.
[49] See *Ideen* I, § 114.
[50] See *ibid.*, §§ 103ff.
[51] *Ibid.*, § 113, p. 228.
[52] See Edmund Husserl, *Erfahrung und Urteil* (Hamburg: Classen Verlag, 1954), edited by Ludwig Landgrebe, §§ 7, 11ff.
[53] *Ideen* I, § 114, p. 233; § 117, p. 242.

believe in it with simple certainty; instead of objectivating the percept I may objectivate the thetic character: "Ashtray – existent." Relative to the simple believing in the ashtray, "existent" is not part of the objective sense, not part of the "predicative noemata." [54] Instead, the thetic character belongs to an entirely different dimension. The ashtray is meant and intended to as round and existent; "round" designates a component part of the objective sense, while "existent" designates something completely distinct. Suppose, furthermore, that I am engaged in the judging, "This is something round," and that I then proceed to judge, "This round something exists." Restated, the first judgment is: "This thing is something round"; the second judgment is: "This meant thing is not only something meant, but also something existent." Determinations such as round, colored, on the table to the left of the inkwell, etc., are predicated of things, that is, of the object "which is intended to"; existence (or non-existence)

[54] To the best of my knowledge, there has been no work in depth carried out on the significance of Husserl's view expressed here for modern philosophy, especially as regards Kant's epoch-making refutation of the ontological argument. As is known, that argument centers around Hume's account of existence in the *A Treatise of Human Nature* (Oxford: The Clarendon Press, 1951). There Hume states that all impressions and ideas are conceived as existent, and from that conception the "perfect idea and assurance of being is deriv'd." This gives rise to a dilemma, namely that the idea of existence is either derived from an impression constantly conjoined with every object of thought, or the idea of existence is the same as the idea of the object of thought (see Book I, Part II, § VI, p. 65). Hume concludes that the idea of existence is not derived from an impression since it would signify that there are cases where two distinct impressions would be inseparably joined. As a consequence, the idea of existence "is the very same with the idea of what we conceive to be existent. To reflect on any thing simply, and to reflect on it as existent, are nothing different from each other. That idea, when conjoin'd with the idea of any object, *makes no addition to it.* Whatever we conceive, we conceive to be existent. Any idea we please to form is the idea of a being; and the idea of a being is any idea we please to form." Anyone who does not agree with this "must necessarily point out that distinct impression from which the idea of entity is deriv'd, and must prove, that this impression is inseparable from every perception we believe to be existent. This we may without hesitation conclude to be impossible." (p. 66)

Kant's answer to Hume is correct: namely, that existence is not a real predicate. But this must be understood, following Husserl, in the sense that "existence" is not just another property among others, in Husserl's language that the noematic thesis is a "character" rather than a stratum of the noema. Not only must the meant sense "existing" not be confused with the objectivated form "existence," but neither must be confused with a property of a thing. Existence or being has nothing at all to do with property. (See *Erfahrung und Urteil*, § 75.) Indeed, to assert the contrary would be, phenomenologically expressed, to assert that there is an objective analogue in the world of the "relationship" of consciousness as intending and its object purely and precisely as intended to. Hume assumes that if existence is anything at all it must be a property in some sense; Kant realizes that this is not the case, but fails to provide a positive answer which Husserl does with the discovery of the noematic thesis. Here we cannot enter further into this problem.

is "predicated" of the object "as it is intended to." [55] By objectivating the senses of the seeing of the ashtray, its shape and color are made thematic for me; but by objectivating the noematic correlate of the believing, existence is made thematic. The object seen, the ashtray, is believed in *as existing*.

Here again objectivation evokes a distinction in dimensions of consciousness,[56] namely between the dimension of noetic theses and thetic characters such as existence on the one hand, and the dimension of manners of presentation on the other hand. If the manner of presentation varies, for example, if the seen ashtray is presented as absent, then there is a correlative variation in the thetic character – the ashtray is believed in dubitatively, uncertainly as only probably existing, or perchance as not existing at all.[57]

Before turning to a development of Husserl's concept of thetic character, it is necessary to note two things in passing. In the first place, it is necessary to distinguish with Husserl doxic positionality from *non-doxic* positionality, doxic thetic characters from *non-doxic* thetic characters.[58] There can be a simply certain liking, or a dubious liking, or an uncertain liking of something perceived, for example. In the case of the simple certain liking of what I perceive, the thetic character is good; in the case of disliking, the character is bad, or evil. We cannot enter into this further here. In the second place, suppose that I am living in the seeing of the ashtray, explicating the shape and color of the ashtray with which I am busied. In no way, however, is this an objectivating of the thetic character the ashtray is posited as having in seeing it. This objectivation only occurs in a new and further act in which I am busied with the "being busied with the ashtray intended to and believed in as existing." Generalized, the implication of this is highly important because it signifies that for every thesis, doxic *or non-doxic*, there is always a possible *doxic* objectivation. As a consequence, doxic intentionality acquires a primacy, being and non-being, finally, reason and un-

[55] See *Logische Untersuchungen*, II, 1, pp. 400ff., especially 435f.; Gurwitsch, *The Field of Consciousness*, pp. 185ff.; Husserl, *Cartesian Meditations*, § 23, p. 56.
[56] However, the distinction is not in *levels:* precisely for this reason Husserl speaks of "modalities" of consciousness; see *Cartesian Meditations*, § 24, p. 58.
[57] *Ideen*, I, § 107, p. 220; § 136, pp. 282ff.; *Cartesian Meditations*, § 26, pp. 59f.
[58] *Ideen*, I, § 114, p. 234; § 115, p. 237; § 117, p. 241; § 121, pp. 250ff.

reason include everything – even valuing and disvaluing, liking and disliking.[59] When the thetic character is objectivated in a new and further doxic act, *ipso facto* there is a new thesis with the previous thesis as the objective sense. Thesis is always, for Husserl, *syn*-thesis:

> As we have said, the multiplicities of modes of consciousness that belong together synthetically and pertain to any meant object, of no matter what category, can be explored as to their phenomenological types. Among such multiplicities are included those syntheses that, with regard to the initial intending, have the typical style of verifying and, in particular, evidently verifying syntheses – or else, on the contrary, that of nullifying and evidently nullifying syntheses. When such a synthesis takes place, the meant object has, correlatively, the evident characteristic *existing*, or else the evident characteristic *non-existing* ... These synthetic occurrences are intentionalities of a higher level, which, as acts and correlates of "reason," essentially producible by the transcendental ego, pertain (in exclusive disjunction) to all objective senses.[60]

Reason is not then an "accidental de facto ability," but always refers to "possibilities of verification." To be sure, to say that objects in the broadest sense "exist for me is a statement that says nothing immediately about evidence; it says only that objects are accepted by me – are, in other words, there for me as cogitata intended in the positional mode: certain believing." [61] But should that acceptance have to be abandoned, for instance, in the further course of experience, then

> we can be sure something is *actual* only by virtue of a synthesis of evident verification, which presents rightful or true actuality itself. It is clear that truth or the true actuality of objects is to be obtained only from *evidence*, and that it is evidence alone by virtue of which an *"actually"* *existing*, true, rightly accepted object of whatever form or kind *has sense for us* ...[62]

That possible doxic objectivating of every thesis whereby an existing object of whatever form, real or ideal, has sense for us, is grounded ultimately in the very nature of transcendental subjectivity.

---

[59] See *Cartesian Meditations*, § 24, p. 58.
[60] *Ibid.*, § 23, pp. 56f.
[61] *Ibid.*, § 26, p. 59.
[62] *Ibid.*, p. 60.

§ 13. The Phenomenological Signification of Sense Reconsidered

One of the chief concerns of the first volume of *Ideas*, and the setting in which the doctrine of noesis-noema is developed, is explication and clarification of the "general thesis of the natural attitude," the "thetic character" or existential sense the world is posited as having. In this connection, Aron Gurwitsch has recast Husserl's concept of the "thetic character" of the noema in terms of a principle of organization.[63] By this I mean that in and through acts of consciousness the world and objects of all kinds are presented – both through single, one-sided perceptual acts and through concatenated systems of acts of all kinds. Presented in and through those acts, objects meant and intended to not only exhibit their properties, qualities, determinations, relations to one another, but they also show themselves as existing (or probably existing, not existing) in specific manners – for instance, as really existing (or as really not existing), as ideally existing (or not ideally existing). Earlier (§ 3) we noted that the "relationship" between noesis and noema is not only *sui generis* but that it also consists in correlation of items belonging to separate planes. Consciousness so understood within the transcendental reduction turns out to be the universal medium of access to the world and objects of the most diverse description, and to their multiple modes of being.

This signifies, among other things, that existence and non-existence, being and nothing, can only be approached indirectly. Most fundamentally to say that consciousness is the (always indirect) access to the general thesis of the natural attitude toward the world signifies that consciousness is most primordially characterized as having a positional-presentational function. Positional presentationality is the basic dimension of the intentionality of consciousness, the basic characterization of consciousness as at or toward the world. At the risk of inviting possible, and perchance even further, misunderstanding of the noesis-noema doctrine, we can introduce a metaphor to express the various descriptive dimensions of intentional analysis involved here.

[63] See Aron Gurwitsch, "The Problem of Existence in Constitutive Phenomenology," *Studies in Phenomenology and Psychology*, pp. 116ff.

Metaphorically, consciousness positionally presenting the world can be likened to a theatre; the audience sits in the darkened area, while the stage is illuminated. Across the dark, the light, the illuminated play is presented. The darkness is consciousness which, by "degrading" itself, making itself dark, allows the light (the play) to be presented. Across the negative, darkness, the positive shows itself – the play (the world). That "positive" is equally a "playing along with the play," a primordial credulity mutually locked into the illuminating presentationality.

This metaphor surely has its inadequacies. But in spite of them and in the first place, it underscores the fact that the world and things, events and others in it are not presented chaotically but instead as always organized, arranged, ordered, standing in a specific context. In the second place, it makes prominent the fact that the relation of consciousness to the world is not a causal one; instead, it is the "relationship" of relevancy and significancy which, in turn, is rooted in the "relationship" of, e.g., perceiving and perceived *as* perceiving and perceived. The positional presentationality of consciousness cannot be reduced to some sort of objective analogue such as the *relation in time* between an event of consciousness and another real event in the world (the percept). The relation of the perceiving and the perceived as such is wholly *sui generis*, which we have tried to express in the metaphor with the expression, "playing along with the play."

Of course the expression is deceptive since, fundamentally, it is not a question of "play" at all. Rather, "serious" presentation of the world as organized, ordered, believed in as having a certain context of relevance and significancy is presentation of the world as existing. "To be," "to exist," signifies accordingly insertion into a specific context dominated by some principle of relevancy and significancy. Two brief examples will suffice to suggest what we have in mind and, at the same time, indicate the nature of Gurwitsch's reformulation of the thetic character of the noema.

Consider the case of "ideal existence," such as the case of numbers. Every number holds a definite place within a systematic context; numbers are presented through certain acts of consciousness, such as those of computation used by the mathematician. Moreover, numbers are presented as existing only with reference to other numbers intrinsically co-present with the given number in a given context – e.g., a certain number system such as the system of cardinal numbers. A second example in the case of "real existence": material things are presented in perceptual consciousness and believed in as spatiotemporally ordered. In this case, that spatiotemporality is the principle of relevancy and significancy. That is to say, for a thing or event to be real, it must occur at a certain place and at a certain time. A basic feature of real existents is that they are presented and believed in as mundane, and the (objectivated) thetic character of such things may be designated as "mundaneity" – equivalently stated, "mundane" is the thesis things and events are posited as having in a spatiotemporal context.

Here we cannot enter further into Gurwitsch's account of the inherent organization of the noema, which is a direct consequence of his critique of Husserl's concept of attention (§ 9, b). Instead the example of real existence leads us to our final consideration of the doctrine of noesis-noema: the concept of "hyletic data."

§ 14. Husserl's Concept of "Hyletic Data"

Of all of Husserl's concepts, that of "hyletic data" is one of the most notorious for causing difficulties in rehearsing and advancing his thought. Nonetheless, the concept of "hyletic data" forms a basic part of Husserl's theory of sense perception, hence of the intentional analysis of real existence.

Although concepts similar to that expressed by "hyletic data" had been employed before the first volume of the *Ideas*, it is there that it receives its clearest formulation. Generally speaking, the concept arose in connection with the analysis of fields of sensuous data within which "*Abgehobenheiten*," prominencies or saliencies, stood out from a background and from one another. But this is only part of the task of the analysis of sense perception. Indeed, it was Husserl's contention that in any concrete perception we can discover a highly stratified structure, each lower stratum founding the stratum above it – whereof the lowest founding stratum belonging to any sensuous perceiving of something physical has, as a component "really inherent" [*reelles Bestandstück*] to the perceiving, what Husserl calls "hyletic data." [64]

Reflective observation of any concrete sensuous perceiving of something material discloses another "really inherent" component, namely an intentive component. The hyletic and intentive components together make up the *"Erlebnisse,"* the "subjective" processes of mental life. Hyletic data, Husserl says, designate the "phenomenological residuum of what is mediated in normal external perception by the 'senses.' " [65] Purportedly uncovered by the phenomenological reduction, they concern what is "mediated" in sense perception, that is, they mediate the founding-founded relationship of the multilayered perceptual structure. An example will help illustrate what is at stake here. In examining fields of sensuous data, such as visual or tactual fields, we find specific differences which stand out, are salient or prominent with respect to each other and their background. It is in referring to the role which they play in sensuous perceivings of physical things that Husserl calls these saliencies "hyletic data." [66] And it is precisely this role in the perception of physical or material things which distinguishes hyletic from other kinds of sensuous data, such as kinaesthesias, somatic data such as muscle tensions, "feelings" of the movement of the body, and the like.[67]

Accordingly, to say that the "physical thing is mediated by the senses" signifies that between the stratum of hyletic data on the one hand, and the founded stratum of the perceiving of the physical thing on the other hand, there lies *still another* stratum founded on that of the hyletic data and founding that of the perceiving of the physical thing as self-same throughout a multiplicity of appearances of it. An example of that intermediate stratum is that which functions as the appearances of physical things in concrete sensuous perceivings. To put the matter in the language of the first volume of *Ideas*, the intentive component is both an "animating" construing of the founding stratum of hyletic data as adumbrations of a multiplicity of, e.g., visual appearances of

[64] *Ideen* I, §§ 85, 97. For a penetrating account of the distinctions involved here, see Rudolf Boehm, "Les Ambiguités des concepts husserliens d'"immanence' et de 'transcendence'," *Revue Philosophique*, IV (1959), pp. 482ff.

[65] *Ibid.*, p. 173.

[66] *Ibid.*, p. 176.

[67] *Ibid.*, pp. 65, 172, 205. See also Edmund Husserl, *Vorlesungen zur Phänomenologie des inneren Zeitbewußtseins* (Halle: Max Niemeyer, 1928), edited by M. Heidegger, §§ 8, 42; in addition, see Edmund Husserl, "Notizen zur Raumkonstitution," *Philosophy and Phenomenological Research*, I (1940), edited by Alfred Schutz, pp. 22ff.

the physical thing *and* a perceiving (a seeing) of the physical thing meant as self-identical throughout those appearances.

Two other things must be noted in this connection. In the first place, hyletic data, that founding stratum of sensuous perceiving and really inherent noetic component, belongs in the realm of original passivity – as early as the first volume of *Ideas* Husserl refers to hyletic data as a case of "intentionality" which does not bestow signification (see above, § 9, a).[68] The other is that the *temporal form* of hyletic data, according to the theory, is that of the intentive component of the noesis.

§ 15. Gurwitsch's Criticism of Husserl's Theory of Hyletic Data

In his *Field of Consciousness*,[69] Gurwitsch explains Husserl's theory of perception as a dualistic one, with the duality obtaining between sense-impressions on the one hand, and intentive acts of apprehension, interpretation, objectivation and apperception on the other hand. Gurwitsch points out, in effect, that if we grant Husserl the distinction between determinations of the physical thing appearing through and adumbrated by noetically construed hyletic data on the one hand, and the hyletic data themselves endowed with adumbration-functions on the other hand,[70] then we must also assert, as Husserl would seem to do, that there is nothing peculiar to the nature of hyletic data themselves which *unambiguously* determines the adumbrations of *this* rather than another sensuously perceived physical thing. Thus, although Husserl first develops his concept purely with regard to the role hyletic data play in a sensuous perceiving, to account for that role he must then regard hyletic data as indifferent to the perceiving in question. In other words, hyletic data remain identical throughout different noetic construings, animatings. We must also add that the distinction between hyletic and kinaesthetic

---

[68] *Ideen* I, p. 172.

[69] Gurwitsch, *The Field of Consciousness*, pp. 265ff. In addition see Harmon Chapman, *Sensations and Phenomenology* (Bloomington and London: Indiana University Press, 1966), Chapter VII. Jean-Paul Sartre should also be mentioned in this connection. However, his critique of Husserl's concept of hyletic data is deeply embedded in his metaphysics, and accordingly presents difficult problems of interpretation into which we need not enter here. Suffice it to say that in *L'Être et le néant* (Paris: Gallimard, 1945), pp. 26f. he rejects Husserl's concept to save the appearances, as it were, of the physical thing as an ideal pole of identity.

[70] Gurwitsch, *The Field of Consciousness*, p. 269.

and other sensuous data disappears if there is nothing peculiar to the nature of hyletic data in virtue of which they play the role they do in sense perception. To account for that role, Husserl must introduce an organization-form extraneous and supervenient to hyletic data: a version of the "constancy hypothesis" which Gurwitsch has elsewhere shown to be false.[71]

Here, again, we cannot develop Gurwitsch's alternative to Husserl's concept, important and original as it is. Clearly Husserl's concept of hyletic data must be rejected. But before rejecting the concept out of hand, or even before reinterpreting it in the light of *philosophically* established results of Gestalt theory, it is worth while considering a Husserlian response to this criticism. In the previous section we noted that, for Husserl, the noetic and hyletic strata have the same temporal form. It is to this feature that we now turn.

§ *16. A Possible Revision of Husserl's Theory of Hyletic Data*

Dorion Cairns has called attention to the fact that at the very beginning of the *Vorlesungen zur Phänomenologie des inneren Zeitbewußtseins* Husserl states that this study deals with the constitution of a pure datum of sensation, i.e., a hyletic datum, and the primary or originally passive constitution of "phenomenological time" underlying active mental life.[72] Thus Heidegger, in

---

[71] *Ibid.*, pp. 270f. It is worth while citing some representative passages from Husserl's writings in this connection in addition to the passages from the first volume of *Ideas*. In the 1912 manuscript published as *Husserliana*, volume 5 (The Hague: Martinus Nijhoff, 1952), edited by Marly Biemel, Husserl says, p. 14, that "die Empfindung steht als Gemeinsames an der Grenze sozusagen der zweiten und dritten Stufe. Auf der zweiten Stufe ist sie Bekundung der Empfindsamkeit des Leibes. Andererseits ist sie auf der dritten Stufe stoffliche Unterlage für perzeptive Auffassungen, z.B. für die materielle Wahrnehmung, hierbei in den doppelten oben besprochenen Auffassungsfunctionen stehend: als kinaesthetische in Funktion des Motivierenden, als darstellende Empfindung in der Funktion des Motivierten ..." Here hyletic data and kinaesthetic data are distinguished and distinguishable only in virtue of their motivating and motivated functions. The implication is that in and of themselves they remain identical whether construed as exhibiting a real physical thing or one's own organism. Again, in the lecture course published under the title of "Phänomenologische Psychologie" (Vorlesungen Sommersemester 1925) [*Husserliana*, Volume IX (The Hague: Martinus Nijhoff, 1962), edited by Walter Biemel], Husserl says that we can "abstract" from the appearance- and adumbration-functions and consider the "pure data of sensation" in and of themselves, p. 165. For the difficulty here, see Gurwitsch's example of perceiving clouds and sky-line, *op. cit.*, pp. 271f.

[72] *Vorlesungen zur Phänomenologie des inneren Zeitbewußtseins*, p. 367.

his 1928 introduction to these lectures, following Husserl in the
first volume of *Ideas*, states in effect that hyletic data and the
noetic components of the *Erlebnisse* have the same temporal
form.[73] In this connection Cairns has also observed that at least
part of the *de facto* course of analysis carried out by Husserl is at
variance with his explicit theory. As a matter of fact, Husserl
begins the actual course of his analysis (§ 8) by speaking of the
temporal form of an auditory sensation – e.g., the sound he
describes is said to have "its *own* time-form." Indeed, Husserl
had earlier referred to the "phenomenologically given" as "the
abstract parts of mental processes which specifically found temporal construings as such and, therefore, found ... the specific
temporal content." [74] The "temporal content," the datum's own
temporal form, is, correspondingly, a founded *noematic* stratum,
and not identical with the temporal form of the noesis in question.

If we carry over the results of Husserl's *de facto* course of analysis into his doctrine of noesis-noema, we have a very different
view than the one usually stated by him both in published writ-

---

[73] This view, already developed in the *Logische Untersuchungen* (V), is found, e.g.,
in the posthumously published lectures; for example, in *Husserliana*, IX, p. 171:
"Der Strom des Subjektiven, also in unserer Sphäre der Strom der subjektiven
Empfindungsdaten, Perspektiven, Erscheinungen heißt als Strom von immanent-
zeitlichen Gegenständen, und selbst zur Einheit einer Zeitgegenständlichkeit sich
zusammenschließend, auch Erlebnisstrom. Alles, was wir aus dieser immanenten
Zeitsphäre als einzeln immanenten Zeitgegenstand, als *ein* Erlebnis herausfassen, ist
Seiendes nur als Strömendes. So jedes Empfindungsdatum, aber auch jede Erschein-
ung *von*, jedes intentionale Erlebnis überhaupt." Likewise, in a manuscript dating
from 1916 and appended to the *Husserliana* edition of the first volume of *Ideas* as
Appendix XXIV (pp. 411ff.), Husserl is even more explicit about this than in the
main text (§ 85 – though the appendix is annexed to § 132).
[74] Husserl, *Vorlesungen zur Phänomenologie des inneren Zeitbewußtseins*, § 1, p. 370.
An example of that "temporal content" is given in § 8, p. 385 (English translation
by James B. Churchill, with an Introduction by Calvin O. Schrag, *The Phenomenology
of Internal Time-Consciousness* [Bloomington and London: Indiana University Press,
1964], p. 44): "In this sinking back, I still 'hold' it fast, have it in a 'retention,' and
as long as the retention persists the sound has *its own temporality*" (the emphasis is
mine). That specific temporal content is, in the terms of *Ideen*, I, the noematic
correlate of an auditory sensing on which is founded the apprehending of world-time.
To be sure, the whole issue is not so simple. In other places in the lectures on time-
consciousness Husserl is consistent with his theory. Though he may at times be
unwitting about the theory, he is not uncritical – the theory often bothered him,
and he seems always to have been aware of the fact that the account of time-constitu-
tion would, or *should*, confirm or disconfirm it (see, e.g., *Ideen*, I, pp. 162f.; the
Introduction of Rudolf Boehm to Edmund Husserl, *Zur Phänomenologie des inneren
Zeitbewußtseins (1893–1917)* [*Husserliana* Vol. X] (The Hague: Martinus Nijhoff,
1966), pp. XXXff.). In other research manuscripts relevant to the lectures on time-
consciousness Husserl seems to realize the absurdity of his theory (e.g., those of
around 1908/09, *Husserliana* X, pp. 333f.).

ings and in posthumously published lectures. Nonetheless, it is one which Husserl had himself developed. Certainly part of Gurwitsch's critique is answered because hyletic data are no longer conceived as "inherently real" components of the concrete perceiving, hence the dualistic theory of perception "officially" promulgated by Husserl falls. Indeed, we no longer need call those components "hyletic data" since, as their different time-form suggests, they are instead constituted as transcendent to the flux of mental processes. The "hyle-morphe" relationship stated in the *Ideas* is vitiated.[75] As a consequence, instead of distinguishing between the construing of sensuous data as adumbrative of appearances of things on the one hand, and perceiving the things themselves through those appearances on the other hand, we must now speak of sensuous perceivings of objective physical things noetically-noematically founded on intendings to sensuous data.

This founding-founded structure is quite distinct from that proposed by Husserl in the first volume of the *Ideas* and, if worked out, provides, I believe, a concept consistent with a Husserlian, if not Husserl's, doctrine of noesis-noema.[76]

§ 17. Conclusion

In this essay we have attempted to state, often in an abbrevia-

[75] Although we cannot develop the consequences here, this would entail, among other things, I believe, revision of many of Husserl's doctrines into which the "Form-Stoff" metaphor is carried (and relativized), and of which the Hyle-Morphe concept is a special case (e.g., Husserl's doctrine of judgment, the theory of language). For the extent of the use of this metaphor, see Robert Sokolowski, *The Formation of Husserl's Concept of Constitution* (The Hague: Martinus Nijhoff, 1964), pp. 54ff., especially pp. 57f. Here we may also mention that Sokolowski attempts to untangle the various versions of Husserl's concept of hyletic data in connection with a discussion of the development of the concept of genetic phenomenology, according to which "sense data and noeses are no longer conceived as two distinct elements; they are now seen to be one immanent reality, one inner flow of consciousness" (p. 211). This is, of course, nothing but Husserl's theory all along – the temporal form is the same for hyletic data and noeses. To go on to say that hyletic data are now but one step in genetic constitution (p. 211) would mean, at the least, that not *all* noeses and sense data are "one inner flow of consciousness" (hence they are still radically distinct from *other noeses* in other steps of constitution). The change would seem to be one of emphasis, rather than of theory. For this see Chapman, *op. cit.*, p. 152.

[76] In my doctoral dissertation, "Husserl's Investigations Toward a Phenomenology of Space" (Graduate Faculty of Social and Political Science, The New School for Social Research, 1964), I attempt to articulate in detail the founding-founded structure in question. However, the presentation there is still infected with Husserl's theory, especially in discussion of the "higher" levels of constitution distinguished.

ted and sometimes simplified way, Husserl's doctrine of noesis-noema as it is stated in the first volume of *Ideas*. At the same time we have further attempted to show how that doctrine must be brought "up to date" with the later writings of Husserl, but nonetheless in line with significant phenomenological criticism of Husserl – here chiefly represented by that of Aron Gurwitsch and Dorion Cairns. This essay makes no pretense of exhausting the possible scope of that criticism, and its positive results need to be more fully formulated. In concluding it is necessary to say, however, that it is my belief that the wide range of revision required of the noesis-noema doctrine, and the radical nature of the criticism it evokes, testify not to the weakness of Husserl's doctrine but rather to its strength and richness.

V. J. McGILL

EVIDENCE IN HUSSERL'S PHENOMENOLOGY

Dorion Cairns has stated the fundamental methodological principle of phenomenology as follows: "No opinion is to be accepted as philosophical knowledge unless it is seen to be adequately established by observation of what is seen as itself given 'in person.' " [1] Sense data, perceived objects, psychic acts, emotions, ideas, and essences, are all given, but the givenness is of very different kinds and orders. Phenomenology differs from empiricism in accepting not only sense-data, but *everything* that is given. However, "it differs far more profoundly from any philosophy that sets up formal definitions and postulates, or material hypotheses, and proceeds by a method of formal deduction – supplemented perhaps by material interpretation and 'verification' ... To take conceptual stuff already on hand and fashion a cloak for objects *in absentia*, then call them in for a partial fitting – that is at best only a way to botch together another ingenious misfit to hang away with how many others in the lumber room of history. The matters judged about must themselves be present from the start, and throughout the entire theorizing process they must never be out of sight." [2]

This challenging formulation by one of the most learned authorities on Husserl's philosophy, serves to introduce the aspect of phenomenology we shall discuss in this paper. The primacy of givenness is Cairns' main emphasis, but we shall mostly be concerned with that givenness which is said to be final, namely, self-evidence (*Evidenz*). Our contention will be that in spite of its

---

[1] "An Approach to Phenomenology," *Philosophical Essays in Memory of Edmund Husserl*, Marvin Farber (ed.), Cambridge, Harvard University Press, 1940, p. 4. [Cf. below, p. 224.]

[2] *Ibid.*, pp. 6–7. [Cf. below, pp. 226-227.]

subtle circumspection and refinement Husserl's account of evidence and self-evidence is open to serious objections.

Searching for Self-evidence

Like other first principles the principle of self-evidence is difficult to define or characterize, and several different accounts can be found in Husserl's writings,[3] all but one of which stir questions and doubts. (1) As we shall see copiously illustrated in what follows, one view simply equates self-evidence with self-givenness, and indeed this might seem *prima facie* quite reasonable. I may doubt that what I perceive in the fireplace is fire; how can I doubt the fiery appearance or appearing? How can I doubt that what I really and truly, and adequately and perfectly see or see is there, is there? One can add adverbs, but the contention that what you claim is there must be there still begs the question. What is self-evident here is only the tautology "If I see A, then I see A," or "If I see that A most certainly exists, then I see that A most certainly exists." Fortunately there are alternatives.

(2) Self-evidence is also interpreted as a complete coincidence of a meaning-bestowing act and the corresponding meaning-fulfilling act. If what I mean is *perfectly* fulfilled, then what I mean lies before me self-evidently.[4] In *Ideas* we have a similar formulation.[5] Self-evidence is coalescence of meaning-bestowing and meaning-fulfillment, under two restrictions. It occurs only when the object on which meaning (*Sinn*) is bestowed is an immanent object, and the fulfillment, or "primordial filling-out" of this meaning is complete, i.e., adequate. To validate a case of "self-evidence" in this sense you would have to certify that your object is really immanent, and not just ostensibly so, and that the fulfillment is adequate, and not just ostensibly so.

By this time Husserl had already distinguished adequate from inadequate self-evidence,[6] and so the general question can be put:

[3] Extended discussions of the subject can be found in Eugen Fink, "Das Problem der Phänomenologie Edmund Husserls," *Revue Internationale de Philosophie*, 2 (1939), and Herbert Spiegelberg, "Phenomenology of Direct Evidence," *Philosophy and Phenomenological Research*, II (1942).

[4] *Logische Untersuchungen*, II, 6 (Halle: Max Niemeyer, 1920), pp. 121ff.

[5] *Ideas: General Introduction to Pure Phenomenology*, English translation by Boyce Gibson (New York: Collier, 1967), § 144.

[6] *Ibid.*, §§ 136, 138.

Are immanence and adequate (complete) fulfillment unmistakable earmarks distinguishing cases of adequate from instances of inadequate self-evidence? One can certainly agree with Husserl that when the object is a transcendent, such as a perceived physical object, which, as he says, can be apprehended fully only in an indefinitely long series of its perspective manifestations, this self-evidence would be impossible. [7] But it would not follow, of course, that self-evidence with regard to immanent objects, which are *not* given perspectively, *can* be certified as adequate – as indefeasible. In fact, there seems to be no effective argument for this conclusion. We can only say something like this: *If* "self-evidence" is so defined as to require an immanent object and adequacy, then *if* you now have evidence about an immanent object, and *if* it is adequate, then you have "self-evidence" with respect to it, *providing that* your appraisal of this evidence – a new act – is also adequately self-evident.

(3) In further search for absolute foundations of phenomenology, Husserl distinguishes between "assertoric self-evidence," which occurs when we "see" something individual, and "apodictic self-evidence," where we "see into" the essence, or what is essential. The former is said to be "impure" whereas the latter is "pure evidential vision," [8] for the reason already mentioned that the individual can only be given in partial perspectives. Our general objection to this formulation is clear from the last paragraph. Of special interest here, however, is the emphasis given such words as "see" and "see into" (*sehen* and *einsehen*) and also "insight" ("*Einsicht*"). They serve to suggest a kind of direct revelation, and the English translation here of "*Evidenz*" by "vision" is in the same vein. But Husserl also describes self-evidence as performance or achievement (*Leistung*), as activity and seeking rather than receptivity. It is both, really and the formulation in the *Logic* [9] embraces the givenness of the thing itself as well as the *Leistung* which uncovers it.

---

[7] *Ibid.* "Impossible," Husserl says, "within the finite limits of experience," and suggests that adequate evidence might be possible even here, as a Kantian regulative idea, an idea of the outcome of an infinite series of possible perspective experiences of a thing. But this would be a very weak sense of "self-evidence," one that he does not endorse.

[8] *Ibid.*, § 137.

[9] *Formal and Transcendental Logic*, English translation by Dorion Cairns (The Hague: Martinus Nijhoff, 1969), § 107.

(4) Husserl's discussion of "the evidence of distinctness" and "the evidence of clarity," valuable in itself, also furnishes another angle and approach to the long sought final evidence. The former is the evidence by means of which the judgment *qua* judgment becomes a distinct judgment, whereas the latter contains the former, but also "the evidence wherein *that* becomes itself given *which the judger wants to attain 'by way of' his judgment* – the judger, that is, as wanting to *cognize*, which is the way logic always conceives him." Although the discussion is generally original and repaying, where it concerns final evidence it is anti-climactic. *"Only a judging with full clarity* as to both judgment and judged-about," Husserl says, "can be *actual present cognition* ..." [10] It is this full and perfect clarity which corresponds to adequate self-evidence, but there is no bell that rings when you have reached it.

(5) A hierarchy of evidences is set up by Husserl, which is anchored *a priori* in "evidences that are first in themselves" and "actually most original," namely, individual judgments,[11] and ultimately in "pre-predicative experience." [12] Moreover, objective self-evidence relating to individuals e.g., perceived objects, has precedence over the self-evidence belonging to judgments as such (*Urteilsevidenz*), "in that it makes the latter possible," according to a posthumous work of Husserl.[13] "All predicative evidences," even those of logic, "must be grounded finally in the evidences of experience (*Erfahrung*)," and are to be clarified in the light of the latter.[14] But this does not at all mean that the evidences of pre-predicative experience are the most adequate, or that the evidences of perceptual judgments are more adequate than those of judgments farther removed from perception, but only that these evidences are most original and come logically first in the order of phenomenological explication. This new and most important theory of the necessary founding of judgments in pre-predicative experience thus does not throw fresh light on the nature of final self-evidence, except in providing that any

---

[10] *Ibid.*, pp. 6of. Italics in original.
[11] *Ibid.*, p. 205.
[12] *Ibid.*, § 86.
[13] *Erfahrung und Urteil. Untersuchungen zur Genealogie der Logik.* Edited by Ludwig Landgrebe (Hamburg: Claassen Verlag, 1964), p. 14.
[14] *Ibid.*, p. 38.

such evidence must be finally grounded in and clarified through the most original evidences of all. Whatever difficulties attach to tracing evidence back to its original source in sense perception, would only further perplex the problem of pinning down and certifying a final self-evidence.

It is pertinent perhaps to note that Eugen Fink, so close to Husserl for years, apparently failed to find the evidence for pre-predicative experience. "There are no pre-conceptual things," he asserts, "if we understand concept strictly in the ontological sense, nor indeed language-free things. There are of course countless things concerning which men have never spoken, but so far as they partake of 'being' they are in the realm to which the power of language extends, which is the openness of being. A little reflection will show that the leading concept of phenomenological method – pre-conceptual and pre-linguistic things – is based on dark and unclarified presuppositions." [15] For all Dr. Fink says Husserl might still be right, for he offers in evidence only an elucidation in terms of the development of Husserl's thought. For phenomenology the question is really: Do you have Husserl's over-all insight and his continuing particular fulfilling insights, or contrary insights? For our part, we cannot see how the logical and explicatory precedence of a pre-predicative stage of experience could be established without *explicit* and *public* consideration of the empirical facts – the facts turned up by genetic psychology, learning theory, studies of pathological disturbances, etc.

(6) It is a pleasure to announce that, after such a lengthy meticulous and indecisive search for a final self-evidence, Husserl came to see that there is no finality. "The possibility of deception," he states, "is inherent in the evidence of experience and does not annul either its fundamental character or its effect ..." [16] This holds "for *every* experience, for every 'experience' in the amplified sense." Even the apodictic evidence of logic and mathematics may prove deceptive. This was a complete reversal of the position insisted on in Husserl's works prior to the *Logic*, as was pointed out by Spiegelberg [17] and others, and could be expected

[15] "L'analyse Intentionnelle et le Problème de la Pensée Spéculative," in *Problèmes Actuels de la Phénoménologie* (Bruxelles: Desclée de Brouwer, 1952), p. 68.
[16] *Logic*, p. 156.
[17] *Op. cit., loc. cit.*, p. 431.

to bring about important changes in phenomenology. We shall now consider some of these changes.

When No Longer Absolute, Evidence Can Be More Adequate

So long as Husserl contended that an absolute and indefeasible self-evidence is attainable about immanent objects, and that prescriptions could be written assuring its attainment, such evidence for an object could not extend beyond that object itself. For in this case the absolute, indefeasible evidence for O would depend on the evidence for O_1, O_2, ... O_n, and on the evidence of O's relation to them – assuming of course that all these evidences could not be included in one Now, which is not difficult to assume. But once the demand for absolute evidence is dropped, this particular difficulty disappears. As Husserl says: "Experience, evidence, gives something existent, and gives it itself: imperfectly, if the experience is imperfect; and *more* perfectly, if ... the experience becomes perfected – that is: amplified in harmonious syntheses." [18] "Perception *alone*," whether external or internal, "is never a full objectivating performance," i.e., "the seizing upon an object itself." It is true that "internal perception" is often assumed to be a seizing upon an object itself, but that is "only because we are tacitly taking into account possible recollection, repeatable at will." [19] Only when recollection has been actualized do we have certainty of this object, a so-called psychic datum. Evidence of its being the object it is requires its identification in time, and its recognition as the selfsame in any recollection. The same is true of "irreal objects" (e.g. $17^2 = 289$); to become evidenced as objects they must be identified in recollection as the same, and "at will," [20] except that they are not individuated *qua* temporal.[21] This evidence, then, does not come at first sight, nor is it pursued in ordinary life. It is the phenomenologist, with his special interest, who ferrets it out, and on a "higher level." "This higher evidence, in turn, can be itself explicated ... only by means of an evidence belonging to a third level; and so on *ad*

---

[18] *Logic*, p. 281. Italics added.
[19] *Ibid.*, p. 157.
[20] It would seem also that the recognition of the expression as a true token of the type would also be involved, and other things as well.
[21] *Logic*, p. 156.

infinitum.'' [22] And the explication and corroboration must always be by way of new "seeing."

It is not surprising, then, that Husserl ridicules the notion of *atomic* evidence on the page following his sudden rejection of *absolute* evidence:

> Evidence [he says] is usually conceived as an *absolute apodicticity*, an absolute security against deceptions – an apodicticity quite incomprehensibly ascribed to a single mental process torn from the concrete, essentially unitary, context of subjective mental living. The usual theorist sees in evidence an absolute criterion of truth; though by such a criterion, not only external but also, in strictness, all internal evidence would necessarily be done away with. [23]

All evidence would be eliminated, Husserl argues, since instead of recognizing that evidence involves strenuous endeavor which may be incomplete or go wrong, the theorist falls back on a mere *feeling* of certainty, which is not evidence at all. The conclusion, however, does not seem to follow. The theorist need not reduce evidence to a feeling of certainty. We should prefer to argue as follows: In so far as evidence is declared absolute, efforts at corroboration are cut off, search for more evidence ceases, and human error and humane correction become impossible. When absolute evidence is rejected, on the other hand, (1) search for further evidence can always continue toward the goal of maximum adequacy, and (2) ontological absolutes disappear. The present moment of consciousness can no longer be seen as self-evidently absolute, as something which could not possibly *not* be, to which everything else is relative.

(1) Nothing could better illustrate the advantages of relinquishing absolute evidence than Husserl's elaborate and discerning account of "horizons," "inner" and "outer." All perceived objects, he held, are necessarily given-*with* inner recesses of complexities, potentialities, and possibilities of variation, not yet determined, or determined only sketchily, but yet as determin*able*. There is the physical object intended, which engages our interest, but implicated in it are inner features and possibilities counted on, which are given only as an empty schema to be filled in by future experience. The *outer* horizon on the other hand, is the frame or milieu of the perceived object, which is

[22] *Ibid.*, p. 159.
[23] *Ibid.*, p. 157.

really as wide as the world, and includes its relations to other objects near and distant. It is not itself the intentional object, but is co-intended emptily or sketchily as the background of the intended object, which could be rendered determinate by a turning-to it (*Zuwendung*). In this case, however, a new horizon would appear. An essential feature of the horizon is that it is always open.

There is also "the horizon of familiarity," which devolves from the pregivenness of things and types. "A table is seen as familiar, as of a type known before, though it is individually new to us. The typically apprehended thing has a horizon of possible experiences, a typicality of still inexperienced, but anticipated features: If we see a dog we immediately see its further traits, its typical manner of eating, playing, leaping, etc. We do not see its teeth now, but we know how they would look." [24] The typicalities of past experience thus give the present one its meaning. The dog is also given as on an immediate ground, a green lawn (say), with trees and sky beyond. There is no end nor boundary, for every object is seen in "the horizon of the world."

It would seem, then, that the evidence for an object O must include a filling-in and confirmation of O's horizons, that if our horizonal anticipations, on the whole, tend to be disappointed rather than fulfilled, we must conclude that the O we saw was not O, after all, not the O we intended. Finally, if we fail to explore O's horizons, which is often the case, we simply take their fulfillment, on the whole, for granted on the basis of past experience with typicalities of the kind involved. The seeing of a house presupposes rooms, ceilings, floors, a foundation, a far side, and proper spatial and causal relations to other things. If it turns out to be merely a façade used in a movie set, or if a man who walks in front of it dwarfs it in size, or if it suddenly starts to flutter in the wind like a flag, then we say what we saw was not a house.

Although the object of "inner perception" e.g., an emotion, is not given in a series of one-sided perspectives, as is the object of external perception, its evidence is also only intimated at the moment, and requires explication of horizonal meanings. Is the emotion what it instantly seems? A great deal is pre-supposed.

[24] *Erfahrung und Urteil*, p. 399.

Much is implicated too when what is apprehended is an "irreal" object like $2 + 2 = 4$, namely, arithmetic and its automatic social acceptance.

Taking as his example occasional judgments which, though occasional, are intersubjectively true or false, Husserl states that both meaning and truth-value are bound to horizons:

> This truth value [of occasional judgments] obviously depends on the relatedness of the single subject's and the community's whole daily life to a *typical specific likeness among situations*, such that any normal human being who enters a particular situation has, by the very fact of being normal, the *situational horizons* belonging to it and common to all. One can explicate these horizons subsequently; but the *constituting* horizon-intentionality, without which the surrounding world of daily living would not be an *experienced world*, is always prior to its explication by someone who reflects. And *it* is the factor that *essentially determines the sense of occasional judgments* – always and far beyond what at any time is, or can be, said expressly and determinately in the words themselves. These horizons, then are "presuppositions," which ... continually determine the objective sense of the immediate experiential surroundings ...[25]

"Presuppositions" is put in quotes because what is meant is not explicit "premise-presuppositions" which logicians are concerned with. Horizons are presuppositions in the sense that they are intended in an indeterminate manner within and along-with the object which is thematic in the intention. They are not mere hypotheses since they are suffused with confirmed expectancies long since reduced to habit.

We may conclude that foregoing the luxury of a fundamental *absolute* evidence has enabled Husserl to evolve his extensive analysis of horizons which extend indefinitely into life-space and into the future, facilitating and encouraging the continuous accumulation of evidence as to the presuppositions of living and of the *Lebenswelt*. The fact that the horizons here and in Husserl's later works are explicitly social, though it does not agree with the reasons given for the *epoché* nor with the "ownness reduction" in *Cartesian Meditations* V, has the same Promethean tendency, and ties in with the next point we wish to make.

(2) "Absolute consciousness," Husserl insists, is the "residuum after nullifying the world," i.e., after suspending belief in its existence. *"The Being of present consciousness ... would not be affected thereby in its own proper existence ... Immanent Being*

---

[25] *Logic*, pp. 199f.

is therefore without doubt absolute in this sense, that in principle nulla 're' indiget ad existendum," whereas *"the world of the transcendent 'res' is related unreservedly to consciousness ..."* Husserl says we have evidence for this and that it is an "insight." [26] The evidence for absolute consciousness is "apodictic," and so also is that for the pure Ego, the transcendental Ego.[27] But Husserl understandably adds that apodictic evidence would not suffice for absolute consciousness, as the foundation of a new science of transcendental phenomenology, since apodictic evidence may not be *adequate* evidence, i.e., completed or completely fulfilled.[28] This evidence must be seen to be apodictic, but there must also be the "insight" that it is *first in itself*, "and precedes all other imaginable evidences." [29] Since these requirements are met in the case of absolute consciousness, it is concluded that "the actual being of the intrinsically first field of knowledge is indeed assured absolutely ..." [30]

Actually, only "the ego's living present" is experienced "with strict adequacy ... while, beyond that, only an indeterminately general presumptive horizon extends ..." [31] It is this living present, then, which invests the world with all its meaning, and to which it is necessarily relative. The world, it is true, is given "originarily," i.e., without mediation, but also with evidence essentially inadequate.[32]

The evidence for absolute consciousness is thus "absolute" in the sense explained, i.e., first in itself and "preceding all other imaginable evidences," and apodictically. It is therefore also "absolute" in the sense we have been discussing throughout this paper, namely, final, complete and incorrigible. For there is no way in which the evidence for "the ego's living present" could be corrected or completed, not with respect to what *exists*. Not by any experience of the world, certainly, for worldly evidence is essentially inadequate; nor by evidence from any "living present," now in the past, for this would have to be linked with

[26] *Ideas*, pp. 136–137, 102.
[27] *Cartesian Meditations*. English translation by Dorion Cairns (The Hague: Martinus Nijhoff, 1969), §§ 8, 9.
[28] *Ibid.*, p. 22.
[29] *Ibid.*, p. 16.
[30] *Ibid.*, p. 23.
[31] *Ibid.*, pp. 22–23.
[32] *Ibid.*, p. 17.

present consciousness by memory, which Husserl admits is dubitable.

This evidence, then, must be entirely *self*-evidence, and impossible to correct or complete. But this is precisely the notion of evidence Husserl rejected in his *Logic*, where he insisted: "The possibility of deception is inherent in the evidence of experience," and "this holds for *every* experience." It becomes obvious that Husserl's evolving philosophy bred two quite incompatible lines of thought. On the one hand, he saw perfect evidence and perfect truth as correlates, so that a failing of the first would mean the loss of the second. On the other hand, he could see that deception is always *possible*. That Husserl was aware and worried is suggested by several remarks, one in the first *Meditation* from which we have been quoting. Speaking explicitly of the *imperfect* evidence obtainable beyond "the ego's living present," he explains how this evidence can be increased in adequacy, and adds: "and the question whether adequate evidence does not necessarily lie at infinity may be left open." [33] But then he marked this sentence in the manuscript "unsatisfactory." And so it was. He surely did not want to imply that the new science of transcendental phenomenology he is founding might be realizable only at infinity.

The point which concerns us here, however, is that the fate of absolute consciousness and related doctrines of transcendental subjectivity, now clearly hangs on absolute evidence. If absolute evidence is rejected, the ontological priority of the present consciousness and of the transcendental ego lose their footing, and no reason remains for holding the world to be a mere dependent and creature of consciousness. For it would not suffice to say: "There is considerable evidence that the world is dependent in this way, but ..." If, on the other hand, absolute evidence is firmly upheld, absolute consciousness, the subservience of the world, and other related doctrines, remain tenable, which is not to say *true*.

There are further consequences of Husserl's "absolute consciousness." For example, his finding that "the ego's living present" is evidenced "with strict adequacy ... while, beyond that, only an indeterminately general presumptive horizon ex-

[33] *Ibid.*, p. 15.

tends ..." [34] seems to imply that other men are mere presump-
tions. Moreover, their existence is strictly relative to my present
consciousness, which invests them with all the meaning they
have. Husserl, of course, has given a great deal of attention to
the charge of solipsism, but his refutations never seem to overcome the initial handicap: the self-sufficiency and sovereignty
of the transcendental ego's living present – an ego which is somehow individuated. In *Meditations* V subtle efforts are made to
solve the problem, but the above doctrines which cause the
trouble are never withdrawn. So we learn that others are "appresented" rather than presented, i.e., intended as something
associated with presented behavior. Like other transcendents,
their existence must be inadequately evidenced and really doubtful.

The self-sufficiency of consciousness is not unrelated to its
alleged sovereignty. If present consciousness is self-sufficient –
capable of existing whether the world does or not, as itself, with
all its presently existing qualities,[35] then, if it is related to the
world at all, it must have a sovereign role. Those who have
followed the evolution of Husserl's phenomenology will agree
that "the transcendental ego constituting the world" first meant
"conferring meaning on it," but increasingly came to mean
actually "creating it."

Noema and Hyle

The phenomenological reduction, or *epoché*, is the methodic
suspension of the natural positing of the existence and characteristics of transcendents. In sense perception, which is the source
and crucial example, we naturally take physical things as real:
we take them and their characteristics for granted. This suspension of natural assent, as Husserl is fond of saying, leaves everything as it was before. There is no prestidigitation: "Now you
see it; now you don't." Only a change of attitude (*Einstellung*).
The phenomenologist, after carrying out the epoché, continues to
see trees *as* growing plants, *as* deriving nourishment through
their roots and from the sun by photosynthesis, and *as* there

---

[34] *Ideas*, pp. 22f.
[35] Or at least a certain kernel of them. See *Ideas*, p. 137.

whether he looks or not. The transcendent ascriptions are there; he simply fails to make them, to go along with them. Why get out on a limb? He merely entertains them.[36]

It is sometimes questioned whether this wholesale abstention from automatic assent to transcendent being is psychologically possible. It is easy, of course, to withhold assent to the premises of a particular argument. But it is quite a different matter to cease to recognize, for what they are, all the things one sees, including one's friends and children, and even one's own hands, as they stand before us ("bodily," and "in person," as Husserl says) in perception. We cannot say it is like a dream where objects and persons do not exist, because in a dream we still *take* things to be real. Nor is it anything like going to a movie, since here one does not withdraw assent from a world one never thought of doubting, nor is it like an illusion we have "seen through," for here we are given a plausible reason for withholding assent. Indeed, it is nothing like any visual experience that comes to mind. It seems possible, then, that the phenomenologist, after he has carried out the epoché, does not really *see*, or *intuit*, what remains, but *infers* what *would* remain if he *did* manage to suspend assent to the whole world. Husserl, however clearly excludes inference from phenomenological demonstration. Conclusions must always be "seen" or intuited.[37] The *epoché*, as Husserl describes it, seems to be a difficult feat, and this much he concedes. It must be performed, however, since it uncovers a vast new field of "pure" experience on which the foundations of phenomenology, and of science in general, can be erected. Once the *epoché* has been executed, and the existence and characters of transcendents removed from consciousness, the possibility of error has also been removed. One must exercise the greatest care, of course. Mistakes are still possible in fact, but they are removable in principle. One can return later to the same immanent object and take a closer look, so to speak. The difficulty of being sure it *is the same*, in view of the lack of intersubjective criteria

[36] Harmon Chapman has made the critical comment that the *epoché* really involves more than suspending assent to the existence of physical things, e.g. a perceived tree; it entails also the suspending of the essence "tree" as well. For the essence includes powers or dispositions which are not directly given, but are transcendent. But how could the essence be suspended? *Sensations and Phenomenology* (Bloomingdale: Indiana University Press, 1966), pp. 129f.

[37] *Ideas*, p. 193.

and corroboration of the difference between *being the same* and *just seeming the same* – so much discussed in recent literature – is never really faced by Husserl.

Husserl expresses great confidence in the fruitfulness of the *epoché*. To the question what "essential phases" this "reduced consciousness," the "noema," will show, he answers: "We can reply to our question as we wait, in pure surrender, on what is essentially *given*. We can then describe 'that which appears as such' faithfully and in the light of perfect self-evidence." [38] He goes on to warn us that what we will find in the noema will be utterly different from what psychologists and physicists talk about. "The *tree plain and simple*, the thing in nature, is as different as can be from this *perceived tree as such* [the noematic tree], which as perceptual meaning belongs to the perception, and that inseparably. The tree plain and simple can burn away, resolve itself into its chemical elements, and so forth. But the meaning (*Sinn*) – the meaning of *this* perception, something that belongs necessarily to its essence – cannot burn away; it has no chemical elements, no forces, no real properties." [39]

It seems that Husserl has already told us in pretty clear language what *"this perceived tree as such,"* i.e., the tree as given in consciousness, is. It is a meaning in the connotative sense.[40] It *has* no properties, but *is* the properties-of, the determinations-of, the tree, plain and simple out in nature. Naturally it cannot be destroyed, and is nothing like the real tree. Thus we must not say that "this perceived tree as such" is a tree, a plant, or that it is blossoming unless we enclose "tree," "plant," and "blossoming" in quotation marks. In favor of this interpretation is the fact that Husserl's discussions of the noema are invariably discussions of noematic *meaning (Sinn)*, and never of particulars. In pointing out that perceptions, judgments, etc., can be retained in the noema, also, he is careful to add: "but only on condition that they be regarded and described as essentialities which they are in themselves." [41] It is also significant that when we perceive an object, e.g., a blooming apple tree, the noema which appears

[38] *Ibid.*, p. 240.
[39] *Ibid.*
[40] This interpretation has recently been put forward by Dagfinn Føllesdal, in "Husserl's Notion of Noema," *Journal of Philosophy*, No. 20 (Oct. 16, 1969).
[41] *Ideas*, p. 240.

in consciousness, can be the same as when we imagine or remember this same tree, though different modes of givenness will qualify the full noema in each case.[42] And finally, this full noema, composed of the *what* of the perceived object, and the qualification as to the mode in which it is given, "is meaning (in the widest sense)," [43] where "the widest sense," is evidently a sense which includes the indication of the mode of givenness, which is perhaps an unusual extension of the word "meaning" (*Sinn*).

This interpretation of the noema may be startling but, on reflection, it appears almost inevitable that it should be found to be *Sinn*. In the first place, the noematic counterpart of the perceived physical tree cannot be spatial, for space is the medium of physical objects, and its properties are explored by physics, which is of course off limits for phenomenological description. For similar reasons, colors, sizes, and other properties of physical things, must be excluded from the noema. But perhaps the noema could have properties *analogous* in some way to those of physical objects. This alternative, however, is certainly excluded by Husserl's repeated rejection of the representative theory of perception. An immediately given representation of the real tree out in nature would "confront us with two realities, whereas only *one* of these is present and possible. I perceive the thing, the object of nature, the true tree there in the garden; that and nothing else is the real object of the perceiving 'intention.' A second immanent tree, or even an 'inner image' of the real tree that stands out there before me, is nowise given, and to suppose such a thing . . . leads only to absurdity," [44] and a vicious regress.

This construal of the noema bespeaks a careful consideration of the alternatives, and the selection of what may well be the best, i.e., the least unsatisfactory of them. But it is hard to believe that the identification of the noema with a meaning (*Sinn*) can be obtained by a "pure surrender" to what "is essentially given," and "in the light of perfect self-evidence," which is what Husserl promised. It looks more like an ingenious *theory* of considerable plausibility, a theory to which he was almost compelled by his direct realism, his firm rejection of the representative theory of

[42] *Ibid.*, p. 244.
[43] *Ibid.*
[44] *Ibid.*, p. 243.

perception, and his conviction that immediacy, and immediacy alone, is adequately self-evident. A more important line of criticism is this: The percept, however it may be described, is always taken to furnish evidence about the perceived physical object, but it is hard to see how a meaning (*Sinn*), by itself, could constitute or furnish such evidence. Husserl's answer could be that this perceptual meaning would, in the case of veridical perception, lead to future perceptual meanings which are harmonious with the first, whereas when perception is illusory, disharmonious meanings would follow. This would be correct *prima facie:* later perceptual meanings do furnish evidence for earlier ones. But when it comes to evidence, you cannot have too much, only too little. We submit that the *meaning* of perceptual takings and judgments clearly does not exhaust the evidence we have for such takings and judgments. Facts supplied by physics and psychology greatly augment this evidence, but these facts are methodologically and enthusiastically excluded from the pure phenomenology of perception. How great the loss entailed by this squeamishness of the *epoché* would be difficult to determine, but we know it is increasing.

If we are mindful that for every noema, there is a corresponding noesis, i.e., for every bestowed meaning there is meaning-bestowal, we immediately feel the need for a stuff of some sort on which the meaning is bestowed. If there is no stuff, then constituting experience – and perhaps also intending it – become equivalent to *creating*. Thus credibility and viability of the noema, as reduced perception, said to be a meaning (*Sinn*), depends on the tenability of the stuff on which the meaning is bestowed.

"The stream of phenomenological being," according to Husserl, "has a twofold bed: a noetic and a material." [45] The material consists of "sensile" experiences, or "hyletic data," e.g. "data of color, touch, sound, and the like," which "offer themselves as material of intentional informings and bestowal of meaning." We thus have "formless materials and immaterial forms." [46] Now these formless materials, the data of color, sound, touch, etc., Husserl warns, must be carefully distinguished from "the appearing phases of things, their color-quality, their roughness, and so

[45] *Ibid.*, p. 230.
[46] *Ibid.*, pp. 226f.

forth, which rather 'exhibit' themselves experientially through their means." [47] He also speaks of "the particular Data of sensation that are 'construed' as Objective colors and sounds." [48] Both formulations suggest a duplication of qualities in perception which, as we have noted, Husserl vigorously rejects. Besides the blue of the perceived physical object there seems to be also a blue sense-datum, by means of which the former is "exhibited." And how could this be if the sense-data are "formless"? It would seem, indeed, that these data of sensation could be neither endowed with qualities nor formless. If formless, they could not be described nor even apprehended; if already informed with color-shape, sound, or other such qualities, there would be no need of an intentionality to so inform them.

Once again we find it unimaginable that Husserl is engaged in simply seeing or intuiting, and then describing, essential features of experience. He seems rather to be grappling with a very difficult but appealing metaphysical construction, as Aristotle once did, and trying to avoid the puzzles it generates. An escape route is not apparent, not for Husserl. It might be held that the pure sense-datum is not a datum at all, but that it can be inferred as an ideal limit of fewer and fewer meaning-bestowals but, as we have seen, Husserl firmly extrudes inference from phenomenological demonstration. The proof is always in the seeing.

In various places and connections, however, Husserl does tell us, at least schematically, how we can get to and seize a pure sense-datum. For example, a resonant violin tone, he says, can be grasped as a real violin tone, and thereby as a spatial, real event, and remain the same tone as I move towards or away from it. If I abstract from the material reality, I can still retain a tonal space phantom, proceeding as from a place in space, sounding through space. Finally, I can set aside the space apprehension, and instead of the spatial, sounding tone, I can take it as a mere sense-datum. Instead of being conscious of a tone which remains the same when I approach and withdraw from it, there appears, when I attend to the sense-datum tone, something continually changing.[49]

[47] *Ibid.*, p. 226.
[48] *Ibid.*, p. 288.
[49] *Ideen zu einer reinen Phänomenologie und phänomenologischen Philosophie*, Vol. II (The Hague: Martinus Nijhoff, 1952), p. 22.

Though experimental controls would be necessary to establish anything, this account rings true, except that we should like to ask what the pure sense-datum tone is like. It is no longer a violin tone, nor anchored in space, nor objective, but it presumably has pitch, intensity, timbre, a certain voluminousness, and duration, including "protention" and "retention," and other features of things in the stream of inner time. Could one, in order to reach the "formless material," also abstract from these characteristics? And what would the tone be like if you could? And one more question: Suppose the noema is *a violin tone (as something actually heard)*. Since this is a meaning, it is out of time. How, then, does it relate to the sense-datum tone, which is certainly *in* time – inner time. Does hearing the tone involve two presentations, or does the sense-datum get absorbed into the timeless perceptual meaning?

Consciousness of Evidence and Evidence of Consciousness

The role of consciousness in phenomenology calls for a second look. It could perhaps be considered one of those basic phenomenological concepts which Eugen Fink calls "operative," as opposed to "thematic." They are used as tools to clarify the thematic concepts, but remain themselves "opaque and thematically unclarified." [50] Consciousness plays an ubiquitous and ever productive role in phenomenology. It is the home of all self-givennesses and self-evidences, and it is said to "constitute" literally everything that is experienced, including even the "[sense-]Data in immanent time, a constituting which goes on with rigid regularity," [51] where "constitute" can mean anything from *confer meaning* on to *create*. Yet like the fairy Godmother in the story it never itself actually comes into view.

We have run into great difficulties, some of them doubtless our own fault, in finding evidence in consciousness to which Husserl points. We cannot discover, to take a fresh example, the giving or constituting of the "Data in immanent time," and do not see how anyone could. It seems more like a theory. We have raised

---

[50] So described by Alfred Schutz, who finds Fink's distinction helpful. "Type and Eidos in Husserl's Later Philosophy," *Philosophy and Phenomenological Research*, XX (1959).

[51] *Logic*, p. 287.

numerous questions of this kind. But the question which we now can no longer restrain is: What is the evidence of consciousness? Whatever evidence is offered turns out to be evidence for something else. This diaphanous, protean, all-productive entity, which is all things to all experiences, never shows itself in person.

Ludwig Landgrebe argued in 1939, a year after Husserl's death, that "consciousness clearly cannot be conceived in the traditional sense as a mere chain of *cogitationes*, succeeding one another in time, ..." and concluded: "One can say indeed that the expression 'consciousness' is a misleading term for this aggregate of [diverse mental] performances (*Leistungen*) and points back to a tradition that Husserl had overcome." [52] Consciousness belongs at best to higher levels of activity. He contended that the concepts of performance and intentionality as performance, which guided Husserl from the first, are the basic ones on the development of which the promise of phenomenology depends.

We think it desirable to go further and, in the interest of clarity and public evidence-gathering, to gradually abandon talk of this universal medium and "occult power" altogether. We can cooperatively assess the evidence for what men do and can do, for their performances and even intentionality, but there seems to be not even "private evidence" for consciousness. Husserl himself saw the advantages of starting out with a common intersubjective world in his last work, *Die Krisis der europäischen Wissenschaften und die transzendentale Phänomenologie*, and also in *Erfahrung und Urteil*, and once this starting-point has been developed with such success, there seems to be no good reason for going back to the *epoché* again, and consigning a final evidence to private construals.

In these concluding remarks we shall permit ourselves another critical approach to Husserl's conception of evidence, since, if it is worth anything, it will strengthen the others. It is an old complaint, and so we may as well begin by citing an expert witness from the tradition of psychology which still explored consciousness. Answering the contention of Karl Bühler and others that thought-processes can be observed in, and described as, data of consciousness, Titchener wrote: "I say that the observers tell us, not what consciousness is, but what it is about ..." E. Dürr,

[52] "Husserls Phänomenologie," *Revue Internationale de Philosophie*, I (1939), p. 297.

who was one of Bühler's experimental subjects, explained: "Over and over again, as I was observing for Bühler, I had the impression ... that my report was simply a somewhat modified statement of the thoughts aroused in me by the experimenter, and that this verbal statement could not properly be regarded as a psychological description of thoughts." [53] Could it be supposed, he asks, that he was giving a psychological report every time he had a conversation with a friend? On the other hand, Woodworth, in *defense* of the observability and the describability of thoughts, insists that subjects should be allowed to talk about (physical) objects, and that when objects A, B, and C are reported in succession, this exhibits "the general course of the thinking process – just as the naming of the towns through which you have driven maps the route you have taken." [54]

More recently L. S. Vigotsky has pointed to the highly schematic character of "inner speech," or thought, as contrasted with spoken language. Compared to the early ego-centric language which it replaces in child development, Vigotsky says, it is like a very economic shorthand or a set of pointers. [55] Some philosophers have found even less articulation, or none at all, in the inner private "world of thought." "If we possess knowledge by acquaintance with respect to mental states of affairs, if there seems to be something 'given,' " Paul Feierabend concluded, "then this is the *result* of the low content of the statements expressing this knowledge." [56]

The purpose of these citations is not to solve intricate controversies with a flip of the pen, but rather to remind readers of some of the currents of research and expert opinion which run against the viability of consciousness as the seat of final, full, and incontrovertible evidence. A satisfactory critique of Husserl's version of this harbor or certainty would far surpass the boundaries of a single paper. Let us bring the present one to an end, in the spirit of phenomenology, by looking into our own con-

---

[53] *Lectures on the Psychology of the Thought-Processes* (New York: Macmillan, 1909), pp. 151, 150.

[54] *Experimental Psychology* (New York: Holt, 1938), p. 785.

[55] *Thought and Language* (Cambridge, Mass.: MIT Press, 1962).

[56] "Materialism and the Mind-Body Problem," in *Modern Materialism*, edited by John O'Connor (New York: Harcourt, Brace, 1969), p. 93.

sciousness, and by making what may appear to be a scandalous, quasi-Ryleian, confession:

If, when thinking, I try to "observe" what is going on, I find practically nothing, except for a few "images," so spectral that I can't be sure; but they are not *thoughts*, in any case. James' "feelings of tendency" are there, perhaps, but I should not know how to describe them. A "readiness" for certain things, perhaps, but my description of it would turn out to be only a verbal report of actions I might undertake. Something would be omitted that I can't *describe*, so I don't want to say I can *observe* this readiness. I would like to say, with Dürr, that I have an *"intimation"* of my thoughts in contrast to an articulation of them, but the intimation would be, again, indescribable. The commom idiom "expressing thoughts in language" seems to me mistaken – as if we tailored our language to our thoughts, trying to match them! I know only that I start talking, sometimes with confidence, other times uncertainly, feeling my way, and that I am sometimes satisfied, and at other times dissatisfied with what I find myself saying. I can sometimes give evidence for thoughts I have expressed, but the evidence I cite is everywhere but in my mind. Even if I could look at evidence in my mind, it isn't clear how I could express it straightforwardly. As is often pointed out, there is no special language appropriate to mental content, and Husserl's language is highly metaphorical, borrowed, as it must be, from intersubjective language.

What do I believe, then, is going on when I sit and think? I should be really worried by my inner poverty if I did not know that I have a brain, and that brain processes can persist in the absence of relevant external stimulation. I have reason to believe, too, that these brain processes are the necessary and sufficient proximate causes of my thinking, whatever this may turn out to be, and that there is no way in which mental, i.e., non-physical episodes, could act upon the nervous system, in any case. If I have often read Husserl with understanding and enjoyment, the main reasons may be that human experience is structured in ways which can be expressed in different philosophical traditions, and that I have a brain and am motivated. I note with a certain dismay how far I have drifted from phenomenology, with which I was once in large agreement, and from the views held, at least in past years, by my long-time friend Dorion Cairns. But I am confident that the vast life-work of Husserl will somehow retain relevance and importance even should the theory of psycho-physical identity eventually turn out to be the best alternative we have.

MAURICE NATANSON

CROSSING THE MANHATTAN BRIDGE [1]

Near the Yiddish Forward sign
A billboard testament
Says in black and white:
The Wages of Sin is Death.
Occasionally, the Sea Beach Express stalls there,
Waiting for a grunt of current
To signal it on to Canal Street.
The tenements, blackened loaves,
Are deserted, the pigeon-coops flown.
Beneath their roofs, an apostate
Announces a red-letter edition for Jews – gratis.
And between the boroughs
The rails tremble and the cars grate.
Below, the river fish circumnavigate.

[1] In a personal communication Dr. Natanson has referred to the occasion for the poem, "Crossing the Manhattan Bridge." During a conversation with Dr. Natanson, Dorion Cairns recalled how good an amateur actress his mother was, and especially how good she was at imitating people in his father's congregation. Dr. Natanson mentioned that his father, Charles Natanson, had been all his life a professional actor in the Yiddish theatre during its golden age. It turned out that Dorion Cairns had known the Yiddish theatre quite well in the twenties, having gone to many plays on Second Avenue. Thus it was more than likely that he had seen Dr. Natanson's father act. "That seethed in me a time," Dr. Natanson wrote; "what emerged – transposed and reconstituted but essentially that totality – is the enclosed poem." (Note of editors.)

HERBERT SPIEGELBERG

HUSSERL'S WAY INTO PHENOMENOLOGY FOR AMERICANS: A LETTER AND ITS SEQUEL

Husserl's Exchange with E. Parl Welch

The two letters here published were discovered around 1963 by Professor Margaret Van de Pitte of the University of Alberta at Edmonton, at that time a graduate student at the University of Southern California, "in a cardboard folder stacked on a shelf with a few others not related to phenomenology" at the School of Philosophy of the University. I am greatly indebted to her for having drawn my attention to this exchange between E. Parl Welch and Edmund Husserl and for additional helpful inquiries. However, her efforts to find out why the forgotten letters had landed and remained there were unsuccessful. One can only surmise that Welch, who at the time was a Ph.D. candidate at the School, had taken them there and never reclaimed them. The two letters were preceded by a separate page with the title "Letter concerning phenomenology by Edmund Husserl in Answer to a Communication by E. Parl Welch."

Welch's letter, which he, through his son, Professor Cyril Welch of Mount Alison University, has kindly permitted me to publish together with Husserl's reply, is printed first, since it throws important light on the content and arrangement of Husserl's reply.

But my main gratitude goes to Professor Gerhart Husserl who gave me permission to publish his father's letter with the exception of passages (indicated in the proper places) which in his judgment are not yet fit for public release.

The Background for Husserl's Letter

Before presenting Welch's letter of inquiry and Husserl's response one might do well to explore the possible reasons for the interest in phenomenology at the California School of Philosophy reflected in Welch's inquiry. One likely hypothesis would be the affinity between the personalistic philosophy of its Director, Ralph T. Flewelling, and the variety of personalism which he seems to have suspected in phenomenology, especially in the "ethical personalism" of Max Scheler. This is borne out by the topic of Welch's dissertation on "Max Scheler's Philosophy of Religion. A Study in Phenomenology" and particularly by its preface. This affinity is of course much less clear in the case of Husserl. But Scheler's tributes to Husserl as the fountainhead of phenomenology were all the more reason to explore Husserl's philosophy.

Welch, whose doctoral committee included Flewelling, had, according to his letter, written to Husserl before in 1932, receiving one "or two" letters in reply. But since none of this preceding correspondence seems to have survived, one can only suspect that it was related to an earlier phase of Welch's thesis project. Welch's new letter of May 9, 1933 was clearly an attempt to secure more specific aid for his Scheler dissertation, though he did not mention his name, which at this time Husserl would certainly not have appreciated.

Why would Husserl write a nine-page letter to a young American Ph.D. candidate, which, according to its date line kept him occupied for four days (June 17–21)? Among the possible explanations the following seem to me singly or cumulatively plausible:

1. Welch introduced himself as "on the staff of the School of Philosophy." Actually he seems to have been merely a research fellow for 1933–1934, whose name does not figure in the university catalogue. To an uninformed European such an introduction could only mean that the writer was at least a "Privatdozent" and as such a "colleague" ("*Kollege*" as Husserl addresses him) far beyond the level of a Ph.D. candidate. From Welch's statement that he was writing a book on the "philosophy of religion of the phenomenological school," Husserl could hardly gather that this was merely the dissertation on Max Scheler, which Welch was to submit in 1934.

2. Some of the questions raised in Welch's letter made Husserl

particularly aware of the problem of the proper introduction to the latest, most radical form of his philosophy.

3. Husserl was particularly anxious to warn Americans about wrong approaches through misleading introductions and his own earlier works, even those translated, and to point out the only possible right way through his latest, largely untranslated writings.

4. Husserl thought of this occasion as an opportunity to promote the academic fortunes of his student-friend Dorion Cairns, in whom he saw the future of American phenomenology, as the end of the letter and its postscript amply show.

The Text of the Letters

A. Letter of Welch to Husserl.

May 9, 1933
Los Angeles, Calif.

Dear Prof. Husserl:

You will probably have forgotten that you honored me with one or two letters in the year 1932, but you may pardon a student of philosophy profoundly interested in you and your work it he ventures to address you once again. I am now on the faculty of the School of Philosophy here at the University of Southern California. Being a thorough-going convert to your movement, and writing a book on the philosophy of religion of the phenomenological school, I find myself in need of your aid on one or two important matters.

I am devoting an entire section to you and your thought in the way of introducing the reader to the general standpoint of Phenomenology. Because of the extreme importance of your thought I am very anxious to present a thorough and adequate description of the philosophy of Phenomenology to the English-reading public. That is the reason I am taking the liberty of enlisting your assistance. There has been but one book devoted to your school, that of Marvin Farber's "Phenomenology as a Method and as a Philosophical Discipline." Although this little work is good, it is by no means adequate or comprehensive. I myself am undertaking the task of supplying the need for a more comprehensive work. Unquestionably Phenomenology has a real and much-needed message for American and English philosophy. Therefore, any help you may be willing to render me will conduce greatly to the enlightenment of our philosophers.

First of all, do you conceive your system as organically connected with any philosophic predecessors? Do you feel it to be absolutely new and unique, or do you believe yourself to have drawn material from some of the great men and their movements, e.g., Plato, Plotinus, and Descartes? If not, how would you define your attitude towards these, and in particular towards Plato's view of essences?

Secondly, how do you deal with the problem of error? I have read your "LU" and the "Ideen," but do not seem to be able to discover just how you would solve this problem. Can there be such a thing as error in the intuition of essences, or in the selection of the essences to be intuited? If so, how are we to know when we err? What standard is one to employ? If you have dealt with this problem somewhere, and I have missed it, could you give me the references?

Thirdly, can you tell me under whom you studied? When do you feel you emancipated yourself from the influence of your teachers?

I believe you will realize the importance of this book to English and American thought. I want to deal with these questions in order to avoid undue criticism of your system. I will print only what you give me permission to print, and shall, of course, gratefully acknowledge your assistance in the Preface.

Believe me

Very respectfully and sincerely yours
E. Parl Welch

B. Letter of Husserl to Welch. (German Original.)

Freiburg, den 17/21.VI.1933

Sehr geehrter Herr College!
(1) In der Unruhe dieser Zeit mit der Revolutionierung unseres

gesamten deutschen Volkes und seines Lebens konnte ich Ihren freundlichen Brief nicht sogleich beantworten.

(2) Es freut mich natürlich sehr, dass meine philosophischen Bestrebungen, die in einer stetigen inneren Entwicklung durch mehr als vier Jahrzehnte zu einer prinzipiell neuartigen philosophischen Methode und damit zu einer völlig neuartigen Philosophie selbst geführt haben, auch in Amerika ein tätiges Interesse erregen. Indessen eben die Neuartigkeit gegenüber aller philosophischen Tradition macht ihre ausserordentlich schwere Zugänglichkeit aus. Es ist eine harte Zumutung für den in der Philosophiegeschichte Stehenden und in ihren Traditionen Erzogenen, diese ganz und gar "einzuklammern" und von ihren Denkweisen durchaus keinen Gebrauch zu machen; und damit auch keinen Gebrauch zu machen von ihren nie radikal herausgestellten Voraussetzungen, den selbstverständlichsten Selbstverständlichkeiten der Welterfahrung und des auf sie zurückbezogenen logischen (wissenschaftlichen) Denkens. Anderseits muss doch von der Tradition und der natürlichen vor-wissenschaftlichen Erfahrung aus (in der jedermann vor der Phänomenologie steht) ein Motivationsweg beschritten werden, der zu der revolutionären "phänomenologischen Reduktion" emporleitet, und es gehört eine ungewöhnliche Konsequenz und Denkenergie dazu, festzubleiben, nicht wieder in die traditionalen Denkweisen zurückzufallen, sich des Neuen wirklich zu bemächtigen, ohne es durch solche allzu versucherischen Rückfälle zu verfälschen. ... Es dürfte aus dieser Situation sich ergeben, dass Sie fehlgehen würden, wenn Sie sich auf irgendeine der literarischen Darstellungen meiner Phänomenologie stürzten ... Es wird keine andere Möglichkeit geben als die, meine eigenen, begreiflicher Weise sehr schwierigen Schriften zu studieren. Hier sind nun für das Verständnis einer Philosophie, die im fortgehenden Werden und selbstbesinnlichem Klären enstand, am allerwichtigsten *die der spätesten und reifsten Periode:* die gleichzeitig entstandenen Schriften "*Formale und transcendentale Logik*" (1929 separat und im "Jahrbuch für Philosophie und phänomenologische Forschung" Bd. X.), sowie die nur in französischer Übersetzung erschienenen "*Méditations Cartésiennes*" (Armand Colin, Paris 1931). *Wichtig* ist auch das "*Nachwort*" zur englischen Übersetzung meiner "Ideen" (am Besten die ein wenig erweiterte deutsche

Veröffentlichung im "Jahrbuch ..." Bd. XI., die auch separat zu haben ist.) [1]

(3) Nun wird Ihnen schon, was ich bisher schrieb, lieber Herr College, fatal klingen, da Ihr Thema eine Einheit der phänomenologischen Bewegung, also so etwas wie eine einheitliche Philosophie dieses Namens voraussetzt, während ich das leugne, nachdem ich lange genug gewartet habe, dass meinen früheren Schülern aufgrund meiner den "Logischen Untersuchungen" nachfolgenden Schriften die Augen aufgehen würden über das, was als eine völlig neuartige und völlig radikale Philosophie im Werden war und ist. So kann man z.B. von der Religionsphilosophie *Schelers* (oder Stavenhagens, oder J. Herings) sprechen, aber mit Phänomenologie in meinem Sinne hat sie nichts zu tun. Denn diese eröffnet mit der phänomenologischen Reduktion eine prinzipiell neuartige Erfahrung, die nicht Welterfahrung ist, und stellt uns damit direkt auf den absoluten Boden, den der "transcendentalen Subjektivität." Dafür blieb leider die "phänomenologische Bewegung" blind. Fast alle Darstellungen und kritischen Äusserungen von diesen Seiten über die Reduktion sind so sinnverkehrend, dass ich Sie nur warnen kann. Es liegt im Radikalismus der phänomenologischen Reform, dass sie vom Urboden der neuartigen "transcendentalen Erfahrung" aus und in Gestalt einer systematischen Analytik der Seinssinn konstituierenden transcendentalen Intentionalität aufzuzeigen unternimmt, wie und in welchen Stufen in dieser die Welt ihren Sinn und ihre Seinsgeltung gewinnt. Die philosophischen Probleme erschliessen sich mit ihrem echten Sinn als transcendental-phänomenologische in einer wesensmässigen systematischen Stufenfolge. Es zeigt sich dabei, dass die religiös-ethischen Probleme solche der höchsten Stufe sind. (Sie sind also als wissenschaftliche nicht so billig zu haben, wie es der im Grunde naive Ontologismus Schelers meinte.) Eben darum schwieg ich mich in meinen Schriften über religionsphilosophische Probleme aus. Doch sind in ihnen und den kommenden Publikationen schon die Wege vorgebahnt, um zu ihnen hinzuarbeiten und die *echten* religions-philosophischen Probleme zu formulieren.

---

[1] [Husserl's footnote:] Lesenswert sind die [in] den letzten Jahrgängen der Deutschen Literaturzeitung erschienenen eingehenden Rezensionen dieser 3 Schriften von A. Gurwitsch und F. [Alfred] Schütz.

(4) Zum Teil liegt die Antwort auf Ihre formulierten Fragen schon im Vorstehenden. Ad 1. Meine Philosophie, bitte ich Sie, nicht ein "System" zu nennen. Denn es ist gerade ihr Absehen, alle "Systeme" für immer unmöglich zu machen. Sie will strenge Wissenschaft sein, die in unendlichem Progress systematisch ihre Probleme, Methoden und Theorien erarbeitet. Was meine *Vorgänger* anbelangt, so habe ich in einem gewissen Sinne viele, ja alle grossen Philosophen der Geschichte, so fern alle, auch die ich nie studierte, mindestens mittelbar auf meine Phänomenologie, wie auf jede Philosophie der Gegenwart eingewirkt haben. Aber seitdem ich im Zuendedenken des misslungenen, (weil nicht in rücksichtsloser Konsequenz durchgeführten) Versuchs der Cartesianischen Meditationen, eine absolut vorurteilslose Wissenschaftsbegründung zustande zu bringen, die phänomenologische Reduktion erreicht hatte, gab es für mich keine Philosophen, von denen ich irgendwelche Ergebnisse hätte übernehmen können. Es gab seitdem für mich nichts, und durfte auch nichts geben, das ich mir nicht auf dem neuen Wege erarbeitet hätte. Und selbst Vorvermutungen müssten sich auf ihm selbst als Arbeitshorizonte vorzeichnen und konnten nur dann als Leitung für die wirklich erledigende Arbeit zugelassen werden.

(5) [2] Meine ganze Entwicklung ist durch den Ausgang von F. Brentano (meinem akademischen Lehrer) bestimmt – von dessen Psychologie, die zum Grundcharakter des Psychischen die "Intentionalität" rechnete. Aber in der Vertiefung in die Correlation zwischen den log. Idealitäten und ihren intentionalen Correlaten (Log. Unt. Bd. II) gestaltete sich mir der Sinn einer intentionalen Psychologie und ihrer analytischen Methode völlig um. Erst nach den L.U. hob sich jedoch der radicale philosophische Unterschied zwischen einer intentionalen Psychologie als positiver Wissenschaft und der transz. Phänomenologie ab.

(6) Welche Rolle mein "Platonismus," mein energisches Eintreten für eine universale Ontologie, also für die Erarbeitung von Wesenseinsichten (für das echte Apriori) in allen Erkenntnissphären, in meiner Entwicklung hatte und welche neue Bedeutung er in der gereiften transcendentalen Phänomenologie gewinnt, darüber wird Sie am Besten meine "Formale und transcendentale Logik" (insbesondere ihr II. Teil) aufklären, obschon darin nur

---

[2] Handwritten insertion in margin of letter.

die "formale Ontologie" in Frage ist. Dank schulde ich für diesen "Platonismus" dem bekannten Kapitel in *Lotze's* Logik, wie sehr seine Erkenntnistheorie und Metaphysik mich stets abstiess. Plotin habe ich nie gelesen, auch die grossen Idealisten nach Kant habe ich nur in Bruchstücken kennen gelernt, also nie eingehend studiert. Jetzt erst, nachdem die Phänomenologie aufgrund meiner Lebensarbeit den sicheren Gang wirklicher Wissenschaft gewonnen hat, (allerdings der grösste Teil meiner konkreten Untersuchungen harrt noch der Veröffentlichung), habe ich ein grosses Interesse auch für sie als meine "Vorgänger." Denn nun kann ich sie als solche *verstehen*, nämlich von meiner Phänomenologie aus und auf sie hin. Im Grunde bin ich zu einem guten Teile Autodidakt. Aber es gibt eben, scheint mir, Wenden der Wissenschaft, in denen es auf Autodidakten ankommt als solchen, die nicht der Versuchung der Gelehrsamkeit unterliegen, Gedanken der Tradition fortzubilden anstatt in deren eigene dunkle Tiefen, in ihre naiven Voraussetzungen usw. selbstdenkend einzudringen. Im Übrigen habe ich vor meinen philosophischen Studien ungefähr sieben Jahre ausschliesslich und berufsmässig Mathematik und exakte Naturwissenschaft studiert und sicherlich von dem Geiste des Radikalismus der Weierstraß'schen Vorlesungen Einfluss erfahren.

(7) Ad 2. Das Problem des *Irrtums* ist auf der ersten Stufe der Phänomenologie beschlossen in der Lehre von der "Modalisierbarkeit" aller Akte. D.h. es tritt auf in der Erforschung des konstitutiven Aufbaus der Welt *im Hinblick auf* die sich immer neu in Intention und Erfüllung vorzeichnende und bewährende Einstimmigkeit des Seinssinnes: eine Einstimmigkeit durch Einbrüche der "Modalisierungen" und durch immer neue "Korrekturen" hindurch. In der höheren Stufe der Phänomenologie wird der Irrtum in eins mit den Fragen des ethischen Lebens, des Lebens in echter oder unechter Menschlichkeit, in letztlicher Befriedigung oder Unseligkeit, (einer individuellen und sozialen Harmonie und Disharmonie) von Neuem zum Problem. Es handelt sich um die allumfassende Problematik, die auch unter dem Titel der universalen Teleologie angesprochen werden kann. Anders ausgedrückt sind es die Probleme der Totalität, der transcendentalen Möglichkeit einer seienden offenen, unendlichen transcendentalen Intersubjektivität, darin beschlossen der Mög-

lichkeit "wahrer Selbsterhaltung" einer jeden, einzelnen und sozialen, Subjektivität im unendlichen Zusammenhang. Die Probleme der "universellen Harmonie," aber auch die der echten "Humanität" gewinnen also als phänomenologische Probleme ihren absoluten, auf die transcendentale Subjektivität bezogenen Sinn. So ist der oberste Abschluss für die Problematik der phänomenologischen Philosophie die Frage nach dem "Prinzip" der in ihren universalen Strukturen konkret erschlossenen Teleologie. Demnach ist das oberste "Konstitutionsproblem" die Frage nach dem Sein des "Überseienden," eben dieses Prinzips, das eine in sich zusammenstimmende Totalität der transcendentalen Intersubjektivität mit der durch sie konstituierten Welt existenzmöglich macht, weshalb man es auch platonisch als Idee des Guten bezeichnen könnte. (Natürlich darf aber hier "Idee" nicht Eidos besagen.) Mit all dem aber bewegt man sich innerhalb der Problematik und der Methodik einer Philosophie als strenger Wissenschaft, der allein radikalen und im höchsten Sinne strengen. Obwohl die oberste Stufe in ihrem allgemeinen Problemsinn sich schon streng vorgezeichnet hat, ist es noch weit bis zur geforderten theoretischen Durchführung in konkret ausgearbeiteten wissenschaftlichen Theorien. Die Phänomenologie ist aber jedenfalls da, als wirkliche Arbeit in lebendigem Werden.

(8) Unter den ganz Vereinzelten, die in den tiefsten Sinn meiner Phänomenologie eingedrungen sind, ist übrigens ein glänzend begabter und sehr ernster Amerikaner, Herr Dorion *Cairns*, der die Energie und Konsequenz hatte, nicht abzulassen, bis er zum wirklichen Verständnis gekommen war. Er hat soeben in Harvard seinen Doktor gemacht und zwar aufgrund eines Entwurfes zu einer Einleitung in die Phänomenologie. Er besitzt zweifellos die dazu erforderliche Reife. Er war schon vor einer grösseren Reihe von Jahren für zwei Jahre bei mir in Freiburg und neuerdings bis letzten Weihnachten wiederum fast ebensolange. Er wird gerne bereit sein, Sie bei allen Verständnisschwierigkeiten zu beraten, falls Sie es wünschen. Ich würde es Ihnen sehr empfehlen. Seine Adresse ist: Dr. Dorion Cairns, 14 Remington Str., Cambridge Mass. USA

...   Mit dem Ausdruck vorzüglicher
                                        Hochachtung
                                     Ihr sehr ergebener
                                                E. Husserl

C. Letter of Husserl to Welch. (Translation.)

Dear Colleague,

(1) In the midst of the unrest of this time with its revolutioniz-
ing of our entire German nation and its life, I was unable to
answer your kind letter at once.

(2) I am of course very glad that my philosophical endeavors
arouse interest even in America; endeavors which in the course
of a constant inner evolution through more than four decades
have led to a fundamentally novel philosophical method and
thereby to a completely novel philosophy. However, precisely
this novelty, compared with all the philosophical tradition,
results in the extraordinary difficulties in its accessibility. It is a
hard imposition on those having their place within the history of
philosophy and educated in its traditions to "bracket" it entirely
and not to make any use of it; and hence also not to make any
use of its presuppositions which have never been radically isolated, of the most obvious obviousnesses of the experience of the
world and of the logical (scientific) thinking based upon it. On
the other hand, it is necessary to make a (well-)motivated approach, starting from the tradition and the natural pre-scientific
experience (in which everyone lives before phenomenology),
which leads upward to the revolutionary phenomenological reduction. And it takes unusual consistency and energy of thought
to remain firm and not to fall back into the traditional ways of
thinking, to really take hold of the new, without falsifying it by
such all too tempting relapses.[3] ... It would seem to follow from
this situation that you would go astray if you rush to any one
of the literary presentations of my phenomenology ... There
will be no alternative to studying my own writings, which are
understandably very difficult. Here, for an understanding of a
philosophy which arose in continuous development and reflective
clarification, the most important writings are those of the latest
and most mature period, i.e., the simultaneously developed texts
Formal and Transcendental Logic (1929), separately and in *Jahr-*

---

[3] In the 23 lines here omitted, except for one sentence toward the end, Husserl
warns the reader of introductions written by some of his former students, especially
those of his Göttingen and early Freiburg period, mentioning specifically one of the
authors of the introductions to Phenomenology to whom Welch had referred in his
letter. H.S.

buch vol. X) as well as the *Méditations cartésiennes*, which have appeared only in French translation. Important is also the Post-script to the English translation of my *Ideen* (its best form is the slightly enlarged German publication in *Jahrbuch*, vol. XI, which is also available separately).[4]

(3) However, [I realize], my dear colleague, that even what I have written you thus far, will sound discouraging to you, since your topic presupposes the unity of the Phenomenological Move-ment, hence something like a unified philosophy of this name, whereas I deny its existence, after having waited long enough for the possibility that as a result of my writings following the *Logische Untersuchungen* the eyes of my former students would be opened up for what was and still is in the making as a com-pletely radical philosophy. Thus, for instance, one can speak of the philosophy of religion of Scheler (or of Stavenhagen or Jean Hering), but it has nothing to do with phenomenology in my sense. For by way of the phenomenological reduction this phenom-enology opens up a fundamentally novel experience which is not mundane experience and thus puts us directly on absolute ground, that of "transcendental subjectivity." Unfortunately, the "Phenomenological Movement" remained blind for this. Al-most all the accounts and critical expressions from these corners about the reduction distort its sense so much that I can only warn you. It is part of the radicalism of the phenomenological reform that it undertakes to demonstrate how and in what stages in this analytics the world acquires its sense and its validity of being, as seen from the ultimate ground of "transcendental expe-rience" and in the form of a systematic analytics of the tran-scendental intentionality which constitutes the sense of being. The philosophical problems disclose themselves in their genuine meaning as transcendental-phenomenological ones in an essential systematic series of steps. On these occasions it becomes manifest that the religious-ethical problems are problems of the highest level. (Consequently they cannot be obtained as cheaply as Scheler's basically naive ontologism believed.) This is precisely the reason why in my writings I kept silent about the problems

---

[4] [Husserl's footnote:] Worth reading are also the detailed reviews of these writings by A. Gurwitsch and Alfred Schütz, which appeared in the latest volumes of the *Deutsche Literaturzeitung*.

of philosophy of religion. However, in these and in my forth-
coming publications the roads are cleared in order to work one's
way toward them and to formulate the *genuine* problems of
philosophy of religion.

(4) In part the answer to your formulated questions is contained in the preceding.

As to question 1: May I ask you not to call my philosophy a
"system." For it is precisely its objective to make all "systems'
impossible once and for all. It wants to be rigorous science, which
in an infinite progression systematically works its way toward
its problems, methods and theories. As far as my predecessors are
concerned, I have in a sense many of them, even those whom I
never studied, have had at least an indirect effect on my phenomenology, as they have had on every philosophy of the present.
However, since the time that, in thinking through the failure
(since not carried through in ruthless consistency) of the attempt
of the Cartesian Meditations to achieve a foundation for science
free of all prejudice, I had reached the phenomenological reduction, there were no philosophers left for me from whom I could
have taken over any results. Since then there was nothing for me,
nor by right could there be anything, that I have not achieved
for myself by the new approach. And in this way even presuppositions had to outline themselves [merely] as horizons for work
and could be admitted merely as directives for really decisive
work.

(5) [Handwritten insertion] My entire development is determined by the stimulation of Franz Brentano (my academic
teacher) – by his psychology which included as a fundamental
character of the psychic "intentionality." However, in penetrating deeply into the correlation between the logical idealities and
their intentional correlates (*Logische Untersuchungen*, vol. II), the
sense of an intentional psychology and of its method became for
me completely transformed. However, only after the *Logical
Investigations* the radical philosophical difference between an
intentional psychology as a positive science and transcendental
phenomenology revealed itself.

(6) What role had my "Platonism," my vigorous plea for a
universal ontology, hence for the achievement of essential insights (for the genuine a priori) in all spheres of knowledge, in

my development, and what new significance does it acquire in the mature transcendental phenomenology? About this point my *Formal and Transcendental Logic* (especially its second part) will enlighten you, although here merely "formal ontology" is under discussion. I am indebted for this "Platonism" to the well-known chapter in Lotze's *Logic*, no matter how much I was always repelled by his epistemology and metaphysics. I never read Plotinus; even the great Idealists after Kant I have come to know only through fragments, hence I have never studied them intensively. Not until now, since, on the basis of my life work, phenomenology has reached the safe course of a real science (to be sure, the large part of my concrete investigations is still awaiting publication), I have great interest even for them as my "predecessors." For now I can *understand* them as such (i.e., from the standpoint of my phenomenology and as tending toward it). Basically I am a self-taught person. However, it seems to me that there are turning points of science where everything depends upon self-taught men as the ones who are not subject to the temptation of scholarship to cultivate ideas of the tradition instead of penetrating by their own thinking into its own dark depths, into its naive presuppositions etc. Besides, prior to my philosophical studies, for about seven years, I pursued exclusively and professionally the study of mathematics and exact science, and certainly underwent influences from the spirit of radicalism of Weierstrass' lectures.

(7) As to question 2. The problem of error is included, on the first level of phenomenology, in the doctrine of the "possible modalization" of all acts. This means that it occurs in the investigation of the constitutive formation of the world with a view to the concordance of the meaning of being foreshadowing and validating itself in intention and fulfillment: a concordance through collapses of its modalizations and through ever new "corrections." On the higher level of phenomenology error, together with questions of ethical life, of the life in genuine or spurious humanity, in ultimate satisfaction and unhappiness (of an individual and social harmony and disharmony) becomes once more a problem. This is a matter of an all-comprehensive set of problems which can also be designated by the title of universal teleology. Put differently, these are the problems of totality, of

the transcendental possibility of an existing, open, infinite transcendental intersubjectivity, and, included in it, the possibility of "true self-preservation" of any single and social subjectivity in infinite connection. The problems of "universal harmony," but also those of genuine humanity acquire, as phenomenological problems, their absolute meaning related to transcendental subjectivity. Thus the supreme terminus for the problems of phenomenological philosophy is the question of the "principle" of teleology disclosed concretely in its universal structures. Hence the supreme "problem of constitution" is the question of the being of "what is beyond being," i.e., precisely of this principle which makes possible in its existence a totality of transcendental intersubjectivity concordant in itself, together with the world constituted by it, which is why one could also designate it Platonically as the Idea of the Good. (But of course "Idea" must here not mean the same as *Eidos*.) But with all this one moves within the set of problems and methods of a philosophy as a rigorous science, the only radical and in the highest sense rigorous science. Although the topmost level has already been strictly outlined in the general sense of the problem, it is still a long way to the postulated theoretical development in concretely worked out scientific theories. But in any case, phenomenology exists, as real work in living development.

(8) Incidentally, among the very rare ones who have penetrated into the deepest sense of my phenomenology is a splendidly gifted and very serious American, Mr. Dorion Cairns, who had the energy and persistence not to desist until he had arrived at real understanding. He just has taken his Ph.D. at Harvard, actually on the basis of a draft for an introduction to phenomenology. Without a doubt he has the required maturity for this undertaking. A considerable number of years ago he was with me in Freiburg for two years, and recently until last Christmas again for almost the same length of time. He will be glad to give you advice in all difficulties of understanding. I would recommend it to you very much.[5] ...

. . .   E. Husserl

---

[5] A handwritten postscript of 12 lines asks specifically whether there could be a place for Dorion Cairns in Los Angeles and reiterates and augments the recommendations given in the previous paragraph. H.S.

Some Comments on Husserl's Letter

The following remarks are to give the readers of the Husserl letter aids for better understanding than the addressee seems to have achieved. I shall begin by commenting on each of the paragraphs in succession, before attempting a final appraisal of the letter in the context of Husserl's development.

1. The initial brief paragraph intimates that the preceding five months since Hitler had come to power had not been easy ones on Husserl, the "non-Aryan," even though as an emeritus he was not directly affected by the first phase of the "revolution." The wording of the paragraph suggests that Husserl, who had not yet stopped identifying with the German nation, being still a naturalized German citizen, though a native Austrian, counted with the possibility that the letter might be read by a censor.

2. The second paragraph is remarkable for the stringency of the demands Husserl makes on anyone who wants to understand his mature philosophy, including the demand to perform a phenomenological reduction by which the whole tradition of philosophy had to be "bracketed." Accordingly he characterizes this reduction as a revolution not yet understood as such by any of the available introductions to phenomenology, for which he gives specific examples. As the only proper approach to this most radical form of his phenomenology he mentions some of his own, at the time still mostly untranslated, writings, omitting the English translation of his *Ideen* of 1913 by W. R. Boyce Gibson, published two years earlier (1931) except for his own Preface, here called a *Nachwort*, and even his article on "Phenomenology" in the 1929 edition of the *Encyclopaedia Britannica*, "translated" and cut down from 7000 to 4000 words by Christopher Salmon.[5a]

3. In the third paragraph Husserl dissociates himself demonstratively from the Phenomenological Movement, to which Welch had alluded, and especially from Max Scheler, actually Welch's primary interest. Husserl makes it clear that until then he had entertained hopes that his erstwhile followers would join his final "revolution," but that they had actually never understood it and especially had failed to see that it led to a new kind of tran-

[5a] For possible reasons see my article "On the Misfortunes of Edmund Husserl's Encyclopaedia Britannica Article 'Phenomenology'," *Journal of the British Society for Phenomenology*, II, 2 (1971), pp. 74-76.

scendental experience which could show how intentionality "constituted" the world, i.e., its "meaning" and "validity," and he intimates that this is true even for phenomenology of religion, of which Husserl tries to give Welch some taste later in the letter.

The remaining parts of the letter seem to follow Welch's two main questions as leads. His third question, that on Husserl's teachers and his emancipation from them, is answered to some extent implicitly when he takes up his predecessors, notably Plato and Descartes.

4. In the fourth paragraph one of the striking things is Husserl's emphatic denial of having developed a system and his claim that he wants to abolish all such systems once and for all. Actually this almost Nietzschean rejection of the will to a system is something that Husserl did not always maintain. From statements in some of his letters and fragments now found in his unpublished manuscripts it appears that Husserl cherished the plan of condensing his final insights into something he himself called a system.[6] Nevertheless, it remains true that he had no intention of rivalling any of the great systems such as those of Aristotle or Hegel, and that he denied any substantial loans from them, claiming that he had reached their conclusions independently by his own method.

5. The hand-written paragraph-length marginal insertion about Franz Brentano, about whom Welch had not inquired, is interesting proof that Husserl did not want him to be forgotten, although he himself had developed his master's "empirical psychology" into a psychology of intentionality and finally into transcendental phenomenology.

6. The sixth paragraph takes up Plato's significance for Husserl's philosophy. Here Husserl makes it plain that in his latest phase Platonism has become subordinated to a transcendentalism for which even Platonic essences are constituted in consciousness. He also admits openly that he had not made an intensive study of post-Kantian idealism, although he had lectured about it. I am not familiar with other texts in which Husserl calls himself self-taught ("*Autodidakt*"), as he does in this letter. This is actually correct in the sense that he had never taken an academic degree

[6] See, e.g., his *Briefe an Roman Ingarden* (Phaenomenologica 25) The Hague, Martinus Nijhoff, 1968, pp. 168f.

in philosophy. It is interesting that in the letter Husserl connects his own radicalism with the lectures of his mathematical teacher Karl Weierstrass.

7. The seventh paragraph tries to answer Welch's question about the problem of error. Apparently this paragraph attracted the special attention of the addressee, since translations of single words are pencilled on top of several German words, not all of them correct ones. Husserl's attempt to account for error in terms of "modalizations" of acts clearly does not treat the traditional problem under its usual name. The expression *Modalisierbarkeit* (possible modalization) does not seem to occur in Husserl's published writings up to that time. However, it can be related to the discussions of modalities of belief in the *Ideen* (par. 100ff.), which also mention the possibility of the transformations of beliefs. Presumably error, though not itself a mode of belief, is to be explained as the correlate of our changing modes of belief, revealing itself when, e.g., our belief in the Ptolemean system has changed into disbelief. However, it is not surprising that this account could not make much sense to the uninitiated. What might have been more helpful is what Husserl suggests by referring to the consonance between intention and fulfillment and the collapses (*Einbrüche*) and emendations (*Korrekturen*) in our constitution of the world. In other words, error occurs in our experience wherever a crisis develops in the normal fulfillment of our intentions and when the lack of fulfillment is followed by a correction, thus revealing our having been in error. However, at this point Husserl turns at once to the situation as it unfolds on higher levels of our experience, including that of religious knowledge, perhaps thinking of Welch's primary interest in philosophy of religion. The injection of the term "teleology," which in Husserl's last phase is closely connected with the conception of a divine goal (*telos*) of all transcendental acts, seems to suggest that error can occur even in areas other than elementary theoretical knowledge whenever a comprehensive totality is at stake. But at this point Husserl seems to have been carried away toward sketching a theory of the principle that stands behind such a teleology, something even above Being, which he finally identifies with the Platonic idea of the Good. There is other evidence in Husserl's last thought suggesting that Husserl's idea of God was

that of an ultimate telos of all transcendental life. But even at this stage he maintains the ideal of phenomenology as a rigorous science, while admitting that at the level of religious consciousness it is still in a rather rudimentary stage.

8. The last paragraph, the recommendation of Dorion Cairns as the American authority on phenomenology with the "needed maturity" to interpret Husserl's own thought implies that others mentioned in Welch's letter do not have it. Was this introduction of Cairns merely an after-thought? This would seem to be a suitable interpretation for the subsequent handwritten post-script, which seems to mean that on re-reading Husserl found the concluding paragraph of the letter itself not yet strong enough. The referral to a live interpreter is certainly well motivated by the preceding paragraph which is anything but easy to understand for a beginner and admits the unfinished conditions of Husserl's own thought. In this sense this recommendation comes as a kind of personal climax to the letter. Whether this means that the whole letter was written with the purpose of making Cairns the official interpreter of phenomenology can no longer be established, but it seems highly likely that Husserl would not have written this letter if it had not given him a chance to make a plea for his favorite American student.

On the Significance of Husserl's Letter

In trying to assess the importance of this letter in the context of Husserl's development one must distinguish between his own perspective and the "objective" place of the letter in relation to his philosophical work.

"Subjectively" one might wonder why no copy of this unusually lengthy letter has survived in the files of Husserl's correspondence as taken over by the Louvain Archives, which comprise not only letters *from* others to Husserl but copies of his own letters *to* others which he seems to have considered important. But the very fact that the letter to Welch was typed, presumably by Eugen Fink, at a time when he continued writing most of his letters by hand, seems significant. So is, in addition to its length, the fact that according to the date line the incubation time for this letter extended over four days. Here was a carefully considered attempt to give directions to an American scholar writing from a new center of philosophy. This challenge gave Husserl a chance of thinking through the whole problem of how to introduce others to the maturest stage of his radical phenomenology, to survey critically the existing introductory literature and to develop some of his own ideas, not only about the problem of error but about his religious teleology.

But what about the objective significance of the letter apart from Husserl's own perspective? What light does it throw on Husserl's philosophy in general or at least on a specific phase in its development? Here one ought to bear in mind that this was the time when Husserl had practically abandoned work on the German version of his *Cartesian Meditations* after having turned them over to Eugen Fink; in this context it is not without interest that in recommending this work to Welch, Husserl mentions merely the French translation, and no longer holds out the prospect of an improved German version. On the other hand the plan of the last work, the *Crisis of the European Sciences*, which was to grow out of the Vienna and Prague lectures of 1935 had not yet been conceived. So Husserl was looking for new and better ways of introducing the public to his transcendental phenomenology. That this new phenomenology represented a radical revolution, not yet sufficiently expressed in his own earlier work was a conviction which Husserl has rarely, if ever, expressed as sharply as in this letter. I am familiar only with one other occasion during the same year, when he warned a student of G. F. Stout, visiting in Freiburg, not only against approaching phenomenology via the history of philosophy but even against his own earlier work. This may well have been the period when he conceived of the radicalism, first announced in his 1922 Lectures at the University of London, as an entirely new type of philosophy, whose first literary expression was the *Formal and Transcendental Logic* of 1929.

My first impression after seeing this letter was that it might well be considered Husserl's "Epistle to the Americans." But on second thought I have come to realize that this would be misleading. As a letter for Americans it certainly does not make any attempt to show the relevance of phenomenology for American philosophers, which Husserl might well have done in view of his admiration for William James as a pioneer of phenomenological seeing and describing. Husserl is simply speaking to a foreign scholar, realizing his difficulty in entering into radical phenomenology and offering him as the only alternative to the study of untranslated text the help of a proven expert, Dorion Cairns.

Thus the message of this letter is really addressed to all those who want to enter Husserl's "most mature" philosophy directly. This was a problem with which Husserl struggled increasingly as he came to realize that in his radicalism he had left behind the entire Phenomenological Movement and had maneuvered himself into a position of nearly solipsistic isolation. Husserl's letter to Welch clearly reflects this realization. It also shows that for Husserl his last period, beginning apparently with the London Lectures of 1922, involved a drastic change in his philosophical development, to which a new approach was indicated. Yet in 1933 all he could suggest was the study of his publications since 1929 with no apparent hope that the German version of the *Cartesian Meditations* would solve the problem. This makes it even more understandable that he was looking for a completely new approach, which did not develop until 1935 with the Vienna and Prague lectures. In this regard the letter to Welch shows Husserl at the half-way mark. He announces the radical novelty of his final phenomenology. But he is still in search of a new road that could make it more accessible to newcomers, if not to old-timers. Obviously there could be no royal road to this phenomenology. But the letter to Welch proves that Husserl had not yet given up hope that there was a way, and that such devoted students as Cairns could show it.

A Sequel to Husserl's Letter

Husserl's correspondence, now in the Archives at Louvain, includes a brief note by E. Parl Welch dated July 20, 1933 acknowledging the receipt of the June letter and thanking him for recommending Dorion Cairns, combined with a request for permission "to publish some parts of your letter, particularly that on the problem of error." On August 31 Husserl answered this request in a brief letter to which I was given access by Professor Cyril Welch, the son of the addressee, in which Husserl, without directly refusing such a permission, advised Welch strongly against such use, mentioning bad experiences he had had on earlier occasions (*"Ich meine, dass Sie vorläufig mit dem literarischen Gebrauch meines Briefes warten sollten"*). This instruction explains to some extent why Welch did not mention this letter at all, neither in his unpublished University of Southern California dissertation of 1934 nor in his later publications on Husserl.[7] Only in two footnotes of the typewritten dissertation did he seem to be referring to it ("in a private letter to the writer") as the source of his information for Husserl's repudiation of Scheler (p. 68) and of his own view that Husserl chose "to remain vague to the point of irritation when questioned upon the matter of error" (p. 339). Otherwise there is no indication that either in his dissertation, submitted almost a year after the date of the letter, or in his later work, Welch made any use of Husserl's substantive advice in the June letter. Anyway, he never referred to Husserl's "latest and maturest work," which Husserl had urged him to consult in preference to his earlier ones. Instead Welch's account of Husserlian phenomenology is based exclusively on the *Logische Untersuchungen*, the *Ideen*, and on the Encyclopaedia Britannica article, along with Marvin Farber's first Husserl book of 1928. Also, according to personal information from Dorion Cairns, Welch had never turned to him for further help and advice, as Husserl had suggested.

Less than two months after Husserl's August letter, i.e., on October 28, the Director of the School of Philosophy at the University of Southern California, Ralph T. Flewelling, sent an official letter to Husserl on Department stationery, which, according to Husserl's letter to Dorion Cairns of November 15, was received only a few days later. Starting with the remark that "we in America have been greatly interested in your work in phenomenology," and describing the philosophical and climatic merits of California, Flewelling closed his letter with this paragraph:

> We are wondering if you could be induced to come to us on a permanent, a part-time, or even a one-year's visiting basis in order to see how you might like it.

[7] *Edmund Husserl's Phenomenology* (The University of California Press, 1939), and *The Philosophy of Edmund Husserl* (Columbia University Press, 1941).

I have been unable to discover any documentary explanation for this amazing invitation to the 74-year-old Husserl, five years after his official retirement. Of course, by October 1933 the true nature of the Nazi revolution, to which Husserl had alluded cautiously at the very start of his June letter, had become sufficiently manifest to make the idea of emigration attractive to all those of "non-Aryan" descent. Thus Flewelling, in his attempt to win such distinguished European scholars as Wildon Carr (known to Husserl as one of the four chairmen of his lecture at the University of London in 1922) and F. C. S. Schiller, both mentioned in the letter of invitation, may well have thought that here was another chance of adding the name of an outstanding European philosopher to the roster of his new School of Philosophy.[8]

But why did Flewelling single out Husserl among all the potential German philosophers, already arriving as refugees in the States, who were in need of asylum? There is no longer enough information available for a definite answer. But there is sufficient evidence to suggest a plausible, if no longer verifiable, hypothesis. Could it have been a mere coincidence that so soon after Husserl's last letter to Welch the School with which he was affiliated issued an invitation to its author? Why was it that Husserl's June letter was found in a special folder with a covering sheet among the papers of the School of Philosophy and not returned to Welch? Why did he turn over his precious letter to Flewelling without asking for its return? Could the main reason have been Husserl's plea for Dorion Cairns as a candidate for a possible opening at the School? And could this plea have turned Flewelling's attention from the recommended novice to the source of the recommendation, Husserl himself? However, apparently Welch himself was not aware of Flewelling's use of his letter, since his obituary article on "Edmund Husserl: An Appraisal" in the *Personalist* (Vol. 21, 1940, pp. 159–168) contains no mention of the 1933 invitation to the School of Philosophy, which published Flewelling's journal.

Husserl's reply to the invitation does not seem to have surviv-

[8] See *The Forest of Yggdrasil: The Autobiography of Ralph T. Flewelling,* edited by W. H. W. Werkmeister and Wilbur Long. University of California Press, 1962, pp. xvii, 113.

ed, either at the School of Philosophy or in the Husserl Archives. But we know a good deal about his reactions and about the very serious thought he gave to the possibility of an asylum in the States. The main source for this knowledge is his correspondence with Dorion Cairns, whom he informed about the invitation in a letter of November 15. Here he declared at once that, while he felt tempted to go for one year, he would not consider doing so without Cairns as his assistant and Eugen Fink as his collaborator (who, however, did not particularly like the idea, as Husserl added). So Husserl asked Cairns for an immediate response about his readiness to join him. A letter by Mrs. Husserl of November 29 mentioned the fact that Husserl had sent a first reply to Flewelling inquiring among other things particularly about the possibility of a teaching assistant in view of his difficulty of expressing himself in English. On December 9 Husserl himself told Cairns that he had made his simultaneous appointment a pre-condition (*Grundbedingung*) for his acceptance. On January 28, 1934 Mrs. Husserl reported to Cairns that there was still no decision as to the assistantship question. Flewelling had written on January 13: "The most difficult question for us would be to take on Dr. Cairns, as we have no notion how much we would have to pay him." But Mrs. Husserl added that any other solution would be "out of the question" and Cairns's assistantship a *conditio sine qua non*.

Cairns's own response to Husserl's original announcement in a letter of January 17 made it plain that he would have been ready to go, although at the time he was even more interested in the possibility of a lectureship at the New School of Social Research, where Husserl had recommended him very strongly to Max Wertheimer (see his letter of December 12 and Cairns' reply of January 12, 1934).

On May 18, Husserl began his letter to Cairns by telling him that the negotiations with Los Angeles had failed. As his chief explanation he named not his age, but the fact that his one basic condition, that of an appointment of Cairns as his aide, had not been met, largely because of lack of funds. Nevertheless, Husserl added that once this obstacle should disappear, negotiations could be resumed in the following year.

All this makes it clear that Dorion Cairns was the key figure in the story of Husserl's invitation to the United States. His place in Husserl's June letter to Welch may have precipitated Flewelling's invitation. And when it came, the failure of a collateral invitation to Cairns was a major reason for Husserl's final "no."

Husserl in America – this possibility was by no means an idle dream.[9] But in view of the short span of four more years he was to live, one may well wonder whether the move to America would have been a wise one, allowing him to work as much or more than he actually did despite the worsening conditions around him. Certainly it would have given Americans better access to him and stimulated interest in his work considerably. In any case, it seems worth recording that Husserl himself seriously considered such a move. The story of this possibility, beginning with the Welch letter, should also not be forgotten in view of its message to all students of his later philosophy in the New World. It also serves as another reminder of Dorion Cairns' key role in the introduction of Husserl's thought to America.

[9] Actually Husserl's ashes came to the States, when after the war Mrs. Husserl, who had kept them with her during the war, joined her daughter Elisabeth Husserl Rosenberg in Arlington, Massachusetts, to whom I am indebted for this information. Only five years later could they be deposited in Mrs. Husserl's grave in Guenterstal near Freiburg.

RICHARD M. ZANER

THE ART OF FREE PHANTASY IN RIGOROUS PHENOMENOLOGICAL SCIENCE

§ 1. In section 70 of the first book of his *Ideen*,[1] Husserl addresses himself to the question of the specific method of apprehending essences – that of "free phantasy." The process involved in disclosing and examining essence, he consistently held in all his works, is in no sense a process of inferring "from an *inductive empeiria*" in the manner, say, of an experimental psychologist.[2] Free variation in phantasy is not at all an "empirical variation," [3] which could only yield inductive generalizations pertaining to a specific class of empirical states of affairs.[4] Variation in pure phantasy as executed systematically in phenomenological reflection

must be understood, not as an *empirical variation* but as a variation carried on with the freedom of pure phantasy and with the consciousness of its purely optional character – the consciousness of the "pure" Anything Whatever.[5]

Over against all forms of actual, positional experience (even in the broadest sense) is

"neutralized" experience, "*as-if experience*," we can also say "*experience in phantasy*," which, with a suitable and freely possible alteration of one's attitudes, becomes positional experience of a possible individual. Naturally, as-if experience has parallel as-if modalities of its primitive mode, as-if certainty of being.[6]

---

[1] *Ideen zu einer reinen Phänomenologie und phänomenologischen Philosophie*, Erstes Buch (Halle: Max Niemeyer, 1913). (Hereafter cited as *Ideen*, I.)

[2] *Formal and Transcendental Logic*, tr. Dorion Cairns (The Hague: Martinus Nijhoff, 1969), p. 211. (Hereafter cited as *F.T.L.*)

[3] *Ibid.*, p. 247; cf. *Cartesian Meditations*, tr. Dorion Cairns (The Hague: Martinus Nijhoff, 1960), pp. 69–71. (Hereafter cited as *C.M.*)

[4] *F.T.L.*, p. 218.

[5] *Ibid.*, pp. 247f.

[6] *Ibid.*, p. 206.

Whatever "free variation," as the central procedure in the phenomenological elucidation of essences, may be, it is clear enough that Husserl strongly urges its rigorous distinction from empirical or inductive variations. Unlike the latter, the former is "released from all restrictions to facts accepted beforehand." [7]

§ 2. Suzanne Bachelard's excellent commentary on Husserl's *Formal and Transcendental Logic* clearly shows the reasons why free phantasy variation cannot be interpreted as a mere empirical varying.[8] Presenting a close reading of the crucial section 70 of *Ideen*, I, and relevant passages from other works, she quite correctly shows the close parallel between the attitude of the geometer and that of the phenomenologist as regards this procedure. Her analysis shows, indeed, apparently

> that the method of mathematical idealization has been the very source of the elaboration of the phenomenological method of investigating essences [9] and that the example which served as starting point for the phenomenological variation has the same role as the particular figure about which the geometer reasons.[10]

The type of procedure in this form of idealization is well-known. In his ongoing thinking, the geometer "operates upon the figure or the model"; [11] he starts with it, but is patently not restricted to its particularity, even though he must from time to time return to it and other actual figures.

The fundamental clue to the geometer's procedure of idealization is the same as that which the phenomenologist utilizes in his elucidation of essences. "Actually, the real datum from which the geometer and the phenomenologist can set out is taken *as an example*. An example as such," Bachelard continues, "is never considered for its own sake, in its individuality." [12] In this, Husserl shows, there are four features vital to a correct understanding of the method.

[7] *Ibid.*, p. 248.
[8] Suzanne Bachelard, *A Study of Husserl's Formal and Transcendental Logic*, tr. Lester Embree (Evanston: Northwestern University Press, 1968), pp. 173–197. (Hereafter cited as Bachelard.)
[9] As is well-known, even Husserl's use of "bracketing" has its mathematical analogue: placing brackets around an expression signifies that the bracketed operations are "put out of play," not "done," but kept in abeyance. Cf. *Ideen*, I, §§ 31–32.
[10] Bachelard, p. 175.
[11] *Ideen*, I, p. 131.
[12] Bachelard, p. 176.

(1) Any particular affair can always be viewed from at least two points of view. On the one hand, I can attend to it *just for its own sake*, in one or another context and mode, concerning myself with "it itself" in its own individuality or uniqueness. But I am free at any moment to *shift my attention* and to regard the affair strictly and purely as an *example* – just as the geometer explicitly does as regards any particular geometrical figure.

(2) I am *free* at any moment to shift my attention to the affair *qua example:* that is, as Bachelard puts it, "The consciousness which deals with the example is a consciousness that one is able to *substitute* another example for this example." [13] In this way, Husserl stresses,[14] the taking of an affair as an example at the same time carries with it the consciousness of the affair's having been "chosen arbitrarily" [*beliebig*], and as such the process is "free" in a complex sense.

First, *any actual or possible instance* of the kind in question could as well serve as the starting point of the variation. Unlike the inductive *empeiria*, free phantasy is in no sense restricted to the "factual," but can begin with any example, actual or possible (indeed, its being able so to begin with *possible* examples is a re-affirmation of the "freedom" in question here).

Second, the procedure is thus *strictly free from* every tie to what actually exists in its starting point as well as in its development.[15] This procedure of becoming freed from actuality is obviously not without its great difficulties. In part, these arise from the intrinsic complexity of the matters being investigated, in part from the enormous effort, as Bergson once said, to "do violence" to the usual, habitual ways of thinking, acting, and doing, and in part to the effort to present the issues in a pedagogically sound and intelligible manner.[16] Most fundamentally, though, the difficulties are rooted in the general thesis of the natural attitude, the "tenacious and often completely hidden presupposition of the

---

[13] *Ibid.*, pp. 176f.

[14] *F.T.L.*, pp. 247f.

[15] Bachelard correctly stresses that "even in the case where actuality is necessarily taken as starting point, it must be recognized that the necessity of this *starting point* should not affect the development of the process it initiates. The necessity of the starting point is not perforce a necessity in principle." (p. 176)

[16] It is not accident, in these terms, that so many of Husserl's works are designed as "introductions."

world's existence-in-itself," [17] thus eidetic affairs and methods seem to be merely empirical and psychological in character and status. Clearly aware of these difficulties,[18] Husserl often was reluctant, as Bachelard remarks, to bring his readers directly into the regions of the transcendentally eidetic, and often seems to mix up empirical descriptions with eidetic ones.[19] He nevertheless constantly warns his readers both of these dangers of misinterpretation, and of the necessary transposition of meaning inherent to the turn to the eidetic and to the transcendental.[20]

A third aspect of the "freedom" appertaining to "free phantasy" must be brought out. It was mentioned that this variation always has the sense of *Beliebigkeit* (free optionalness). This signifies that though one is constantly free to start with any actual or possible example, and indeed to continue through all possible pertinent variations, *there is no need* to do so. We are free, in other words, to break off at any moment: the optionalness inherent to free variation signifies a "remarkable and extremely important consciousness of 'and so forth according to option.' " [12] Hence, one is not only free to begin anywhere, to move freely from one to another variant, but also the process "implies the consciousness of a fundamental potentiality, a consciousness that one can continue without actually being obliged to do so," [22] as opposed to the process of empirical variation. It is precisely because of this *"fundamental character of the act of viewing ideas"* [23] that the phenomenologist is able to ascertain what he is all along after in his variation:

> ... all the variants belonging to the openly infinite sphere – which includes the ⟨initial⟩ example, as "optional" and freed of all its factualness – stand in a relationship of synthetic interrelatedness and integral connectedness; more particularly, they stand in a continuous and all-inclusive synthesis of "coincidence in conflict." But, precisely with this coinciding, what necessarily persists throughout this free and always-

---

[17] Bachelard, p. 192.
[18] Cf. *C.M.*, p. 76.
[19] Cf. *C.M.*, pp. 69–71.
[20] Bachelard is right (although I shall disagree on one crucial point in this): "Husserl's concessions to the demands of pedagogy in no way alter the principle of the distinction between transcendental phenomenology and intentional psychology." (p. 194; cf. also *C.M.*, §§ 16 and 35, and *F.T.L.*, Ch. 6.)
[21] Husserl, *Erfahrung und Urteil*, red. u. hrsg. von Ludwig Landgrebe (Hamburg: Claassen Verlag, 1954), p. 413. (Hereafter cited as *E.U.*)
[22] Bachelard, p. 178.
[23] *E.U.*, p. 422.

repeatable variation comes to the fore: the *invariant*, the indissolubly identical in all the different and ever-again different, the *essence* common to all, the universal essence by which all "imaginable" variants of the example, and all variants of any such variants, are restricted. This invariant is the ontic essential form (apriori form), the *eidos*, corresponding to the example, in the place of which any variant of the example could have served equally well.[24]

(3) What Husserl expresses here brings out the third vital feature of free variation: namely, whatever may be one's point of departure, and with regard to no matter which problem, the shifting of attention in viewing an affair as an example is equivalent to a *sui generis* transposition of attitude which "brings to the fore" the *eidos* – that is, that by virtue of which a freely chosen example, as any other actual or possible example, is what it is; or, that without which it would not be what it is. The "shift" which inherently brings into play the "free optionalness" (the "and so forth" idealization) belonging "essentially to every variation manifold," [25] is a specific and fundamental modification of the natural attitude, an attentional focusing on the region of the eidetic which governs "a universe of conceivability (a 'pure' allness), in such a manner that the negation of any result is equivalent to an intuitable eidetic impossibility, an inconceivability ..." [26]

(4) In so far as this method alone opens up the region of pure eidetic forms, of the pure conceivability as such, *it is itself something which has its own essential character*. That is, the explication of the method of free variation is in no sense the description of some empirical fact whose validity would therefore only be a matter of probability. To put the matter differently, the method was one found in mathematical idealization generally, geometry in particular (as Bachelard noted). But, our focusing on it as found therein was one which of necessity took it *as an example*. As such, the delineation of its features was not a description of a "matter of fact" but rather of an eidetic affair. Thus, as Husserl emphasizes,

The universal validity of the eidetic method is unconditionally necessary; it is a method that can be followed, no matter what conceivable object is taken as an initial example; and that is the sense in which we

[24] *F.T.L.*, p. 248.
[25] *E.U.*, p. 413.
[26] *F.T.L.*, p. 249.

meant it. Only in eidetic intuition can the essence of eidetic intuition become clarified.[27]

It would thus be as drastic a mistake to think that mathematical idealization is the only genuine "free variation" as it would be to interpret this method as merely an empirical technique practiced by empirical psychologists. This is by no means to deny that there are manifold connections and parallels between free phantasy as practiced phenomenologically and as found in mathematical idealization, and even between the former and empirical variations and inductions. It is to stress only that the specifically phenomenological method is not reduceable to empirical induction, nor is it precisely like the procedures used by geometers and mathematicians. Indeed, it is to say even more: phenomenological elucidation and explication discloses the essential features of both of those other procedures, and *its own as well*.[28] It is in this sense that Husserl conceived phenomenology as the "science which has the unique function of criticizing all the others and itself at the same time ..." [29] Phenomenology, he later wrote, "is nothing more than *scientific self-examination* on the part of transcendental subjectivity ...," [30] that is, is the philosophical discipline of criticism and self-criticism, carrying out "the most extreme *radicalness in striving to uproot all prejudice*." [31]

§ 3. As already noted, Bachelard sees the method of free phantasy as being "parallel" to, and even having its "very source" in, the procedure of mathematical idealization. Although she goes on to deny that she has "claimed to reduce phenomenological thinking to these mathematical 'antecedents,' " [32] and notes Husserl's claim that phenomenological philosophy is "a genus of investigation that in a certain sense gives to them all a new dimension," [33] she nevertheless lays considerable stress on the "parallel." That Husserl was himself an accomplished mathemat-

[27] *Ibid.*, p. 249.
[28] Cf. *F.T.L.*, pp. 245f.
[29] *Ideen*, I, § 62.
[30] *F.T.L.*, p. 273.
[31] *Ibid.*, p. 276.
[32] Bachelard, p. 180.
[33] Husserl, "Philosophy as a Rigorous Science," in Husserl, *Phenomenology and the Crisis of Philosophy*, tr., notes and Intro. Quentin Lauer (New York: Harper & Row, 1965), p. 74, note a; Bachelard, p. 180. (This essay cited hereafter as *P.C.P.*)

ician doubtless gives credence to this interpretation, as does also his heavily formalistic style of philosophizing, and his life-long concern for displaying the foundations of logical and mathematical cognitions.

There is, in other words, a good deal of evidence to support such an interpretation. But this is, I think, a temptation to be rigorously avoided, on pains of failing to appreciate precisely the genuinely universal validity of the method of free phantasy. As Husserl himself emphasizes in many places (among the most noteworthy, the passage cited above from *Formal and Transcendental Logic* [34]), the methods of logic and mathematics are to be understood strictly *as examples*, freely chosen from among many other equally possible ones. To explicate this method *starting from* the attitude of the geometer – as Bachelard notes, indicatively for her own interpretation, *"ex abrupto"* in section 70 of *Ideen*, I [35] – in no sense justifies her claim, from which, of course, she is obliged to retreat only a few pages later. Indeed, if one turns to that crucial section, one finds a number of critically important points for the full understanding of the *eidos* of free phantasy. Although Bachelard notes several of these passages, she curiously fails to mention one which can only be regarded as quite anomalous on her interpretation. It is to those passages that I now want to turn in order to bring out what I think is a highly important dimension of this method, thereby hopefully correcting a number of misunderstandings of the full character of the truly seminal discovery in his conception of free phantasy variation.

§ 4. Pointing out that freedom in eidetic inquiry "necessarily demands operating in phantasy," [36] Husserl also makes it quite plain that such free phantasy variation functions strictly for the critical (and self-critical) *clarification* of eidetic affairs; its operation serves solely to elucidate the essentially possible, impossible and to make manifestly clear what is in principle actualizable. In no event can it serve to establish factual truth or falsity. The evidence disclosed in the experience of free phantasy pertains to

[34] *F.T.L.*, p. 249.
[35] Bachelard, p. 174; *Ideen*, I, p. 131.
[36] *Ideen* I, p. 131.

clarification (and its various modalities), not to validation.[37] As Bachelard expresses the point,

> to be precise, if we treat it [any particular individual] as an example and not as an actual datum considered for its own sake, the individual loses its noxiousness [its factuality] and enables the "exercising" of the phantasy through which perfect clarification is attained.[38]

But what is requisite for such phenomenological clarification? Precisely that one "fertilize one's phantasy by observations in originary intuitions that are as abundant and excellent as possible." [39] Husserl goes on to stress, in a highly suggestive passage, how this is to be understood:

> An extraordinary amount of profit can be drawn from what is presented in history, but to an even richer extent from the expressions of art and especially of poetry. The latter are, to be sure, products of the imagination, but in respect of the originality of their new creations, the abundance of detailed features and the uninterruptedness of the motivations involved, they greatly excel the productions of our own phantasy and beyond that, through the suggestive medium of artistic presentations, become easily transformed into completely clear phantasies when cognitively apprehended.
> Thus, if one prefers paradoxical expressions and already understands the multiple senses of the term, one can actually say, in strict truth, that *"fiction" is the vital element of phenomenology, as it is of every other eidetic science*, that fiction is the source from which the knowledge of "eternal truths" draws its nourishment.[40]

However much, with Bachelard, one can easily see parallels between free phantasy and mathematical idealization, it seems that from this remarkable passage it is clearly misleading to conceive that "parallel" as closely as to make of Husserl's method little more than an analogue, in the manner of Descartes, of mathematical procedures. Indeed, speaking of the new apriori science of pure eidetic description he has sketched in his *Ideen I*, Husserl emphasizes that very point:

> Here we have one difference (though not the only one) between the whole manner of this new *apriori* science and that of the mathematical disciplines. These are "deductive" sciences, and that means that in their scientifically theoretical mode of development mediate deductive knowledge plays an incomparably greater part than the immediate axiomatic

[37] *Ibid.*, p. 132, also §§ 73–75.
[38] Bachelard, p. 177.
[39] *Ideen* I, p. 132.
[40] *Ideen* I, p. 132; Bachelard does not quote the passage pertaining to art and poetry, nor the phrase asserting that fiction is the "source" of all "eternal truths."

knowledge upon which all the deductions are based. An infinitude of deductions rests on a very few axioms.

But in the transcendental sphere we have an infinitude of knowledge previous to all deduction, knowledge whose mediated connexions (those of intentional implication) have nothing to do with deduction, and being entirely intuitive prove refractory to every methodically devised scheme of constructive symbolism.[41]

This new science concerns, not the "factual data of [the] inner sphere of intuition, but ... the essence, inquiring, that is, after the invariant, essentially characteristic structures of a soul, of a psychic life in general." [42] Precisely that inquiry into the essential, the invariant in every actual and possible affair taken as an example of some essential kind or sort,[43] must necessarily proceed by means of free phantasy variations; and that "way" [Weg] to what is essential is a matter of "fiction," of the imagination.

§ 5. It would seem, then, that the method of free variation has, as Husserl insists, a privileged position in the development of the pure eidetic science of philosophical criticism. That method has both a *systematic* and, following from that, a central *pedagogical* function and place. Because of this double character, it is necessary to emphasize that the pedagogical function of phenomenological discipline is by no means an accident – Husserl does not, I submit and hope to show shortly, merely "make concessions" to the demands of pedagogy, as Bachelard argues,[44] but to the contrary the pedagogical task is quite essential to that discipline of criticism. A case can be made, in fact, for the thesis that the misunderstanding of the properly eidetic character of phenomenological statements and claims arises precisely from a misunderstanding of this pedagogical dimension. If that case can be made, then it becomes possible to show that part of the real force of Husserl's method of free phantasy is that it requires a reconceiving of the relationships between the eidetic and the empiric.

To make this entire case requires first bringing together several strands of the previous discussion: the sense of "exemplification"

---

41 Husserl, "Author's Preface to the English Edition" of *Ideen*, I: *Ideas: General Introduction to Pure Phenomenology*, tr. W. R. Boyce Gibson (New York: Collier Books, 1962), p. 6.
42 *Ibid.*, p. 8.
43 *F.T.L.*, p. 246.
44 Bachelard, p. 194.

as it is pertinent to the method of free phantasy, and the interplay between "phantasy" and "freedom." Second, the pedagogical function must be laid out, if only schematically here. Third, the specific kind of reconception of the relationships between the eidetic and the empiric can be suggested. Finally, it should then be possible to see clearly the sense of "fiction" as the prime "way" to and "source" of phenomenology.

§ 6. That every actual or possible particular individual (whether "real" or "ideal") can be considered either "for its own sake" or "as an example" is plain enough. *How* or *why* this is so is just as plainly a crucial issue, but it is one which does not directly concern me here; indeed, only a full genetic and constitutive phenomenological explication could unravel that issue, and such a task considerably exceeds this analysis. What is germane is to determine more precisely the sense of the method which begins with "taking some affair as an example."

Quite in general, this procedure involves a *shift of attention*, an explicit and deliberate refocusing of one's "attitude" toward or preoccupation with some affair, but in a quite specific way. For, although we commonly advert to one or another affair in the course of our experience "for its own sake" (with one or another kind of concern – valuationally, memorially, volitionally, perceptually, and so on), it is just as usually the case that our lifeworldly experiences of objects are, as Schutz has shown in depth,[45] *typified*, such that the objects and events within the world of daily life are already *types* for that stratum of our lives. Furthermore, the course of our experience shows a constant shifting back-and-forth between regarding these affairs "for their own sake" ("this is my dog, 'Irving'") and "as types" ("he is a mixture of this and that breed"). Judging from Schutz's studies, we only rarely achieve an apprehension of an affair "for its own sake"; for the most part, our dealings with the "things" in the lifeworld are usually in terms of typifications of one or another kind and to one or another level of typification (from anonymity to rela-

[45] Alfred Schutz, *Collected Papers*, Vol. I (ed. Maurice Natanson), e.g., essays on pp. 3–47, 48–66, 207–259, and 287–356; see also his *The Phenomenology of the Social World*, tr. George Walsh & Frederick Lehnert, intro. George Walsh (Evanston: Northwestern University Press, 1967), §§ 15, 16, 19, 36–40. (*Collected Papers* cited hereafter as *C.P.*)

tive familiarity, which itself has its own specific forms of typification as well).

Hence, to speak of the "shift of attention" inherent to free phantasy is to say that several crucial "steps" must be accomplished. On the one hand, it requires a *step of making explicit the type as type*, however unclarified the specific content of the "type" itself may be initially. Only if I explicitly advert to the type as type does the specific individual itself "come to the fore" as something "for its own sake"; and only following on that explicit apprehension of the "thing itself" (*as* an "itself," an individuality over against the "type" through which it is commonly experienced) does it become possible to refocus my attention on the specific individual affair *as an example* of the still unclarified type itself.

In slightly different terms, if, as Schutz argues, our everyday knowledge of the lifeworld is a system of constructs of its typicality,[46] whose prime characteristic is its taken for grantedness (or, as he puts it, its implicit use of the *"epoché of the natural attitude"* [47]), then to advert to an affair as "itself" and hence not typified, requires, first, an explicit apprehending of the type itself and then, an explicit focusing on the affair "for its own sake." The explicit grasping of the affair as an example, then, involves necessarily two *"Ich-Akte"* in Husserl's specific sense,[48] an explicit being busied with the affair *as* an exemplification.

In still different terms, the "starting-point" of free variation must be seen as essentially presupposing the effectuation of the phenomenological epoché and reduction, following on which the specifically *eidetic* epoché and reduction can then be effected. The validity of the method of free variation always rests on the apprehension of the intentionality of consciousness and its intended correlates. It is from the apprehension of the noetic-noematic character of any actual or possible experience that the method of free variation begins. Thus, to speak phenomenologically of beginning from affairs taken as examples is always a short-hand: it is intentional experiences with their intended noematic-objective correlates that are to be taken as examples for free phantasy variation. Only because of that "disconnection" and its subse-

---

[46] Schutz, *C.P.*, I, pp. 7–27.
[47] *Ibid.*, p. 229.
[48] *Ideen* I, § 115.

quently established "attitude" (the epoché and reduction) can one properly characterize free phantasy as leading to the originary intuition of essences. Hence, free variation is not simply a procedure of progressively clarifying the typification-constructs intrinsic to lifeworldly experience; that is merely the first step of ego-advertence which, if it goes no further, remains strictly empirical in its force. What is requisite is the apprehension of the affair, not merely as typified or "for its own sake," but as an exemplification of some essential kind – and this signifies nothing less than the apprehension of specific individuals in respect of their *being-intended "as examples" of some eidos.*

§ 7. The sense of "freedom" and "free optionalness" has already been indicated above. Closely following Husserl's works, Bachelard stressed that this *Beliebigkeit* signifies (1) a consciousness that one is able freely to substitute one example for another, or that any actual or possible example can serve as the point of departure, (2) that eidetic phantasy variation is a "freeing from" all factuality, and (3) that the method does *not* oblige one to run through all possible cases in order for the invariant (the *eidos*) to be made to "stand out" as such (due to the essentially appertaining consciousness of the "and so forth according to option" which Husserl stresses), this consciousness of "potency" being intrinsic to the method.

That these characteristics are essential to the method is unquestionable. There is, however, another, somewhat dialectical feature inherent to free phantasy which needs to be brought out. The concretely existing philosopher is at any moment "free," just as is the geometer, to vary his examples in any manner which is pertinent to his specific problem at hand; he can "choose arbitrarily" which examples he shall make use of. This "consciousness of freedom," Bachelard points out, "is discovered specifically in phenomenological varying. The varying is a free varying." [49] But, to be precise, just what does this "consciousness of freedom" and "optionalness" inherently require?

In the first place, it is plain that if I as a phenomenologist am "free" to begin with any arbitrarily chosen example, I am thus free solely to the extent that I can also *refuse* to choose "this" as

[49] Bachelard, p. 176.

opposed to "that" example. Indeed, it is essential to this freedom that I be able to refuse to engage in the analysis in the first place. Husserl in a way recognized this when he insisted that I be free at any moment to *break off* the process of variation – a move which may, of course, itself be subject to a negative critique, to the effect that I did not perchance vary widely enough to warrant some particular conclusion (I am always, Husserl insists, subject to error regarding eidetic affairs).

This negative feature is obvious enough, although its full ramifications would require much further study.[50] But, in the second place, the possibility of refusal – which is essential to the "freedom" in phantasy variations – has its positive aspect as well, and it is here that I find a most important dimension to free phantasy. Very early in his career, Marcel came across this dimension, although in a somewhat cumbersome way. Writing in his *Metaphysical Journal* about what it is to think something as true, as verifiable, he went on to say,

> The fact is that truth is only possible for thought when it liberates itself from the conditions of time and space [i.e., one may say, from factuality] ... Such thought cannot without contradiction posit itself as existing; and that is equivalent to saying that it is free.
> Freedom, which is the condition of all verification, cannot itself be thought save as radically unverifiable, that is, as liberated from the conditions of existence which an object must satisfy if it is to be an object of verification (determined as truth) [i.e., a factuality] ... the pure activity about which we are speaking is only capable of appearing to a reflection that itself bears on the conditions of the possibility of the true ... It is pure reflection, then, that introduces the idea of this activity – which is equivalent to saying that it brings it into being and creates it, because it itself is the very activity in question and is only capable of thinking itself as identical with it. *The act by which I think freedom is the very act by which freedom comes to be* ... Thought creates itself when it thinks itself; it does not discover itself, it constitutes itself.[51] [My emphasis.]

He was to return to this idea time and again in the course of his life, affirming again (later calling this "pure reflection" *pensée pensante* or "second reflection") that such a reflection "*is free from the moment that it is freeing.*" [52] This "*interprétation libéra-*

---

[50] As Marcel has done, e.g., in his *Being and Having*, tr. Katherine Farrer (New York: Harper & Row, 1965), and other works.

[51] Marcel, *Metaphysical Journal*, tr. Bernard Wall (Chicago: Henry Regnery Co., 1952), pp. 3of.; also pp. 41–43, and 113. (Hereafter cited as *M.J.*)

[52] Marcel, *Du Refus à l'invocation* (Paris: Librairie Gallimard, 1940), p. 73. (Hereafter cited as *R.I.*)

trice," as Pietro Prini calls it,[53] later becomes regarded by Marcel as the crux of an "ascending dialectic" [54] by means of which I who first thus free myself gradually apprehend "the purest reaches of myself"; [55] I thus find myself "in the presence of the central mystery of our being. Because freedom is ourselves ..." [56]

In many respects, the philosophical distance from Husserl to Marcel is so vast as to make any effort to bring them together seem far-fetched indeed. Still, there are points of remarkable convergence; as William E. Hocking has stressed, the philosophical works of these men represent "an aspect of the broadened and heightened empiricism which may well be, in its completion, the major achievement in epistemology of the present century." [57] Without pretending here to interpret Marcel, nor even to elaborate on the passage cited above, what I want to suggest is that Marcel there hit upon a vital positive aspect of a phenomenon to which Husserl, too, has pointed in his conception of free phantasy. That dimension is precisely the *creative, indeed self-creative*, character of that special type of reflection whose contexture is the "consciousness of freedom" and of "optionalness" which are essential to free phantasy variation – hence, of the disclosure of essences. There are several components of this which can now be brought to the fore.

§ 8. In the first place, while it is doubtless true that eidetic research necessarily demands the use of variation in free phantasy in order to determine what stands out as invariant (the *eidos*), and that "any variant of the example could have served equally well," [58] there is always the pertinent question concerning *how one can at all begin this process at the outset*. It has been pointed out that its initiation presupposes two specific acts of ego-advertence – toward the type qua type, and toward the individual "for its own sake." But that by no means answers the

[53] Pietro Prini, *Gabriel Marcel et la méthodologie de l'invérifiable* (Paris: Desclée de Brouwer, 1953), p. 79.

[54] Marcel, *Être et Avoir* (Paris: Fernand Aubier, Editions Montaigne, 1935), p. 247. (Hereafter cited as *E.A.*)

[55] *R.I.*, p. 91.

[56] *Ibid.*, p. 78.

[57] William Ernest Hocking, "Marcel and the Ground Issues of Metaphysics," *Philosophy and Phenomenological Research*, XIV (1954), p. 441.

[58] *F.T.L.*, p. 248.

question, for then it can be asked, Why or how does it happen that the ego-advertence itself occurs? That is, what "frees" the self from its rootage in the taken for grantedness of daily life (or: what makes it possible to practice the epoché on the "epoché of the natural attitude" itself)? What releases the self from its "naivity"? What is the *genuine source* of this "freeing"?

After the bulk of his own inquiries had been completed, Marcel wrote, in the "Author's Preface" to the English translation of his early *Metaphysical Journal*, of an "intuition ... [which] is not something that lies at our disposal, something we have, but rather it is a source, in itself inaccessible, from which we set out to think. It is what I have called a blinded intuition; moreover, it is also a 'forefeeling' or premonition ..." [59] The ground for what Husserl calls the "consciousness of freedom," is, i.e., I would now suggest, precisely that "source, in itself inaccessible," or what Marcel earlier called the "pure reflection," the "act by which I think freedom," which is "the very act by which freedom comes to be" and is "free from the moment that it is freeing." This act, as I have suggested elsewhere, is the most fundamental expression of that root phenomenon of human life, reflexivity – the condition *sine qua non* for every cognitive endeavor, of whatever kind,[60] and is, as Marcel says, the "central mystery" of human selfhood.

In the second place, these considerations shed an unexpected light on Husserl's otherwise quite peculiar remarks in section 70 of *Ideen I* – remarks which, he notes with marked sarcasm, "should be particularly suitable for a naturalistic ridiculing of the eidetic mode of cognition." [61] *Strictly*, as he says, " *'fiction' is the vital element of phenomenology, as it is of every eidetic science,* [it] is the source from which the knowledge of 'eternal truths' draws its nourishment." [62] Precisely because of this, he insists in the same section, as we noted, that it is essential for phenomenologists that they "fertilize" their phantasy, and this has its prime source in the presentations of history, but even more in those of art and poetry. These comments, underscored by Husserl him-

[59] *M.J.*, p. x.
[60] Richard M. Zaner, *The Way of Phenomenology: Criticism as a Philosophical Discipline* (New York: Pegasus Press, 1970), especially chapter 4.
[61] *Ideen* I, p. 132, footnote.
[62] *Ibid.*, p. 132.

self, make sense, I have suggested, only if one takes Husserl quite seriously and literally; that act which frees itself by being freeing, by which freedom itself comes to be, and which, Marcel contends, is a "radical opting," is exactly the core of *artistic creativity* and hence of "fiction." That Husserl is not proposing that phenomenological inquiry be equivalent to artistic creation is plain; what he is asserting is that there is not only a profound connexion between these, but moreover that the latter is at once the fundamental, vital element, and the ultimate source, of phenomenology and every other eidetic science. The "fertilization" of one's phantasy, his imaginative powers, speaks directly to what the phenomenologist can, and indeed must, *learn* in order to carry out his proper task – the turn to fiction is thus directly pedagogical in this sense. But there are still further dimensions to this pedagogical function.

In the third place, once having "freed myself" through this creative and self-creative act, *matters are never again the same for me*. Having once truly apprehended the taken for granted typifications of which I make use in my daily life, having caught myself in my own correlative self-typification, having achieved what Berger calls a "precarious vision" of myself,[63] the world, its objects, events, other persons, and I myself, are no longer experienced by me in quite the same way. Having once truly grasped an affair, or a person, in its own uniqueness as such, neither it, he, nor I remain the same. By the same token, the more I *practice* this "freeing" act, the less is it possible for me simply to live as I have been before – a phenomenon which, although well-known, does not seem to me to have been sufficiently appreciated in its phenomenological consequences. Similarly, however, the continual practice of phenomenological free phantasy variation shows the very same thing: in short, there is a *fundamental developmental function* to the artful practice of phenomenologically rigorous science. It is in this sense that it is necessary, I think, to understand Husserl's emphasis on the necessity for "fertilizing one's phantasy" by the careful and attentive study of history and the arts, not so much for their own sake (however otherwise important this is) but for the sake of becom-

---

[63] Peter L. Berger, *The Precarious Vision* (New York: Doubleday & Co., 1961), especially Part I.

ing increasingly able at transforming these into "completely clear phantasies" with a view toward the rigorous, cognitive explication and articulation of eidetic impossibilities and possibilities and, correlatively, conceivabilities and inconceivabilities, which are the prime aim of the discipline of philosophical criticism. So to speak, the careful advertence to "fiction" tends to increase one's imaginative abilities to conceive alternatives, other possibilities – in brief, to "enlighten" one – and the systematic practice of phenomenological free phantasy in turn enhances one's abilities to conceptually grasp with increasing clarity the eidetic structures embodied in "fiction."

Only through the rigorous practice of this art of apprehending, through free phantasy, completely clear phantasies (i.e., essential possibilities and impossibilities) and grasping in them the essential features they embody, can the phenomenologically disclosed region be secured in its rightful sense. What is disclosed thereby is precisely "transcendental subjectivity" or what I have called the full phenomenon of reflexivity – which, as Bachelard rightly emphasizes,

is not a chaos of intentional mental processes. It is not even a chaos of intentional types each one of which has an organization relating to a species of intentional objects. The intentional types are themselves grouped into an organized structure. These types in their totality form an *ordered* system. The task of transcendental phenomenology then consists in carrying out in a systematic fashion the different constitutive investigations corresponding to these intentional types.[64]

Thus, with the progressive development of free phantasy variations, the transcendental field itself becomes progressively displayed in the full "coincidence in conflict" of which Husserl spoke. What this signifies is that the "invariant" or universal essence "comes to the fore" and can be grasped as such. With this elaboration of the ordered system of invariants, finally, an ordered body of knowledge, of acquired and reiterable cognitive possessions, becomes progressively actualized.

§ 9. In as much as my own initial act of achieving a "precarious vision" is already a free act (fundamentally connected to, or even a part of, one's power of imagination [*Einbildungskraft*]), a grasp-

---

[64] Bachelard, p. 192.

ing of my own typifications and my own coordinate social and socialized typifications, and am thereby led to grasp, however minimally the initial glance may be, myself as being freed by that free act, "what is ultimately at issue," Maurice Natanson points out, "is a philosophic upheaval, the self-discovery that makes philosophy at all possible." [65] In a way, one may say, I in effect am a party to my own freedom – and just for that reason am I able at any moment to deny, betray, degrade, or lose my own freedom.

But this philosophic upheaval has a dialectical counterpoint. The apprehension of myself in my typifying constructs is at the same time *the apprehension of the coordinate other person* fundamentally as "like myself," as *alter ego*. That is, the system of typicality constructs taken for granted, as Schutz frequently said, as the unquestioned, but always able to be questioned, matrix of social life, is *necessarily a shared system*. It is not experienced by me as "my private affair"; "the" world is for my lifeworldly experience "our" world, a "common" world of reciprocal and mutual interaction. The grasping of typifications is *eo ipso* not only a precarious vision of myself but of the other as well, in a new way – namely, *as* typified and typifying, and hence as able to "free" himself in the freeing act of reflection by virtue of his own transcendental dimension of reflexivity. I recognize that I have all along been simply operating in terms of taken for granted assumptions regarding others (and the objects and events of the social world in general), and included in this complex set of assumptions is that the other, I have been assuming, has been similarly operating in terms of similar typifications regarding me (and the objects and events in "our" world). I recognize that I have assumed that he has assumed, and that he has been assuming that I have assumed ...

What, in other words, this "upheaval" signifies is that my very grasping-recognition of the other as *alter ego can*, but need not necessarily, have the import of a kind of creative mutuality, a freeing of the other for his own self-recognition and "upheaval." As Marcel expresses it, in recognizing and responding to the other as a person ("Thou"), "I help him in some way *to be free*, I

[65] Maurice Natanson, "Introduction" to Maurice Natanson (ed.), *Philosophy of the Social Sciences: A Reader* (New York: Random House, 1963), p. 6.

collaborate in his freedom . . . on the other hand, it is qua freedom
that he is truly *other*," [66] as I am truly myself only qua freedom.
Prini gives a succinct formulation to this mutual collaboration:
"I find myself and I 'am' in the other, as the other finds himself
and 'is' in me, both of us being the active mediators of our truest
personality." [67]

Precisely the same point can be put in more technical phenomenological terms. In so far as the phenomenological investigator
makes epistemic claims concerning the eidetic affairs he has gained access to by means of his free phantasy and optionalness, these
claims have by essential necessity a double character.[68] On the
one hand, they are claims of knowledge. As such, their inherent
sense is that they themselves are essentially open to critical
inspection, and criticism is an intrinsically co-subjective or dia-
logical process of questioning and responding. The root of this
mutual engagement is the free consent by persons to take up the
invitation to quest and respond in pursuit of that which would
end the pursuit – i.e., the truth which frees *from* ignorance
and *for* wisdom. It is the character of epistemic claims in general
that they leave themselves open to critical examination at a
variety of levels, that they are in this sense invitations to critical
dialogue. One need not take up the invitation; but if he does,
he necessarily engages himself in the questing and the responsibility inherent to that – responsiveness to continuous searching,
and responsibility (answerability) for his questions and re-
sponses.[69] In such terms, criticism (phenomenological philosophizing) is an *essentially free and freeing act*, one in which the
philosopher collaborates in his own and in the other's freedom,
and vice versa, as Marcel's analysis of "appeal" (questing) and
"response" ("answering"), grounded in what he calls "*disponibilité*," shows with great insight.[70]

On the other hand, as Dorion Cairns has concisely expressed it,

[66] Marcel, *E.A.*, p. 154.
[67] Prini, *op. cit.*, pp. 109f.
[68] Cf. Zaner, *The Way of Phenomenology*, Prologue, for a fuller treatment.
[69] I have pursued this further in my article, "The Phenomenology of Epistemic
Claims: And Its Bearing on the Essence of Philosophy," in Maurice Natanson (ed.),
Phenomenology nd Social Reality: Essays in Memory Alfred Schutz (The Hague: Martinus Nijhoff, 1970).
[70] Cf. Marcel, *Homo Viator*, tr. Emma Crawford (Chicago: Henry Regnery Co.,
1951), pp. 21–23; and *R.I.*, Chapter 2.

every phenomenological judgment is at one and the same time
an epistemic claim and a communicative guide, an assertion about
some state of affairs and a guide to others:

> The matters judged about must themselves be present from the start,
> and throughout the entire theorizing process they must never be out of
> sight. They must be observed and explicated in their self-given intrinsic
> sense and judgments must be produced that derive their entire content
> immediately and continuously from them.
> In their communicative function, phenomenological statements *are
> intended to help the person addressed to bring to selfgivenness for himself,* to
> grasp, explicate, and compare the very matters in question, to attach to
> the words a signification deriving solely from his own observations, and
> to see the statements as evidently confirmed (or cancelled) by the matters
> themselves ... Strictly phenomenological statements are to be used as
> guides for observation, much as one might use a previous observer's
> descriptions of a landscape as an aid in distinguishing its features while
> all the time it lies before one's eyes.[71] (My emphasis.)

In a way precisely analogous to that of the explorer (whethe-
Columbus, astronauts, or scientific discoverers), whose stater
ments about "what lies at hand" are simultaneously epistemic
claims (having one or another doxic modality) and communicative guides (*meta-hodas*) to the "landscape," so do the phenomenologist's critical claims have that dual status. *"Method" is
strictly correlative to "knowing."* Indeed, as could be shown,[72] an
immanent component of every specifically epistemic claim (or the
epistemic dimension of any other claim – valuative, volitional,
etc.) is the *co-subjective accessibility* of the affairs about which
the claim is made. Every such claim includes the supposition that
others, if they are properly "guided" and if they exercize caution
and follow the requisite steps, will be able to "see for themselves"
the affairs judged about and to "see" whether they are *as* alleged.
Since, as Descartes, Husserl and others have insisted, I am not
always "wide-awake," alert, and am indeed "infirm" in some
respects – as are others – *all* phenomenological claims are necessarily *subject to deception,* to revision, to modification, and even
to denial.[73] Hence, even eidetic claims have the epistemic status
of *tentativeness,* requiring unending critical inspection by oneself

[71] Dorion Cairns, "An Approach to Phenomenology," in Marvin Farber (ed.),
Philosophical Essays in Memory of Edmund Husserl (Cambridge, Mass.: Harvard
University Press, 1940), p. 7. Cf. below, p. 227.
[72] Cf. above, footnote 69.
[73] *F.T.L.,* pp. 155f.

and others.[74] The phenomenologist is always, in Merleau-Ponty's phrase, a "perpetual beginner" in that sense.

§ 10. But at the same time, just because of the interlacing of these mutually free because freeing acts inherent to free phantasy, because every phenomenological statement is necessarily dual (epistemic and communicative/methodological), there is an *essential pedagogical as well as self-augmentative* feature to the method of free phantasy. To the extent that free phantasy variation requires the artful ability to imagine variational alternatives and modifications, the more and better one is able to imagine, the more adept he becomes at practicing this difficult procedure. Hence, Husserl's insistence that one must "fertilize" his phantasy, especially through the study of artistic productions, and that fiction is the "vital element" in all eidetic sciences, acquires a still deeper dimension than already mentioned. It is by no means a mere "concession" to pedagogy, any more than teaching is a mere concession to learning. Nor is it at all peculiar that such a seminal philosopher should have had such persistent concern to view so many of his major works as "introductions" to phenomenology – each of them from a different perspective. They are, clearly, philosophical "cartographies" – explorer's "maps," at once epistemic probings and soundings, and methodological and communicative guides for others. Although hardly without his own profound and lively "children," Husserl is very much of a socratic "mid-wife" – indeed, perhaps just because he himself gave birth to so much, his mid-wifery shows important differences from that of Socrates, but that circumstance does not at all belie the "educative" function of his labors. What the phenomenologist in effect does is to make explicit just what we in our daily lives, in art, in science, and in every human engagement, do all along, but without usually being expressly cognizant of it. As Cairns remarks,

... as deliberately practiced and critically justified, [the active grasping of generic natures or essences] presupposes reflective inquiry. But as a naive "method" it has always been practiced by everyone. To paraphrase Locke's aphorism: God has not been so sparing to men to make them barely able to grasp individuals and left it to Husserl to make them able

---

[74] Cf. Cairns, p. 13; cf. below, p. 233.

to grasp essences. It should be emphasized that, according to the phenomenologist, reflection and the observing of essences are not his prerogatives but the *de facto* practices even of the narrowest empiricist. "The
truth is that everyone sees 'ideas,' 'essences,' and sees them, so to speak,
continuously; they operate with them in their thinking and they also
make judgments about them. It is only that, from their theoretical 'standpoint,' people interpret them away." [75]

The phenomenologist, as establishing and working expressly
within an autonomous discipline of philosophy – criticism and
self-criticism carried out radically – brings this "operative use"
to the fore, and by so doing *makes it possible* for others to do so
likewise (i.e., his free-because-freeing act is one which "collaborates" in the similarly freeing act of others). As such, the
pedagogical-educative function of phenomenology is one of its
essential components. "Teaching" and "learning" (asking-saying-
listening-responding – i.e., dialogue) are eidetic components of
the discipline of critical philosophy.

§ 11. Bachelard points out, correctly, that there is an always
present danger in interpreting Husserl psychologistically. There
are, she contends, two main reasons for this "falsification":

> In the first place, it is difficult to eliminate, in a radical and definitive
> manner, the tenacious and often completely hidden presupposition of the
> world's existence-in-itself [i.e., the general thesis of the natural attitude] . . .
> On the other hand, even when we are conscious of the transcendental
> character of the Husserlian analyses, we are from time to time bound to
> recognize in these analyses empirical descriptions which insidiously lead
> us to their psychological interpretation. Actually, taking into considera-
> tion the difficulty of this type of analysis, Husserl often hesitates to bring
> us immediately to the level of properly eidetic analyses. Hence he conducts
> his investigation, even in the heart of the transcendental sphere, in an
> empirical manner, and only by a second step does he transpose his anal-
> yses into eidetic analyses. [76]

On the first point Bachelard makes there can be little to quarrel
with: our rootage in the natural attitude is, in Santayana's succinct phrase, an "animal faith." That we are nevertheless able
to bring this entire attitude itself to explicit, attentive focus is
well-attested to already, but the difficulty of maintaining this
focus is never to be underestimated. As has already been sug-

---

[75] *Ibid.*, p. 13; cf. below, p. 233. The quotation is from *Ideen* I, § 22.
[76] Bachelard, pp. 192f.; she notes *C.M.* as a case in point.

gested, a prime way of securing this sphere is the careful fertilization and practicing of one's phantasy.

But as regards Bachelard's second point, I am convinced that there is considerable room for dissent. In the first place, if it were really the case that Husserl or other phenomenologists (Merleau-Ponty would certainly be a relevant case in point) engage in "empirical descriptions" *qua empirical*, then it would be obviously true to hold that, minimally, Husserl and others mix levels of analysis unpardonably, openly inviting a psychologistic reading of their analyses. That there is, as Bachelard says, a great risk in such a reading (indeed, it would be a false reading) is doubtless true, of course; but the *risk* should never be confused with the *supposed* actual practice of empirical variations and statements. Husserl is much too clear and consistent on just this point,[77] as we have seen, and even Bachelard emphasizes. It is not at all the case, I submit, that Husserl engages in empirical descriptions *qua empirical* in the usual sense attached to that term by him and by other philosophers. This brings me to a second point.

The point is a very simple and straightforward one: what may appear to be "empirical" descriptions and statements are, properly understood, *pedagogical or communicative guides*. The "risk" lies, not in Husserl's supposed "concessions" to pedagogy, as Bachelard holds, nor in his sometimes alleged falling into empirical descriptions, but rather with the phenomenologist's readers and auditors. What must never be lost from view is not only the dual character of phenomenological statements but as well the fact that "since every *fact can be thought of merely as exemplifying a pure possibility*," [78] the phenomenologist's statements (descriptive explications of the eidetically true), while they may and often do *begin* with "actualities" ("facts," empirical affairs), they by no means can be taken as having their bearing on, or as being justifiable by, these actualities. To think so is to miss precisely the very sense of free phantasy variations. The beginning with any actual (or possible) example, in order to carry out the task of phenomenological explication of essences, to determine the eidetically invariant, in other words, is to a considerable extent

---

[77] Cf. *C.M.*, pp. 32, 131, 142–144, and passages from *F.T.L.* already cited.
[78] *C.M.*, p. 71.

pedagogical in significance, not at all meant as having empirical
status or import.

An alternative way of expressing the point at issue is found in
Marcel's seminal work, *Le Mystère de l'être*. Speaking of his own
procedure, Marcel points out how his method was always one of
attending to examples in the rich soil of human life. In this way,
he writes, his method consists "in proceeding from life toward
thought and subsequently redescending from thought toward life
in order to attempt to illumine the latter." [79] At one level, the
method of free phantasy variation, although more formalized and
rigorously employed by Husserl, consists in deliberately focusing
on, descriptively explicating and comparing actual and possible
examples *dans le milieu de choses*. To interpret such a procedure
as a kind of inductive *empeiria*, however, makes about as much
sense as taking the fictionally developed characters in a novel as
empirical and statements about such characters as epistemic
claims about actually existing human beings. And precisely here
is the point toward which I have been pushing throughout: the
phenomenologist's claims emerging from free phantasy variation
are in no sense empirical inductions or generalizations; free phantasy ("fiction") is their source, not empirical observations as
usually understood.

§ 12. Nevertheless, the method Marcel indicates does have another level to it, one which is not usually noticed and which can
help articulate my final point about free phantasy: namely, not
only does the latter yield, when systematically practiced, insight
into eidetic affairs, it also *invariably functions to illuminate, or
"bring to the fore" the structures of actuality [Wirklichkeit]*. It is
just at this point that we find, not only an important dimension
of its pedagogical function, but also the necessity for reconceiving
the relationships between the eidetic and the empiric. Husserl, it
is true, strongly asserted the radical difference between these, as
in the following characteristic passage:

> the positing of the essence ... does not imply any positing of individual
> existence whatsoever; pure essential truths do not make the slightest assertion
> concerning facts; hence from them *alone* we are not able to infer even the
> pettiest truth concerning the fact-world.[80]

[79] Marcel, *Le Mystère de l'être*, Vol. I (Paris: Aubier, 1951), p. 49.
[80] *Ideen* I, § 4.

Indeed, as was already noted, his comment concerning the ridicule which naturalists could and would doubtless make regarding his belief that fiction is the vital element in phenomenology merely underscores his emphatic stress on the radical difference between the two regions. Still, several matters strike me as forcing the reconception of the "difference" itself.

In the first place, Husserl's systematic attack on absolutism in philosophy, especially on the questions of truth and evidence,[81] clearly shows that a central part of his criticism is to call into question the very meaning of the *"apriori,"* and therefore also the eidetic. It must be recognized, he insists, that *every such claim is essentially subject to deception*, modification, revision and even denial – in short, continual criticism. It thus becomes necessary to distinguish between the *epistemic modality* of claims (certainty, probability, doubtfulness, etc.) and the necessity inherent to every claim that it remain *open to continual criticism*. Hence, simply because one contends that some statement is apriori by no means signifies that it is exempt from critical revision, rejection, etc.[82] A prime distinction, then, is between "dogmatic" (or "naive") and "critical" in Husserl's sense – and this distinction *cuts across* that between "apriori" and "aposteriori." It is, it could be suggested, in view of his conception of criticism and dogmatism (as brought out in *Ideen*, I, and radicalized in *Formal and Transcendental Logic* especially) that Husserl then conceives the region of the apriori as essentially an *ideal*, and strictly rejects "the usual, fundamentally wrong, interpretation of evidence ... as an *absolute apodicticity*, an absolute security against deceptions – an apodicticity quite incomprehensibly ascribed to a single mental process torn from the concrete, essentially unitary, context of subjective mental living." [83] "What if," he goes on to suggest,

each and *every* truth about reality, whether it be the everyday truth of practical life or the truth of even the most highly developed sciences conceivable, remains involved in relativities by virtue of its essence, and referable to *"regulative ideas"* as its norms? What if, even when we get

[81] *F.T.L.*, §§ 79–80, 105–107.
[82] Cf. Richard M. Zaner, "Reflections on Evidence and Truth in the Theory of Consciousness," in Lester Embree (ed.) *Lifeworld and Consciousness: Essays in Honor of Aron Gurwitsch* (Evanston: Northwestern University Press, 1971), where I have treated these issues at greater length.
[83] *F.T.L.*, pp. 156f.

down to the primitive phenomenological bases, problems of relative and absolute truth are still with us, and, as problems of the highest dignity, *problems of ideas* and the *evidence of ideas?* It is high time that people got over being dazzled, particularly in philosophy and logic, by the ideal and regulative ideas and methods of the "exact" sciences – as though the In-itself of such sciences were actually an absolute norm for objective being and for truth ... But to rush ahead and philosophize from on high about such matters is fundamentally wrong; it creates a wrong skeptical relativism and a no less wrong logical absolutism, mutual bugbears that knock each other down and come to life again in a Punch and Judy show.

To judge in a naive evidence is to judge on the basis of a giving of something itself, while continually asking what can be actually "seen" and given faithful expression – accordingly it is to judge by the same method that a cautiously shrewd person follows in practical life wherever it is seriously important for him to "find out how matters actually are." That is the beginning of all wisdom, though not its end; and it is a wisdom we can never do without, no matter how deep we go with our theorizing – a wisdom that we must therefore practice in the same fashion when at last we are judging in the absolute phenomenological sphere. For ... it is essentially necessary that naive experiencing and naive judging come first ... Though further reflective inquiry always follows ... still this pure intuiting and a faithfulness to its pure contents are involved again and again, are continual fundamental characteristics of the method ... When we follow this procedure, we have continuously anew the *living truth from the living source, which is our absolute life,* and from the self-examination turned toward that life, *in the constant spirit of self-responsibility.* We have the truth, then, not as falsely absolutized, but rather, in each case, as within its *horizons* ... that is to say, in a living intentionality (called "evidence of it") ...[84]

Without trying to unpack the full and central significance of this important passage (which I have attempted elsewhere [85]), what stands out is not only that Husserl can never be accused of either naivity (i.e., engaging in merely empirical statements) or of absolutism (appealing to some *ab extra* source or criteria to secure eidetic claims – whether Descartes' divine veracity or the "self-evident" criteria of logic, or any other), but also that the very sense of "apriori" has undergone a fundamental reconception. "Truth" is always within "horizons," no matter how fundamental the analyses become; that is to say, as I have expressed it, "tentativeness" or "open availability" (Marcel's *disponibilité*) turns out to be *a formally necessary characteristic* of every epistemic claim, most especially eidetic ones. Just as one may claim apriori that some statements are never more than empirical and probable, so one may claim tentatively that other statements are

[84] *Ibid.*, pp. 277f.
[85] See above, footnote 82.

apriori and eidetic – where "tentativeness" in no way is synonymous with "probable" or "empirical." But "tentativeness" is also, I have suggested, fundamentally connected to the essentially pedagogical function of critical philosophy. This brings me to a second point in this connection.

Precisely because of the "illuminative" character of eidetic statements as regards actualities, because the "wisdom" of the "shrewd person" anxious to "find out how matters really are" is a wisdom which carries over into all theorizing whatsoever, because every truth is intimately connected to "living intentionalities" within our very "life" and carry with them the necessity for absolute "self-responsibility" – it becomes necessary to reconceive, not simply the apriori, but the aposteriori (claims about actualities) as well and therefore their relationships. In the first place, to the precise extent that that "practical wisdom" mentioned carries over into every theorizing, every theorizing, when executed with the same caution and precision, reflects back upon that very "practical life." This "return" I have called, following Marcel, "illumination" or the "pedagogical function" of phenomenological thinking. It has seemed to me that Husserl's conception of free phantasy and the centrality of fiction points in just that direction. There seems to me a remarkable analogue between the kind of procedures used by the artist (and especially the poet and the novelist) and those used by the critical philosopher in Husserl's sense. The explicative elucidation of essences has as its counterpart the illumination of actuality – just as a particularly fertile and imaginative creative artist can, through fiction, reveal certain subtle and eidetic features of human experience and at the same time illumine (fictionally) the actual life and lifeworld of the sensitive reader.[86]

How much more there is to this mere hint remains to be seen; it does seem to me highly suggestive, however, for the phenomenologist. If nothing else, the emphasis on phantasy and fiction, so long as they are systematically converted into clear phantasies and thence into fertile concepts embodying eidetic truths (always tentatively held "until further notice"), helps to correct several

[86] I have made an initial, exploratory effort in this direction: see Richard M. Zaner, "Awakening: Toward a Phenomenology of the Self," in F. J. Smith (ed.), *Phenomenology in Perspective* (The Hague: Martinus Nijhoff, 1970), pp. 171-186.

deeply erroneous misreadings of phenomenology, and Husserl's work in particular. He is neither a mere empirical psychologist, nor a mere mathematician, anxious to construct consciousness in conformity with either empirical data or mathematical idealizations. That much is evident; the rest is up to further phenomenological labor.

APPENDIX

DORION CAIRNS

AN APPROACH TO HUSSERLIAN PHENOMENOLOGY [1]

The peculiar character of Husserlian phenomenology lies not in its content but in the way the latter is attained. Whatever its sense, an account is phenomenological in the Husserlian sense if, and only if, it is produced "phenomenologically." Mere acquaintance with the doctrines of Husserlian phenomenologists is therefore not acquaintance with Husserlian phenomenology as such. To be acquainted with an account as phenomenological in the Husserlian sense, one must also know Husserlian phenomenological method.

The theory of this method is itself phenomenological in the Husserlian sense – and this indicates that Husserlian phenomenological method, in some form, is prior to Husserlian phenomenological methodology as well as to the rest of Husserlian phenomenological theory. Nevertheless, methodological knowledge is an instrument for improving method deliberately; and improved method leads to improved theory in general and improved methodology in particular. In view of these facts, there is a reason for making Husserlian phenomenological method the central theme of an essay addressed partly to non-phenomenologists, and there is also a reason for not beginning such an essay with an exposition of Husserlian phenomenological methodology

---

[1] Published under the title, "An Approach to Phenomenology," in *Philosophical Essays in Memory of Edmund Husserl*, edited by Marvin Farber (Cambridge, Mass.: Harvard University Press, 1940). What I publish here is not a reprint. I have corrected a few orthographical, punctuational, or stylistic errors, I have deleted the translation of two sentences in Husserl's *Ideen* ..., I. Bd., § 22 – two sentences to which Husserl himself objected, and one sentence of mine; I have appended this footnote and one other new one; I have, above all, altered the terminology again and again, to make it more nearly in accordance with my present (and, I believe, greatly improved) usage. But I have changed neither the essay's structure nor its sense; though today (thirty years later) a few opinions expressed in the essay are opinions to which I no longer adhere unqualifiedly.

in its more developed form. The latter can be understood only after the method in its rudimentary form, and certain results of rudimentary method, have been grasped.

To be sure, an adequate understanding of any purposely employed method includes an understanding of what the one using the method sets up as the thing to be actualized by its means. The goal of Husserlian phenomenological activity is always knowledge, but the initial conception of knowledge – like the initial method and the theory of method – undergoes a change, because of cognitional results actually attained. There is, therefore, an analogous reason for not attempting to state the specifically Husserlian phenomenological ideal of knowledge at the beginning of the present essay.

I

The fundamental methodological principle of Husserlian phenomenology may, I think, be initially formulated as follows: *No opinion is to be accepted as philosophical knowledge unless it is seen to be adequately established by observation of what is seen as itself given "in person." Any belief seen to be incompatible with what is seen to be itself given is to be rejected. Toward opinions that fall in neither class – whether they be one's own or another's – one is to adopt an "official" philosophical attitude of neutrality.*

When this principle is first presented, or adopted either implicitly in practice or explicitly as a maxim, its sense derives not only from an already acquired familiarity with the difference between awareness of something as itself given and awareness of something as not itself given, but also from accepted traditional theories. Perhaps the most striking instance of this difference, and surely the instance most emphasized by current traditions, is the difference between sensuously perceiving a thing and being aware of a thing – otherwise, e.g., in remembering or expecting it, or in sensuously perceiving or imagining something *else* as depicting or as symbolizing it. Obviously, the sense of the principle also derives at first from a like familiarity with the difference between an opinion that merely formulates what one grasps as itself given and an opinion that goes beyond, or conflicts with, what one grasps as actually given "in person." And here too the accepted tradition plays its role.

But vague familiarity and traditional concepts do not provide the principle with such clarity and definiteness as are necessary if it is to be applied to all opinions with certainty and precision. It might be expected that this defect should be remedied by contriving a set of defining postulates or rules of procedure. The principle itself demands, however, that traditional and habitual opinions about self-givenness and the other matters referred to in it be tested and, if necessary, corrected by *original observation*.

II

Something like the Husserlian phenomenologist's fundamental maxim, as initially stated, would probably be acknowledged by empiricists, at least qua empiricists. But empiricism imposes a restriction. The empiricist, as such, accepts a belief as philosophical knowledge only when it is somehow known to be adequately established by observation of *individual* affairs. Indeed, some empiricists give the maxim an even more restrictive interpretation, in accordance with which they refuse to accept "the perception of the operations of our own minds within us" as a form of observation by which genuine knowledge may be established. To them, only opinions known to be adequately established on the basis of "sensation" of sensuous perceiving are officially acceptable, "scientific" knowledge.

The Husserlian phenomenologist asserts that any empiristic restriction of his fundamental principle leads one to ignore or "officially" reject matters of which one is in fact aware as themselves given "in person," matters that are "data" in the very sense that spatio-temporally individuated matters (including those sensuously perceived) are data. He contends, furthermore, that this assertion of his can be verified according to the above-stated methodological principle, and that therefore any statement to the effect that only individual things are observable (as themselves given) is a statement observably *incompatible* with what is itself given – a stated opinion that must be rejected in accordance with his fundamental principle. Such opinions, far from being based on original observation, not only go beyond but actually conflict with observable data.

Sensuous perceivedness, to consider it first, is indeed contrasted, as a form of "original self-givenness," with, e.g., the "meant-ness" of a physical thing as represented by a (perceived, remem-bered, or imagined) picture or symbol, or even as directly meant in a clear recollecting of a physical thing itself as past-perceived. More than that, it is (in a quite precise sense) the "basis" for all other types of givenness. Still it is, in itself, only that manner of original self-givenness *peculiar* to individual objects of a certain kind, e.g., to individual physical things, their individual shapes, individual colors, etc., and to their individual durations and changes in worldly space-time. One can be, and often is, aware of things of *other* kinds as themselves given – in other manners, to be sure, but "given" in precisely the same sense.

The Husserlian phenomenologist finds not only that non-sen-sible things and their determinations may be themselves given and grasped but also that the self-givenness of a self-given thing may be itself given and seized upon – moreover, that the generic similarity of the specific sorts of self-givenness peculiar respec-tively to sensuous data and data of other kinds is likewise some-thing that may be itself given and observed. Thus, when he speaks of them all as "data," as "given," or even as "seen" or "perceived," he is – at least in his own opinion – indulging in no mere metaphors.

In short, the fundamental maxim of Husserlian phenomeno-logy requires that empiristic restrictions be rejected because they conflict with or lead one to ignore strictly self-given, observable, and – as we shall see – intersubjectively verifiable "matters them-selves." It is not perchance in the name of an alleged but un-observable Absolute nor even in the name of alleged necessary conditions for the possibility of experience or knowledge, condi-tions that allegedly cannot themselves be experienced "data," that the Husserlian phenomenologist rejects empiricism. Rather is it solely in the name of matters whose self-givenness the empiricist overlooks or resolves officially to ignore.

Although Husserlian phenomenology differs thus from empir-icism, it differs more profoundly from any philosophy that first sets up formal definitions and postulates, or material hypotheses, and proceeds by a method of formal deduction – supplemented perhaps by material interpretation and "verification" – more or less according to the example of an incompletely understood mathematics or mathematico-empirical physics. To take conceptual stuff already on hand and fashion a cloak of theory for things *in absentia*, then call them in for a partial fitting – that is at best only a way to botch together another ingenious misfit to hang away with how many others in the lumber-room of history. The matters judged about must themselves be present from the start, and throughout the entire theorizing process they must never be out of sight. They must be observed and explicated in their self-given intrinsic sense; and judgments must be produced that derive their entire content immediately and continuously from them.

In their communicative function, Husserlian phenomenological statements are intended to help the person addressed to bring to self-givenness for himself, to seize upon, explicate, and compare the very matters in question, to attach to the words a signification deriving solely from his own observations, and to see the statements as evidently confirmed (or cancelled) by the matters themselves. Whatever verbal definitions or deductive arguments may be contained in a Husserlian phenomenological discourse are quite ancillary to this purpose – or out of place. Statements that are strictly phenomenological in the Husserlian sense are to be used as guides for observation, much as one might use a previous observer's description of a landscape as an aid in distinguishing its features while all the time it lies before one's eyes. In other words, their purpose is to assist the reader to knowledge that fulfills the Husserlian phenomenologist's own criterion. Assistance is useful not only because some observations are intrinsically difficult but also because prejudices are likely to induce one to overlook or explain away what is actually there to be seen. The Husserlian phenomenologist's appeal to "immediate" inspection is not made on the assumption that a Husserlian phenomenological proposition need only be understood for its truth to become evident forthwith. The truth of an opinion is seen "immediately" only when its coincidence with a given fact, as judged on the basis of the very matters entering into it, is seen. And often it is a long and hard road to a position from which one *can* see the truth of an opinion – "immediately."

III

Not all empiricists would restrict the sphere of philosophically acceptable self-givenness to what is given sensuously. Locke spoke, as a matter of course, about perceiving such "actions of our own minds" as "perception, thinking, doubting, believing, reasoning, knowing, [and] willing." He did not consider it incumbent on him to vindicate the existence of "reflection," "that notice which the mind takes of its own operations and the manner of them." In recent years, however, it has become important to defend the view that such mental processes as Locke enumerated are indeed perceptually self-given and that processes of reflecting, in which these "actions" are perceived, are themselves given reflectively.

Locke apparently thought of reflection only as a perceptual process, in our terminology a process in which one is aware of something as itself given "in person." But not every awareness of something as one's own mental process is an awareness of it as thus perceptually given. For example, one may not only perceive but also remember, expect, or phantasy something as one's own mental process. The Husserlian phenomenologist, imitating Husserl's terminology, applies the name "reflection" to any awareness of something as one's own mental process or as a determination thereof. He accordingly speaks not only of reflective perceiving but of reflective expecting, judging, etc., just as he speaks of non-reflective or "straightforward" perceiving, expecting, etc. Reflective and straightforward perceivings are both called "perceivings" because the original self-givenness of a mental process seized upon reflectively is, as such, observably like the original self-givenness of a thing seized upon straightforwardly, though their specific manners of original self-givenness are observably different.

But those who imitate Husserl's usage do not restrict the name "reflection" to awareness of one's mental processes and their really immanent determinations. The name, as they employ it, also covers awareness of something *as* an object of one's mental life. Usually one is busied with things not *as* objects of one's mental life but only as things. If a thing is itself given, one is usually busied with it not *as* something given but as having certain thing-determinations. As I look about, I see physical things, their shapes, colors, etc., and usually occupy myself – cognitively, aesthetically, practically – with physical things only as having physical thing-determinations, not as things believed in, seen, liked, etc. Sometimes, however, one does pay attention to things *as* believed, *as* things given, *as* liked – in brief, *as* intended to in one's awareness of them. And this paying of attention to the usually ignored status of things *as* intended to is contrasted terminologically as "reflection" with one's usual "straightforward" paying attention only to things.

The deliberate application of the fundamental principle of Husserlian phenomenological method requires paying attention not to things simpliciter *but to things as intended to* and, more particularly, to their self-givenness or non-self-givenness. That is to say, it requires reflective rather than straightforward observation. To be sure, one can and frequently does establish one's beliefs by straightforward observation of what is itself given, without making its givenness one's theme. But straightforward observation, even when it does not in fact go beyond what is itself given, is not "phenomenological" in a Husserlian sense of the word. The exclusively reflective character of all Husserlian phenomenological inquiry deserves emphasis, if only because, according to a perhaps more common usage, pure straightforward descriptions (without construction or explanation) are also called "phenomenological." There is an important difference, however, between simply describing a thing and describing the sense that a thing is intended to as having – between ascribing to an (in fact presented) thing certain (in fact presented) thing-determinations and saying that a thing is presented as having certain determinations that are also presented. Husserl sometimes expressed the difference by saying, in effect, that straightforward description is description of things *per se* whereas his phenomenological description is description of *intentional objects*. Once the difference itself has been grasped, this convenient manner of speaking should not be misleading. It is apt to mislead, however, if one fails to see that the terms "thing *per se*" (or "thing *simpliciter*") and "intentional object" are names for one and the same thing, only paid attention to in different manners. In the straightforward attitude one ignores the thing's being intended to, being believed in (or believed), etc., being paid attention to, etc., and lives in one's intending to, one's believing in (or believing) the thing *per se;* in the reflective attitude one pays attention to *the same thing's* being intended to.

No matter how one may be busied straightforwardly – believing, doubting, denying; liking or fearing; perceiving, phantasying, willing – no matter what the object of one's concern is meant as being – a stone, an atom, an adjective, an angel, space or time, or even the world itself as a concrete whole – always one can adopt a reflective attitude and concern oneself with the thing *as* what one is, or was, busied with straightforwardly, *as* what remains intended to in this manner or that, as having such and such thing-determinations. When one does so, one is attending the "intentional object," the same thing qua object of one's mental process.

From this it should be clear that the dual terminology does not indicate an epistemological dualism. Intentional objects are not things somehow "in one's mind," nor are they intermediaries between mental processes and the things themselves. They are the things one's mental processes intend to, the things with which one perhaps deals cognitively, emotionally, volitionally; they include all the things that one correctly means as existing in the real, intersubjectively accessible world. Things *per se*, things pure and simple, are, on the other hand, not alleged things transcendent of the realm of intentional objects, but these same intentional objects as they are meant straightforwardly, without regarding their being intended to.

Our usual attitudes and mental activities are not reflective, but that does not mean that reflection is practised only by Husserlian phenomenologists. Reflection, and even reflective perceiving, are the occasional practices of everyone, including those whose historically understandable prejudices make them oblivious to reflection and its data as soon as they adopt a theoretical attitude. And from this it follows that reflection, though essential to Husserlian phenomenologizing, is not its sufficient differentia.

IV

We have seen that the fundamental principle of Husserlian phenomenological method requires that one's mental processes, as themselves given in reflective perceivings, be acknowledged as genuine data. We have seen also that, to apply that principle, one must regard all things reflectively as intentional objects, i.e., consider them in their status as somehow intended to in one's mental processes. Any thing of which he is aware serves the Husserlian phenomenologist as a clue to the mental processes in which it is intended to. Following this clue, he attempts to bring to clear self-givenness the really immanent determinations of the process and correlatively the manner of givenness – perhaps self-givenness – of the thing *as* intended to in that process. In this attempt he is applying his fundamental principle – and doing so in the only manner that can bring to original self-givenness the matters of which the principle speaks, and thus lead to its original clarification.

So far, we have centered our attention on individual matters: primarily on things intended to as individuals and on individual processes intending to them. But it is to be observed that some things are straightforwardly meant as not being individuals. Indeed, they are not only meant but sometimes themselves given and grasped as such. An individual thing is intended to not merely in its individuality, as having individual parts and standing in individual relationships to other individual things. It is also intended to and may be explicitly seized upon *as* an individual (an instance of that *category*), as an instance of a *specific sort* of individuals, as having parts of *specific sorts*, etc. Furthermore, these "categories" and "specific sorts" may be not only thus co-intended to but also directly paid attention to for their own sakes and grasped in their original self-givenness on the basis of a clear perceiving or phantasying of at least possible instances. Thus, e.g., a thing may be intended to and clearly given as a possible, and perhaps an actual, instance of *color in general*, as having a quality that is an individual instance of *brightness in general*, and as standing in an individual relationship, that is an instance of *similarity in general*, to other individual instances of color And. color, brightness, similarity – these general kinds – may themselves be presented and seized upon. Indeed, it is only on the basis of the original givenness and seizedness of the kind as well as the individual that one can judge "with original insight": this is an instance of color; this has a brightness; this is similar to that in brightness; this instance of color belongs to this instance of surface; etc. And only when one has thus judged with original insight can one seize upon, as originally self-given, the state of affairs itself: that this is a color, that it is bright, etc. Moreover, general kinds themselves can be judged *about* just as individuals can – they can be identified, distinguished, named, and, in short, "treated" in all the manners necessary to justify one in calling them "things," despite their non-individuality.

Straightforward seizing upon, observing, and judging about generic and specific things that are themselves given are not, however, Husserlian phenomenological activities. The Husserlian phenomenologist as such observes and describes color in general *as* intended to, *as* seized upon, in its manner of being given, etc., not color in general *simpliciter*. And, correlatively, he describes the mental processes in which color in general is variously intended to, seized upon, judged about, etc. He observes that the generic and specific pure "essences" instanced by individuals straightforwardly intended to are, in a strict sense, themselves given; he describes the manner of their straightforward givenness, and the straightforward method of seizing upon them and judging with evidence about them. But he himself, qua Husserlian phenomenologist, practices the observation of only such generic and specific pure essences as are instanced by *reflectively* given individuals, i.e., by his own mental processes and their intentional objects. Reflectively seized upon individual processes of sensuous perceiving provide him with the basis for seizing upon the specific pure essence instanced by any sensuous perceiving as such; processes of visual perceiving function as a basis for seizing upon the more specific pure essence instanced by any visual perceiving; and processes of seizing upon individual things as themselves given, whether sensuously or nonsensuously, function as a basis for seizing upon the generic pure essence instanced by any perceiving. The same is true, *mutatis mutandis*, for reflectively seized upon mental processes of whatever kind. Similarly, the intentional object as such, in its sense for the mental process, in its manner of being given, believed, doubted, valued, etc., is a basis for seizing upon the generic or specific pure essences instanced by any intentional object, any givenness, any objective sense, any intentional object intended to as an individual thing, etc.

Though other egos cannot directly examine my individual mental processes, each of them can examine his own and confirm or refute my statements about the generic pure essence of any mental process, etc. If there is anyone who has anything like what I have and call "perceiving," it is *ipso facto* an instance of the genus of which my perceiving is an instance, and he can seize upon that *same* genus on the basis of his processes even as I seize upon it on the basis of mine.

Active seizing upon generic pure essences, whether they be instanced by straightforwardly or by reflectively seized upon individual processes, is at first practiced naively. But when it has been practiced, individual mental processes may be themselves seized upon reflectively and used as a basis for grasping their specific pure essence and, correlatively, the pure essence of the self-givenness peculiar to things seized upon as specific pure essences. On the basis of such an original seizing upon the pure essence of the process and the pure essence of what it accomplishes as an original seizing upon essences, one then may practice it not naively but as a deliberate and critically justified method.

Thus, as deliberately practiced and critically justified, it presupposes reflective inquiry. But as a naive "method" it has always been practiced by everyone. To paraphrase Locke's aphorism: God has not been so sparing to men to make them barely able to seize upon individuals and left it to Husserl to make them able to seize upon pure essences. It should be emphasized that, according to the Husserlian phenomenologist, reflection and the observing of pure essences are not his prerogatives but the *de facto* practices even of the narrowest empiricist.

But it would not be correct to say that *all* judgments based on the observation of pure essences exemplified by reflectively given matters are phenomenological in the Husserlian sense. Indeed, it would not be correct to even say, conversely, that *all* judgments that are strictly phenomenological in the Husserlian sense are based on observation of pure essences. The observation of one individual mental life provides a basis not only for seizing

upon the generic pure essence it exemplifies but also for making
Husserlian phenomenological judgments of existence, most notably, the judgment that this individual mental life itself is not
only essentially possible but also exists as an actual instance of
mental life. And this turns out to be anything but trivial, since
it is the basis for every other Husserlian phenomenological judgment of existence.[2]

V

The present flux of mental life, as reflectively observed, is not
simply a process of being actually busied now with this thing,
now with that. The intentional objects of my actual believings,
valuings, and willings are singled out from an intentionally objective background that is all the while meant as there, to be paid
attention to.

No matter how intendings to things may vary, as I live actually
now in perceiving, now in remembering, in judging, liking, willing – straightforwardly or reflectively – always there goes on, at
least automatically, a continuous simple believing-intending to
"the world" as the concrete individual nexus in which all particular individuals intended to are intended to as having their actual
or possible being. The course of mental life may bring doubting
or disbelieving of some previously believed in detail in the objective sense of this world, but the latter as a whole is still simply
believed in – only as somehow otherwise, or perhaps otherwise,
than was previously believed. If I am busied with matters that
have the sense of not being temporally individuated, still the
individual world is at least automatically co-intended to and itself given – though incompletely, as having more to it than

---

[2] *Footnote appended in November, 1970, to the passage beginning:* "Indeed, it would
not be correct even to say ...": According to Husserl's *Ideas* ..., "Introduction"
and "Book I," what I wrote in these sentences is terminologically incorrect. Fully
expressed, the title of that would be: *Ideen zu einer rein⟨ deskriptiven, rein eidetischen,
transzendental-⟩ reinen ⟨oder transzendentalen⟩ Phänomenologie und ⟨zu einer trans-
zendental-⟩ reinen ⟨oder transzendental-⟩ phänomenologischen Philosophie [Ideas Pertaining to a ⟨Purely Descriptive, Purely Eidetic, Transcendentally⟩ Pure ⟨or Tran-
scendental⟩ Phenomenology and ⟨to a Transcendentally⟩ Pure ⟨or Transcendental-⟩
Phenomenological Philosophy].* None of the judgments of existence referred to in the
sentences to which this footnote is appended would belong in a Husserlian phenomenology itself as Husserl conceived such a discipline when he was writing his
Ideas ..., "Introduction" and "Book I." Each of them would belong rather in some
other philosophical discipline, *founded on* such a *Husserlian phenomenology.*

presents itself – and, by their sense, these non-individual things have their varied types of "ideal" being, essentially in relation to the individual world of individuals, e.g., as pure essences *exemplified* by actual or possible world-individuals, as facts ultimately "about" world-individuals, as cultural affairs ultimately "embodied" in individual physical things or processes in the world. Thus, in a broad sense, they too are all intended to and perchance originally given, as worldly things.

In particular, when I busy myself reflectively with this mental life, it is at least co-intended to, like any individual process to which I pay straightforward attention, as a process in the world; and when I seize upon the pure essence exemplified by this mental life, it is at least automatically intended to as the pure essence exemplified by an individual process possible in the world. Indeed, even when I am not busied with this mental life or its intentional objects as such, but paying attention straightforwardly to "outside" affairs – still there goes on an intending to this intending to the world as an intending itself *in the world*, as an actually existing part of the actually existing individual nexus in which all actually existing particular individuals occur.

The "being in the world" that this mental life always automatically accepts itself as having is a determination that is always at least partially self-given and capable of being seized upon whenever I advert to it. Thus, e.g., causal-functional relationships between straightforwardly perceived changes in this physical organism and reflectively perceived changes in mental processes are continuously given and belong to the familiar, simply believed-in style of the world that is intended to and partially itself given.

However, even in this, its original self-givenness, the sense of this mental life as "in the world" is a sense it has *only by virtue of its essential character as intentive to the world*. It is, as it were, a necessary *reflex* effect on this mental life produced by its own essential nature as intentive to the world. Its given status as intentive to the world is in this way *fundamental* to its given status as in the world to which it is intentive.

The Husserlian phenomenologist, as I have seen, is always reflectively orientated toward this mental life and toward things to which it is intentive *as* things to which it is intentive. In order to seize upon the above-stated intentional structure clearly, the reflecting Husserlian phenomenologist adopts as his fixed policy an attitude of neutrality, or self-restraint, vis-à-vis his own continuous believing in, and otherwise taking a position toward particular intra-mundane things intended to and towards the world as a whole.

This means, in the first place, not only that he seizes reflectively upon the believedness, etc., of what he is actually busied with but also that, for purposes of investigation, he "officially" dissociates himself from his actual positions and regards their intentional objects *purely* as "what I believe in," "what I see," etc. In the second place, it means not only that he makes explicit and seizes upon the believedness of the continuously, even if "only tacitly," automatically, believed-in intentionally objective world as a whole, but also that he actively dissociates himself from this fundamental and continuously validated belief. Thus the world and *all* intra-worldly things, in the broadest sense, are regarded purely as "what is believed-in," "what is meant," etc. This fixed policy of dissociation from all believing, valuing, and willing – automatic as well as actional – is then maintained *in his reflective seizing upon mental processes*. That is to say, reflectively he not only makes explicit and seizes upon the continuously believed-in, self-given sense of mental processes as "in the world," but he also regards this sense of these mental processes *purely* as part of "what is believed in," "what is itself given." Thus, e.g., the experienced status of these mental processes as in causal-functional relations with this physical organism, and, more fundamentally, as a process in world space-time, are regarded by the Husserlian phenomenologist purely as "what is experienced."

If I am successful in maintaining this attitude, I *find*, over against the whole world, including this mental life as a process in it, this mental life in its more fundamental status purely as this continuous process of believing in the world and in this believing as itself a process in the world. In its status "apart" from its essentially necessary being in the world, this mental life is, if you will, an "abstraction," but not in the sense of being an abstract *part of the world* that now I merely think of and seize upon "regardless" of everything *else* in the world – perhaps as evidently existing even if nothing else "in the world" exists.

When the Husserlian phenomenologist applies the epithet "transcendental" to this mental life purely as a process of intending to and "having" the world, and speaks of this mental life in its status as *also* in the world as "phenomenal," he must exercise vigilance not to be seduced by the habitual associations of such language, not to mean by the different words something more – or other – than the difference in "status" that is actually itself given and grasped in reflection. In particular he must be careful not to think of "transcendental" mental life as, so to speak, existing in an "other world," or as a realm concretely apart from the world. He must not be misled by the traditional associations of the world "phenomena," as applied by him to himself and this mental life as in the world, and to the whole world and all other intramundane things. He must reject any suggested contrast of phenomenon with noumenon, with its relegation of the experienced world to the status of an appearance relative to some alleged unexperienced reality.

A further pitfall, not easily avoided at the outset, is the tendency to think still of the "relationship" of transcendental mental life to the world as analogous to the real relationship of phenomenal mental life to other processes in the world – to think, let us say, of the intentional "relationship" between, on the one hand, a transcendental process of perceiving a physical thing and, on the other hand, the physical thing itself, as analogous to the real relationship between the "same" process, as an event in the world, and the physical thing. The difficulty has its roots in the fact that, in the world, perceiving and perceived are not only "related" *as* perceiving and perceived but also as realities in space-time, with real spatiotemporal relations. There is some sense in asking how soon after a change takes place in the perceived physical thing a change in the perceiving (as an event in the world) takes place. The question would, however, be absurd if asked concerning the perceiving as transcendental and the thing as phenomenal. The "relationship" of mental life *purely* as intending and things *purely* as intended to is utterly *sui generis;* it has no real analogue. Mental life as in the world not only has this "relationship" to the world but also has real relationships to other things in it, and this is a chief source of the confused strife among the various types of idealism and realism. Only after the peculiar dual status of mental life as pure transcendental intending (to the world) and as phenomenal mental life (in and intentive to the world) has been clearly seen, can the confusion be dissipated and the historic enigma solved.

The general structure of mental life as itself given in reflection *to one who dissociates himself from his own believing in the world and in the status of mental life as itself in the world* may be said to be the first theme of strictly Husserlian phenomenological inquiry. The "transcendental" possibility of the reflexionally given mental life as a clearly possible instance of the pure essence, transcendental mental life, is, at first, simply accepted as itself given. And this is the *only* "assumption" of Husserlian phenomenology, even at the outset, since the being intended-to, the givenness, etc., of the world qua phenomenon is implicit in the essential nature of transcendental mental life, even though the world intended to is not itself a really immanent part thereof. In analyzing this transcendental mental life as intentive to the world and the world as something to which this transcendental mental life is essentially intentive, Husserlian phenomenology is presupposing neither the existence nor the possibility of the world, as every other philosophical inquiry must do, at least tacitly.

* * *

Thus, in attempting to carry out the fundamental methodological principle stated at the beginning of this essay, the Husserlian phenomenologist comes upon a self-givenness that, in a clear but not easily expressed sense, is "prior" to every other self-givenness, and is able to discover and verify by direct observation the fundamental presuppositions of all natural inquiry – without involving himself in the otherwise inevitable circularity of assuming their validity as its own basis and as the justification of the method itself.

It is at this point that a genuinely philosophical inquiry can really *begin:* as a "transcendental phenomenology." As its inquiry progresses, it develops its own peculiar problems and method, in accordance with the gradually discovered nature of "the matters themselves" – always following the maxim that only what is seen to be itself given is to be accepted as genuine knowledge.

DORION CAIRNS

THE IDEALITY OF VERBAL EXPRESSIONS [1]

I

We who are in this room are hearing sounds, coming from my mouth. We perceive them as natural processes, like the sounds that come from brooks and engines. But the sounds now coming from my mouth are perceived as also having particular functions that merely natural processes lack. Seeing my body and hearing my voice, we are also aware of me, as willing the sounds and giving expression to thoughts which I wish to communicate. Thus we are apprehending the sound of my voice as manifesting certain psychic processes and embodying verbal expressions of certain senses.

Sufficiently minute examination will show that at least five things are involved in any case of overt verbal expressing:

1. Something psychic, which is manifested.
2. Some sense, which is expressed.
3. The verbal expression of the sense.
4. Something physical, which embodies the expression and also manifests the psychic process of thinking the expressed sense.
5. Some thing or things, that the verbally expressed sense is about.

For example, when I say "My hat is gray," (1) my psychic

[1] A paper read at the meeting of the Eastern Division of the American Philosophical Association, University of Pennsylvania, Philadelphia, December 27, 1940, and printed in *Philosophy and Phenomenological Research*, I (June, 1941), pp. 453–462. As in the case of the previous essay, "An Approach to Husserlian Phenomenology," what I publish here is not a reprint. In this case too I have corrected a few punctuational or stylistic errors and altered the terminology repeatedly to make it more nearly in accordance with my present usage. In this case, furthermore, I have substituted my published translation of a long passage in Husserl's *Formale und transzendentale Logik* for the translation of it contained in the paper as printed in *Philosophy and Phenomenological Research*.

judging is manifested and (2) the sense of my judging is expressed by (3) the verbal sentence, which, in turn, is embodied in (4) the sound that I produce. This sound is also a manifestation of my judging and of my willing to produce such a sound. Finally, (5) my hat and its color are things that the sense of my judging is about.

In this paper the verb "express" and its derivatives express an unusually restricted sense. We often say that psychic states and processes are *expressed* by words or by somatic behavior. Here, however, I shall speak only of the sense of, e.g., a judging, an asking, a commanding, or a wishing, as expressed. (Expressible senses, I should maintain, are not psychic, not moments or contents really immanent in thinkings.) It should be noted that, though all physical embodiments of expressions are also manifestations of psychic processes, it is not the case that, conversely, all such manifestations are embodiments of expressions. On the other hand, it is proper to speak of even the non-physical overt effects of psychic processes as manifestations. For example, not only the sounds I make but also the overt expressions embodied in them are manifestations of psychic processes.

What is manifested is always a psychic reality. Its manifestation may be, but need not be, a physical reality. The thing or things that the expressed sense is about may be any kind. But expressions and expressed or expressible senses are not and never can be realities, if by "realities" one means things that are spatio-temporally individuated. I hasten to add that expressions and expressible senses are nevertheless not nonentities. They are observable, distinguishable, repeatedly identifiable *somethings;* about them one can ask sensible questions and make intersubjectively verifiable judgments. Thus they satisfy every legitimate criterion of objective existence, despite their non-reality, their *ideality* (as Husserl called it).[2]

Prevailing motives for doubting or denying the existence of ideal formal and material universals are also operative against the belief that expressions and what they express are ideal existants. It is likely, therefore, that my exposition has been heard with something less than full and universal assent. Perhaps the statement that verbal expressions, as ideal entities, are distinct

[2] Cf. pp. 248-50, *infra*.

from their real embodiments has been the least acceptable. However that may be, I shall restrict myself to an attempt to show
(1) that expressions are not real but ideal and (2) that they are
neither classes nor formal or material universals.

II

Within the real world, we find concrete things and abstract
thing-determinations that are intrinsically relative to the psychic
activities of psychophysical things. Figuratively speaking, such
things and thing-determinations make up a stratum that overlies
a substratum of things and thing-determinations *not* thus relative
to actional psychic processes. Let us call the upper layer "culture"
and the lower one "nature." We find nature as a spatiotemporal
order of real individuals, real individual things, processes, states,
qualities, relations. Among these natural individuals we find some
that are psychophysical or, more precisely, each normal individual human being finds himself and other animals as natural
things among other natural things.

On the other hand, the determinations of things as familiar or
strange, useful or useless, finished, half-finished, or spoiled, their
determinations as tools or monuments, as slaves or pets or kings –
all such determinations are intrinsically relative to psychic activities and belong to the cultural stratum of the world. A stone is
naturally a real thing with a particular shape, size, rigidity, and
color. It may also be a real paperweight or a real hammer, but
only culturally, i.e., in relation to psychic activities of someone
who uses (or might use) it to some intended end. Thus the realm
of individual reality contains cultural as well as natural determinations. At the same time, the cultural stratum of the world
contains more than just the *real* cultural determinations of real
things. It also contains non-real things; among them – verbal
expressions.

If a particular real collocation of marks on a sheet of paper
embodies an expression, that is a cultural fact. The marks are
embodiments, not naturally but culturally, though obviously
they can embody a particular expression only because they have
natural determinations of some particular kind. Having such
natural determinations, the marks can also be a real cultural

embodiment of a particular ideal cultural thing, a particular expression.

A particular collocation of marks or sequence of sounds is "real" in that it can have only one spatiotemporal locus. To be sure, we say "This is the cry I heard last night. These are the very stripes I saw on that other zebra." But, when we say this, we in fact mean either that two cries at different times, two sets of stripes on different zebras, are quite alike or, perhaps, that the very same cry has been sounding without interruption and that this zebra has appropriated the other's hide. A real individual thing may spatially extend, temporally endure, and spatiotemporally move; but it cannot be "repeated" at different places or times. This holds, in particular, for real things that are embodiments of expressions.

On the other hand, an expression itself is identifiable as identically the same expression "in" any number of real individual embodiments. If I suspect that you do not seize upon my words, I shall repeat them, repeat the very same words. In repeating *them*, however, I shall be producing new real sounds, *like* the sounds that I produced before but not the same individually. As a matter of fact, I should attempt to produce new sounds that differed from the earlier ones, in respects that would improve the embodying and make it easier for you to seize upon the selfsame unvaried words. (Such repetition, incidentally, is not the procedure to which I should resort if I believed that, while seizing upon my words, you failed to seize upon the sense that they express for me. In that case it would seem futile to repeat the same words; and I should therefore cast about for others to express the same sense or at least a sense that is roughly equivalent.) Again, to borrow and elaborate an illustration from Husserl,[3] one unique language composition may be embodied a thousand times, perhaps in book-form; and, on the first page of any "copy," there will be marks very similar to those on the first page of any other "copy" – a thousand similar but numerically distinct real individual configurations, each embodying the very same sentences.[4]

---

[3] Cf. *loc. cit., infra.*

[4] That words and sentences, whatever their positive nature, are not physical things, is a fact frequently denied, at least by implication. The following is quoted

III

A sensuously perceived thing is presented as having more natural determinations than are actually presented or could become presented in the course of an actual – and therefore limited – exploration. On the other hand, when a thing embodies an expression, only a few of its natural determinations are the immediate basis for its embodying function; and these are among the ones actually presented or easily brought to self-givenness in a familiar manner. It is rarely or never the case, however, that *all* the presented determinations of a thing are immediately involved in embodying an expression. For example, in speaking an identical English sentence on two occasions, one may vary the loudness of one's voice, or the speed with which vowels and consonants succeed one another, without thereby changing any natural determination directly involved in embodying the sentence.[5] The difference in the natural sounds manifests a difference within the realm of the psychic, but the expressed sense, the things referred to, and the expressive sentence – each of these may remain identical and quite unchanged.

Obviously, then, neither the whole concrete natural thing nor all its presented individual determinations can be identical with the expression. But, one might ask, may it not be that the expression is identical with (rather than "embodied" in) the real determinations just referred to as "directly involved in the embody-

only because it is the most concise and unequivocal recent statement of a contrary opinion that has come to my attention:

"A sentence is a group of words, and words, like other symbols, are in themselves physical objects. ... Sentences when written are thus located on certain surfaces, and when spoken are sound waves passing from one organism to another. ... Sentences, therefore, have a physical existence." (Morris R. Cohen and Ernest Nagel, *An Introduction to Logic and Scientific Method*, New York, 1934, p. 27.)

[5] "It is to be noted, too, that any sign or symbol, taken merely as an object, is of great complexity, but that it is only certain features of signs which are symbolically significant. Take ... the word 'man.' It does not matter how large or small this word is written, or what the color of the ink is, and there may be a good deal of difference in the shapes of the letters, as in the handwriting of different persons. All these features are symbolically irrelevant; although they might, of course, be given meaning in some usage – in maps and in bookkeeping, for example, color has a notable significance. There will, however, in the case of any symbol, always be an enormous variety of aspects which are to be neglected, and only a small number selected to represent what is to be meant by a symbol." (Clarence Irving Lewis and Cooper Harold Langford, *Symbolic Logic*, New York and London, 1932, pp. 311f.)

I regret having failed to discover these words of Professor Langford's before reading this paper.

ing"? If that were the case, any change in those determinations would be a change in the expression. As a matter of fact, however, even determinations that exercise an immediately embodying function can always vary to some extent while the embodied expression remains identical and unchanged "in" all its variant real individual embodiments. Though a lisp, a stammer, or a foreign accent affects immediately embodying determinations, identically the same words may be spoken either normally, lispingly, haltingly, or in a voice with foreign intonations. Similarly, in the visual sphere, one and the same word may be printed in broken or unbroken type. Indeed, the same word may be even spelled (and misspelled) in various manners and yet be the self-same word "in" all its diverse embodiments. In short, because even the immediately embodying individual moments of a real embodiment may vary while the expression embodied remains constant, the latter cannot be identical with any real individual determination or with any complex of real individual determinations of a real thing.

IV

Now, if we bear in mind a certain modern formula for exercising the world of ideal formal and material universals, we shall expect that, at this point, a similar device will be brought to bear against the alleged ideality of verbal expressions. We ought therefore to consider whether, after all, there *is* any self-identical thing such as, e.g., *the* sentence "My hat is gray." Perhaps there is only a plurality of similar real individual sounds or collocations of marks on pieces of paper. Perhaps what we have referred to as "seizing upon *the* sentence" is in fact seizing upon a real individual sound or spatial collocation (or some real individual determination of such a sound or collocation) as a member of a particular class of real things.[6] To be sure, such a hypothesis would have to allow for the fact that expressions, *qua* expressions, are

---

[6] "It has often been pointed out that a word, strictly so called, is not a particular entity, but is rather a class or collection of entities which resemble one another in certain respects." (Lewis and Langford, *op. cit.*, p. 311.) However Professor Langford apparently does not share the tacit assumption that a word must be either a "particular" entity or a class. Cf. p. 10, n. 9 *infra*. (As used by Langford, "particular" is obviously equivalent to "individual" as used in this paper.)

cultural things. It would be obviously incorrect to maintain that, e.g., the word "hat" is no more than "any" individual member of a class of purely *natural* sounds or spatial collocations. To seize upon a natural configuration simply as a member of a particular class of natural configurations is not tantamount to seizing upon it as even a possible embodiment of an expression. And, even if some hypothesis of the type just mentioned were correct, still such apprehension would not be tantamount to seizing upon a natural individual configuration as one of many, each of which is "the" expression.

However, even when the hypothesis is refined to account for the cultural determinations of the real individuals that are involved in any case of overt expressing – even then the hypothesis is untenable. It is refuted by the evident givenness of an expression itself, in its unitary identity, when one actually seizes upon it, e.g., on the basis of perceiving two or more numerically distinct real individuals that embody it. The object of such a grasping is observably distinct from the thing seized upon when one apprehends a real individual as a member of a class. The difference between the two seizings is analogous to that between seizing upon a unitary ideal formal or material essence, in respect of which two or more real individuals are alike, and seizing upon a real individual as a member of a class by virtue of the fact that it has a particular individual characteristic. (E.g., the difference between seizing upon the ideal material essence, *loudness*, in respect of which two individual sounds are alike, and seizing upon an individual sound as a member of the class of loud sounds.)

V

Are we then to identify the identical expression with some complex of ideal formal or material essences exemplified in each real individual that functions as a basis for seizing upon the identical expression? Is what I have called the relation of a single embodied expression to its many embodiments not merely analogous to but identical with the relation of an ideal formal or material essence to the (actual and possible) real individuals making up its extension?

An affirmative reply would at least be compatible with the

given identity of the expression as embodied in a number of distinct and perhaps dissimilar real individuals. And yet, unless I am mistaken, there is also an observable difference between seizing upon an ideal essence *exemplified in* something and seizing upon an expression as *embodied* in something. If I examine the two psychic processes reflectively it seems to me that I am performing an act of one kind, when I seize upon an identical ideal universal essential structure as exemplified in two collocations of marks, and an act of an observably different kind, when I seize upon an identical ideal sentence as embodied in each of the collocations. The acts seem to differ precisely in that the ideal things upon which they respectively seize are fundamentally different. To be sure, the two collocations of marks must exemplify a particular ideal universal material structure, if they are to function as bases for seizing upon a particular sentence. It does not seem to be the case, however, that, when I turn my attention from the real individual marks (or their real individual shapes) to the sentence, I am *ipso facto* turning my attention to the universal shape exemplified in the real marks (and by their individual shapes). In both cases I am indeed turning from a real to an ideal thing, but they seem to be fundamentally different ideal things. Is the difference merely that what I call "a verbal expression" is an ideal universal overlaid with a particular cultural significance, which makes the universal itself, e.g., the universal shape, a verbal expression? That is a plausible doctrine, but there are facts with which it is hardly reconcilable.

Though verbal expressions are like formal and material universals in not being spatiotemporally individuated, i.e., bound to a single spatiotemporal locus, they differ from such "eidetic" universals in being parts of a stream of cultural history and susceptible to historical vicissitudes. The kind of verbal change immediately relevant to our problem is obviously not semantic change but the kind exemplified by changes in syntax, word-division within a sentence, inflexion, spelling, pronunciation, and letter formation. Such changes involve corresponding changes in the range within which natural individuals may vary and still function, at a particular time in cultural history, as embodiments of identically the same verbal expression. Now, if the verbal expression were an eidetic universal exercising a cultural function, then such a change would be the gradual shifting of a single function from one universal to another. There would be no single self-identical expression, undergoing historical changes. This consequence, however, conflicts with such observable facts as the psychic act of seizing upon a single word as identical throughout historical changes in its pronunciation or spelling. To be sure, we must then ask ourselves whether the word, as self-identical throughout its historical changes, is not perhaps a higher material universal, under which stand, as ideal species, "the" word as pronounced or spelled at various stages in its history. It is easy to see, however, that this suggestion conflicts with the fact that I do seize upon the word itself as *something identical that has undergone changes* throughout its historical lifetime. It would be only slightly more incongruous if one tried to account for the identity of a human being throughout his life by appealing to the fact that *infant*, *child*, and *adult* are quasi-specific sorts, all falling under the one generic kind, *human being*.

VI

We are, I trust, already far removed from identifying an expression with its real embodiments but, having introduced the concept of history, we are tempted to clinch the distinction between them by pointing out how different the history of an expression is from that of its real embodiments. The latter are, let us say, similar sets of marks on several sheets of paper. Each embodiment has its individual history. *Qua* natural thing it discolors, fades, and finally disintegrates. *Qua* cultural thing, it may be stored in a library, thrown away, worn as an amulet, or perhaps read from time to time. Meanwhile, the history of the ideal expression itself is, at most, only *influenced* by the several fates of its real embodiments. As member of successive generations write and rewrite the same expression, it preserves its identity but it also changes. It may even be said to grow old – and, eventually, those who knew it in its youth might hardly recognize it, supposing they were still alive to meet it in its worn down and contracted old age. The possible vicissitudes of an expression, however, are quite different from the natural decay of a manuscript, the wearing out of a phonograph record, or the dying away of a sound of speech.

Returning to tie the threads of our unfinished argument, we cannot fail to note an appearance of paradox in the thesis that, on the one hand, verbal expressions undergo changes while, on the other hand, they lack spatiotemporal individuation. Without question, this appearance will remain until we have seen and analyzed the peculiar relation of ideal cultural things in general, and verbal expressions in particular, to space and time. Meanwhile, the suspicion that we have already made a fundamental mistake is reduced when we note that there are indeed other things besides verbal expressions that exhibit the same remarkable pair of characteristics. Consider, for example, a traditional melody or folk dance. One must distinguish the *one* melody or dance from its *many* real performances at various times, in various places. *The* melody, *the* dance, is also something "ideal," embodied in its numerous real renderings. And such ideal things also undergo historical changes without losing their identity.

Because verbal expressions are not unique in combining ideality with mutability, it is convenient to have a common name for things exhibiting this pair of characteristics. Following Husserl's suggestion, one may refer to them appropriately as *ideal individuals*, thereby contrasting them, on the one hand, with *real individuals* and, on the other hand, with *ideal universals* and ideal expressible senses. While it appears to be the case that there are genuine things belonging in each of these four categories, the so-called Platonic doctrine of *real universals* is apparently false.

VII

With the exception of some details, all the views developed in the present exposition have been set forth or at least indicated by Edmund Husserl:

> The uttered word, the actually spoken locution, taken as a sensuous, specifically an acoustic, phenomenon, is something that we distinguish from the word itself or the declarative sentence itself, or the sentence-sequence itself that makes up a more extensive locution. Not without reason – in cases where we have not been understood and we reiterate – do we speak precisely of a reiteration of the *same* words and sentences. In a treatise or a novel every word, every sentence, is a one-time affair,

which does not become multiplied by a reiterated vocal or silent reading. Nor does it matter who does the reading; though each reader has his own voice, his own timbre, and so forth. The treatise itself (taken now only in its lingual aspect, as composed of words or language) is something that we distinguish, not only from the multiplicities of vocal reproduction, but also, and in the same manner, from the multiplicities of its permanent documentations by paper and print, parchment and handwriting, or the like. The one unique language-composition is reproduced a thousand times, perhaps in book form: We speak simply of the *same* book with the same story, the same treatise. And this self-sameness obtains *even with respect to the purely lingual composition;* while, in another manner, it obtains also with respect to the sharply distinguishable significational contents, which we shall shortly take into account.

As a system of habitual signs, which, within an ethnic community, arises, undergoes transformation, and persists in the manner characteristic of tradition – a system of signs by means of which, in contrast to signs of other sorts, an expressing of thoughts comes to pass –, language presents altogether its own problems. One of them is the just-encountered *ideality of language*, which is usually quite overlooked. We may characterize it also in this fashion: *Language has the Objectivity proper to the objectivities making up the so-called spiritual [geistige] or cultural world, not the Objectivity proper to bare physical Nature.* As an Objective product of minds, language has the same properties as other mental products: Thus we also distinguish, from the thousand reproductions of an engraving, the engraving itself; and this engraving, the engraved picture itself, is visually abstracted from each reproduction, being given in each, in the same manner, as an identical ideal object. On the other hand, only in the form of reproduction does it have factual existence in the real world. The situation is just the same when we speak of the Kreutzer Sonata, in contrast to its reproductions *ad libitum.* However much it itself consists of sounds, it is an ideal unity; and its constituent sounds are no less ideal. They are obviously not the sounds dealt with in physics; nor are they the sounds pertaining to sensuous acoustic perception, the sounds that come from things pertaining to the senses and are really extant only in an actual reproduction and the intuiting of it. Just as the one sonata is reproduced many times in real reproductions, each single sound belonging to the sonata is reproduced many times in the corresponding sounds belonging to the reproductions. Like the whole, its part is something ideal, which becomes real, *hic et nunc,* only after the fashion of real singularization. Now it is quite the same in the case of all verbal formations; and the ideality in their case is not solely an ideality of what is expressed in them – however great a rôle the expressed may also play. To be sure, our ascertainments do concern verbal formations *also* as sense-filled locutions, concrete unities of verbal body and expressed sense. But they concern such formations even with respect to the verbal corporeality itself, which is, so to speak, a *spiritual corporeality.* The word itself, the sentence itself, is an ideal unity, which is not multiplied by its thousandfold reproductions.

The fundamental treatment of the great problems that concern clarification of the sense and constitution of Objectivities belonging to the cultural world, with respect to all their fundamental types, including language, makes up a realm by itself. Here it is to be noted only that, for the logician, language is of primary importance solely in its ideality, as the identical lingual word, the identical lingual sentence or complex of sentences, in contrast to the actual or possible reifications: precisely as the aesthetician's theme is the particular work of art, the particular sonata, the particular picture, not as the transient physical complex of sounds or as the physical picture-thing, but as the picture itself, the sonata itself – the properly aesthetic object, corresponding to the properly linguistic object in the parallel case.[7]

Professor Weiss has called my attention to a passage [8] where Peirce contrasts "one and the same word" with its many "single instances" or "Replicas." There can be no doubt that Peirce is referring to what I, following Husserl's terminology, have called the distinction between the word and its "real individual embodiments." [9] In that same passage Peirce also says that the word is "a general type which, it has been agreed, shall be significant." At first blush, this looks like the theory considered and rejected in Part V of this paper. However, a more extensive examination of his *Collected Papers* has inclined me to believe that what Peirce refers to as a "general type" is not what I, again following Husserl, have referred to as an "eidetic (formal or material) universal." In any case, it seems fairly certain that Peirce's theory of the nature of verbal expressions is not identical with the one *advocated* here, though he agrees on the fundamental fact that verbal expressions are not real individual things.

---

[7] Edmund Husserl, *Formal and Transcendental Logic*, translated by Dorion Cairns (The Hague: Martinus Nijhoff, 1969), pp. 19–21.

[8] *Collected Papers of Charles Sanders Peirce*, edited by Charles Hartshorne and Paul Weiss (Cambridge, Mass.: Harvard University Press, 1932), 2.246, pp. 142f.

[9] Obviously, Professor Langford is referring to the same distinction when he says: "The word 'man' has many different instances, written and spoken, and the word itself cannot be identified with any one of these instances" (*op. cit.*, p. 311). He concludes that the word "must be regarded either as a class made up of them (sc., its many different instances) or as an abstract entity after the fashion of a universal" (*loc. cit.*). In its apparently deliberate vagueness, the phrase "after the fashion of a universal" could be understood broadly enough to cover the possibility that words are *not* universals but individuals, *like* universals in being ideal.

DORION CAIRNS

PERCEIVING, REMEMBERING, IMAGE-AWARENESS, FEIGNING AWARENESS [1]

This paper is about four kinds of mental processes. I call them, respectively, "perceiving," "remembering," "image-awareness," and "feigning awareness."

I shall describe examples, with a view to bringing out generic features of each kind and distinctive features of certain species. I shall compare examples of one kind with examples of others, in order to bring out similarities and differences, and prevent confusions. I shall also attempt to show certain relations between species of one kind and species of another.

The paper is offered as an example of Husserlian phenomenologizing. The general account that emerges from it is phenomenological, in a Husserlian sense of the word, and agrees with the account that might be gathered from Edmund Husserl's writings. But I shall not follow the letter of any of his statements. Rather I shall present a free description of certain mental phenomena as I see them, thanks to the fact that Husserl points out their essential and distinctive features. The immediate purpose of the paper is to induce its hearers to examine phenomena of the sorts described and, by their own observations, clarify and verify (or, perhaps, correct) the presented descriptions.

If I turn my attention to my mental life, perhaps the easiest thing to discriminate in this flux is a current of *sensuous* perceivings. Not only sensuous perceivings as such, but also some of their species, are easy to note and distinguish.

First, I find tactual perceivings: Feeling these coins in my pocket; feeling the shape and the hardness, now of this one and

[1] This previously unpublished manuscript of Dorion Cairns was first delivered as a lecture read to the Philosophy Seminar, McGill University, 21 February, 1962. It was revised by the author in November, 1970, for publication here. [Note of the editors.]

now of that one. Or again: Feeling the floor under my feet, and feeling its solidity. Then, passing over various sensuous perceivings that we often lump together with tactual perceivings, I hasten to mention the epistemologists' favorites: *visual* perceivings. For example: seeing this room, the walls, and particular people and things in it; seeing the shape and the color of this thing or that thing.

Auditory perceivings are likewise easy to find and to discriminate from sensuous perceivings of other sorts: Hearing an automobile passing by outside; hearing the noise of its motor.

Having mentioned three out of five, we may as well complete the traditional list. *Olfactory* perceiving: smelling a rose and its fragrance. And *gustatory* perceiving: tasting a sip of wine and its dryness or its sweetness.

Different modes of sensuous perceiving are often found in combinations: *Feeling and seeing* this coin and its shape; *smelling and tasting* the sip of wine; *hearing* and at the same time *seeing, feeling*, and *smelling*, the new automobile.

If we compare normal examples of the various mentioned sorts, we shall find that, much as they differ, there are some respects in which they are alike. Each is *an awareness of some physical reality as itself presented*, as *given* (so to speak) *"in person,"* simultaneously with the awareness of it. In short, each is a *perceiving* of some physical reality.

But, though each is an awareness of some physical reality as *itself* presented, each is a perceiving of this reality itself *through* an appearance, or through appearances. Frequently the appearance or appearances through which the reality itself is perceived goes unnoticed. It stands out, however, and attracts attention in case the reality is perceived as the same through *different* appearances, or as *un*changing through a *changing* appearance, or as changing in a manner that *differs* from the manner in which the appearance changes, or the like. Let me illustrate!

There may be a tactual perceiving of the *shape* of a coin as the *same*, whether the coin be felt with a bare hand or with a gloved hand; but when the two perceivings are compared, the two *appearances* of the shape stand out as *different* from one another.

I see some things in this room as unchanging; but there are changes in the perspectival *appearances* through which I see them, when I perceive my organism as moving about or my eyes as opening wide and then shutting: This draws my attention to the perspectival appearances, which otherwise might be seen *through* without being noticed. And something similar is true in the case of auditory, olfactory, and other modes of sensuous perceiving. Always the physical realities are themselves presented *through* appearances.

And these intermediary appearances *too* are *presented;* they too are presented, moreover, as simultaneous with the perceiving in question. They too, in short, are sensuously *perceived* – are felt, or seen, or heard, or the like – in the same sense in which the physical realities are. But they are not *terminal* objects of the sensuous perceivings; and, as a rule, when we speak of what is perceived, we refer to the terminal objects of a perceiving – which are, in the case of normal perceivings, physical realities. (We shall examine a few anomalous perceivings shortly.)

In the case of an *active* (as distinguished from an *automatic*) sensuous perceiving, we may say that attention is ordinarily *focused* on a terminal object – a concrete physical thing, or its color, or the brightness of its color, let us say – but that attention *can* be focused, instead, on some intermediate appearance, through which the terminal object is perceived.

But it is possible to shorten the focus of attention still further and thus find *fields of sensation* – a field of *tactual* sensation, a field of *visual* sensation, and others – in each of which particular sensa, particular data of sensation stand out from a background. As the name "data" suggests, these sensa are indeed *given*, themselves *presented*. But they are no more *truly* given, no more *truly* themselves presented, than are the physical realities and the appearances *through* which the physical realities are perceived. We may indicate the situation by saying that, on the *basis* of sensa which stand out in fields of sensation, physical realities are perceived through appearances. The perceiving of the physical realities includes presentive awarenesses of all three: the sensa, the appearances, and the physical realities. Or, to describe the situation more precisely, we may say that a sensuous perceiving of something physical includes three strata of presentive awareness. The lowest of these strata is a presentive sensing of sensa in some presented sensuous field or other; the intermediate stratum, a presentive awareness of appearances; the highest stratum, a presentive awareness of physical realities.

Though a sensuous perceiving is indeed an awareness of things as themselves *presented*, it is also an awareness of *more* than is itself presented. Seeing an opaque solid includes awareness of it as having an unpresented side and an unpresented interior. Hearing an automobile is awareness of something as having more to it than is heard. And so it is in every other case. We may describe this by saying that any sensuous perceiving includes an *apperceiving* and that what is presented in a sensuous perceiving *appresents* something else. The presented front appresents the rear of the opaque object; the presented glow of the merely *seen* fire appresents its warmth; and so forth.

Moreover, what is itself presented may be presented more or less clearly and, in a correlative sense, the perceiving may be more or less clear. But some degree of clarity is essential to what I call "perceivings." If an awareness of something is utterly obscure, I do not call it "a perceiving of it."

When I turn my attention to my mental life, *I find* sensuous perceivings. That is to say, I am *reflectively* aware of *them* as themselves presented, as given "in person," simultaneously with my awareness of them. Obviously this reflective awareness of them is not sensuous: I do not *feel* them in the sensuous sense of the word; nor do I *see* them with my eyes. In short, I do not perceive them sensuously; but I do *perceive* them somehow: in that I am aware of them as themselves presented while they are going on. But sensuous and reflective *perceivings* are not the only mental processes that I can reflectively perceive when I turn my attention to my mental life.

Rememberings are almost as easy to find and discriminate as sensuous perceivings. We could run through our list of examples of the latter and find, in many cases, a corresponding example of remembering: *Remembering* a certain coin and its hardness – as previously *felt*. *Remembering* this room and some of the people and things in it, *as I first saw them*, when I was coming in. The phrases "as previously felt" and "as I saw them" point to an essential feature: Any *remembering* is a more or less *clear* awareness of something *as previously perceived in some specific manner or manners* – for example: sensuously or, more specifically, tactually. And, still more specifically, in the case of something sensuously perceivable: it is remembered as previously perceived through *appearances* of certain sorts. Thus the concrete or full *object* of awareness, in the case of a remembering, includes a past *perceiving* of the thing remembered. Let me illustrate.

I am now remembering a sunset that I once saw from a mountain-top, above the clouds. I pick up my past mental life at some long past moment; and now, as the saying goes, I relive for a while a past perceiving. What is being remembered is not just the setting sun and the sea of red clouds beneath; it is the past visual perceiving of sun, and clouds, and other people around me. One brief stretch of the remembering happens to be clear enough for me to shorten the focus of my present memorial attention and clearly remember a sequence of changing appearances through which I saw the scene. Like the physical scene itself, these perspectival appearances are remembered now as past. They are not *present* appearances, through which I *remember* the past scene; they are *past* appearances through which I saw it. The sunset, the perspectival appearances, the seeing – *all* these I am now aware of as things past. Only the remembering is present; but it is a present remembering of the sunset *as previously seen*, and seen through those appearances.

Perceivings and rememberings are obviously not the only things that I find when I turn my attention to the present flux of my mental life. They are not, that is to say, the only modes of awareness that I can *perceive* reflectively; and, similarly, they are not the only ones that I can *remember*. I may perceive, for example, a present expecting to perceive the bottom of this table (if I do such and such); and, a few moments later I may remember a past expecting to see the bottom of this table. In itself, an expecting to see the bottom of the table is a completely obscure awareness of the bottom of this table; and, correspondingly even a remembering of such an *expecting* does not involve remembering the bottom of this table. The remembering of something is an awareness of it as previously *perceived*, not an awareness of it as somehow meant in a past, *non-perceptive*, awareness.

Enduring things can, of course, be simultaneously perceived and remembered. After many years I see an old acquaintance again and, at the same time, remember him as he looked when

I last saw him. This is more than merely recognizing him. I may recognize someone – that is to say, see him and be aware of him as someone I've been before – without at the same time remembering him as I saw him before. But, in the case of a simultaneous sensuous perceiving and remembering, the present *perceiving* of the thing has such a structure as we described a while ago; and the complete *object of* the present remembering is a *past* perceiving that has such a structure. Besides all this there may be, as in our last example, an awareness of identity between something now *perceived* and something now *remembered* as previously perceived.

But even a bare perceiving of something, without remembering it, and without recognizing it, includes a memorial awareness of it. Any perceiving is a process – that is to say: it has temporal *extension*, and is made up of partial extents, each of which is a perceiving. But, every later extent is an awareness of what is perceived in it as identical with or other than something perceived in the just previous extent. Thus it is not only a perceptive awareness of what is perceived in itself but also a *memorial* awareness of something as perceived in the just previous extent. This memorial awareness, and the identifying or distinguishing based upon it and the present perceiving, do not involve any activity on my part; they go on *automatically*. And they are necessary to the awareness of a continuous perceiving. But something similar is necessary also to the awareness of a continuous awareness of any sort. Thus, for example, every later extent of a remembering includes an automatic memorial awareness of the just previous extent of the remembering and a likewise automatic identifying of what is being remembered *now* with what was being remembered *up to now*. The memorial awarenesses involved here are not *re*-memberings, not *re*-collectings; they are rather, so to speak, original *"memberings,"* original *"collectings"* of past awareness, in such a fashion that any extent of awareness, however short, is clear awareness of a more extended continuum of awareness. No analysis of mental processes of any sort can make them fully intelligible without clarifying such *primary* memorial awareness and bringing out the similarities and differences between it and that secondary memorial awareness which I call "remembering" or "recollecting."

On the basis of even our present hasty and inadequate examination, however, we may note certain important similarities and differences between perceivings and rememberings or between perceivings and memorial awarenesses of any sort. They are similar in that each is a more or less clear awareness of something as *presented*, as given, so to speak, "in person." And in this they differ from any *completely obscure* awareness of something – as, for example, merely *appresented* or merely *represented*. But a perceiving differs from a memorial awareness in that a perceiving is a clear awareness of something as presented simultaneously with this clear awareness; whereas a primary memorial awareness or a remembering is an awareness of something as presented in an earlier perceiving.

We shall continue our examination of perceiving and remembering. Before we do so however, let me introduce the third theme of this paper: image-awareness. As we shall see, an image-awareness is even more complex than a perceiving or a remembering, since it *includes* either a sensuous perceiving, or a remembering of something as sensuously perceived, or some other awareness with a structure like one or the other of these. Thus image-awarenesses belong to *different sorts;* and the image-awarenesses that belong to what we may call the primary sort include a *sensuous perceiving*. Let us consider a few examples.

Someone perceives something sensuously – perhaps visually, perhaps tactually, perhaps in both manners – as a concrete physical reality with a more or less clearly given shape. At the same time he takes this thing to be an image of something else – perhaps an angel, perhaps some saint or other, perhaps a certain man – the late John Doe – whose name, let us suppose, is to be carved beneath the image.

To say that the perceiver takes the perceived thing as an image of something else is to say that he has a complex awareness of two things: a *presentive* awareness of the perceived thing and, founded on that *presentive* awareness, a *non*-presentive awareness of something else – in our example: an angel, or a saint, or the late John Doe. This whole complex awareness is what I call an image-awareness. The lower stratum is a sensuous perceiving of a physical reality – an awareness which, as we have already seen, itself includes at least three strata of awareness. Its higher stratum is a non-presentive awareness of something else, as *depicted* by and, in this specific manner, *represented* by the presented physical reality. Relative to the thing he is aware of as *depicted*, the thing the person in question is aware of as presented is for him a picture, an image, of the depicted thing.

The awareness of the depicted thing may be an awareness of it as existing now, or as existing in the past, or as existing in the future. It may be – as perhaps in the case of the angel, an awareness of it as existing at no time. In the case of the late John Doe, it is, of course, an awareness of the depicted thing as existing in the past. But it is no more a *remembering* of John Doe than it is a *perceiving* of him. In case the person who has an image-awareness of John Doe also remembers John Doe, while seeing what he takes to be an image of him, the two simultaneous awarenesses of John Doe differ observably in structure and in quality.

The image-awareness has at least four strata: it is a presentive awareness of sensa, a presentive awareness of an appearance, a presentive awareness of a physical reality and, over and above all that, a non-presentive awareness of John Doe. The remembering, on the other hand, is a *presentive* awareness of John Doe as previously perceived – that is, as the terminal object of a *past* awareness that had a structure like that of the *present* awareness of the physical thing which is taken to be an image. Moreover, the remembering involves no awareness of a mediating image.

One further point about this example: The physical thing is perceived as having *more* to it than is presented – and (to use a term introduced earlier) this "more" is *ap*presented by what is presented. That is to say, more explicitly: there is a non-presentive awareness of it as *present with* what is presented. The *ap*-presentation which is combined with any sensuous presentation of a concrete physical reality is different from *representation*. In an awareness of something as representing something else, e.g., as an image of something else, that which is meant as *re*presented is not meant as present with the representative.

Awareness of an image in a mirror is another image-awareness of the *primary* sort: It includes a *sensuous perceiving*, although, to be sure, this sensuous perceiving is anomalous.

It occasionally happens that, for a time, I see certain things as realities, and then take them – the same things – to be images in a mirror, of whose presence I was previously unaware. If I compare the two parts of this mental process I find that the latter part differs from the earlier in two respects. The things seen in the earlier part as *realities* are now seen as *phantoms*, and in addition to this, they are now taken as *images* of other things. A visual phantom may be defined as something that can be perceived visually, but not tactually. And mirror-phantoms have these further characteristics: that they can be seen only behind a mirror and that, while they can be seen as approached by and approaching my organism and other physical realities, the phantoms are always seen on the far side, and the realities on the near side, of the mirror. Visual phantoms are not appearances through which other things are seen. On the contrary they are like physical realities in being terminal objects, which themselves are seen through appearances and on the basis of data of sensation. The *appearance* of a phantom chair behind a mirror may change while the phantom-chair itself is seen as unchanging. Nor would mirror phantoms be images, in our strict sense of the word, unless they were *taken to be* images of other things. For example, images of realities or perhaps images of *other phantoms* – phantoms, so to speak, of the second degree, seen behind a phantom mirror which is seen behind a real one.

Now it frequently happens that when a phantom is seen behind a mirror and taken to be an image of a reality, this reality itself is perceived too. In such a case we have, as in the case of the late John Doe, two awarenesses of the same reality. In both cases there is, on the one hand, an awareness of something as depicted and, on the other hand, an awareness of the same thing as presented. Only now the latter is a perceiving of it, not a remembering of it.

Just as I can *perceive* a physical reality or a phantom and take it as an image of something else, so I can *remember* a physical reality or a phantom, and take it to be an image of something else. Obviously this *secondary* type of image awareness is more complex, since remembering is more complex than perceiving.

We shall examine still other sorts of image-awareness; but first we must consider our fourth main kind of mental process: *feigning* awareness.

Perceiving, remembering, and the sorts of image-awareness

that we have already examined are what may be called "un-feigning awarenesses"; but every genus or species of unfeigning awareness has as its *counterpart* a genus or species of feigning awareness. Thus perceiving has what may be called "quasi-per-ceiving" as its counterpart in the realm of mental feigning; remembering has what may be called "quasi-remembering" as *its* counterpart; and an image-awareness that includes a perceiv-ing has as *its* counterpart, an image-awareness that includes a quasi-perceiving. Let us begin with feigning awareness of the kind I call "quasi-perceiving."

Right now I am feigning to myself seeing a large black cat walk slowly across the room. He comes over; I feel his fur, hear him purr; I see him stretch and walk away. In everyday discourse I should say that I was *imagining* a cat. But for purposes of accurate description and discrimination among kinds of aware-ness, this manner of speaking will hardly do. What went on in my mental life was a feigning awareness of *a cat* as itself present-ed, a quasi-perceiving of a real individual cat in person. I was not seeing something *else* and taking it to be an image of a cat; nor was I *quasi*-seeing something else and taking it to be an image of a cat. In short, this was not a case of *image*-awareness of any sort. My cat-awareness was no more and no less complex than a non-feigning cat-perceiving. Structurally it was, in fact, the pre-cise counterpart of unfeigningly perceiving a cat; it was a *modifi-cation, not a complication,* of seriously perceiving a cat.

The like is true of quasi-remembering. I cannot remember see-ing Caesar cross the Rubicon. But I can, and now I *do, feign* to myself such an awareness. It is as though I were remembering having stood, two thousand years ago, on the bank of some little stream in Northern Italy, and watched the Roman general wade across it. This *quasi*-remembering is observably different in struc-ture from seeing a physical reality or a phantom, and taking it to be an *image* of Caesar crossing the Rubicon. It is different also from *remembering* something and taking it to be an image of Caesar crossing the Rubicon. And, yet again, it is different from *quasi*-seeing or *quasi*-remembering a reality or a phantom and taking it to be an image of the scene. In short, *it too* is no *image*-awareness but rather the structural counterpart, in the realm of feigning, of a genuine remembering.

As I have already indicated, image-awarenesses that have, as their lower strata, quasi-perceivings and quasi-rememberings are indeed possible. But structurally they are more complex than rememberings or quasi-rememberings, and, a fortiori, more complex than perceivings and quasi-perceivings.

We have considered four principal kinds of mental process: perceiving, remembering, image-consciousness, and feigning consciousness. Comparison of examples has made it apparent that the four kinds are not co-ordinate. Each of the first two has its feigning counterpart; and image-awareness based on perceiving or remembering has as its counterpart image-awareness based on quasi-perceiving or quasi-remembering. Indeed, if we were to examine still other kinds of awareness, we should find the same parallelism of non-feigning and feigning in every case. Thus a judging has as its counterpart a quasi-judging. I cannot judge that Bordeaux is the capital of France. But I can and do quasi-judge this when I follow and understand the statement.

Similarly, in the spheres of emotion and volition: I do not love the girl next door. But I can feign to myself loving her, just as, a while ago, I feigned to myself seeing a cat. And the actor playing Hamlet does not will the death of the king – any more than he believes the king is behind the tapestry. At most he *plays at* willing the king's death.

Leaving aside all feigning awareness, we find that perceivings and rememberings are alike in being awarenesses of things as themselves given; whereas an image-consciousness is not an awareness of the thing depicted as something itself given. We chose as examples of image-awareness, only examples in which the depictive thing is presented or quasi-presented. But a thing can be obscurely meant and taken to be an image; in which case the image-awareness is completely obscure – obscure, not only as an awareness of something depicted, but also as an awareness of something as depictive.

Furthermore, let me repeat that image-awareness is not the only sort of non-presentive awareness. The awareness of a thing as symbolized by a symbol, the awareness of a judgment merely as expressed by a sentence, the awareness of anger, merely as expressed (in quite a different sense) by a frown – all these are non-presentive and, in this respect, similar to the awareness of something as represented by an image.

Finally, let us note that, although perceiving and remembering are structurally quite different from image-awareness, certain analogies between them make it natural to speak of perceiving or remembering in terms more appropriate to image-awareness, and *vice versa.*

In being quite distinct from one another, the *appearance* through which a thing is sensuously perceived and the perceived thing itself are like picture and depicted. Furthermore the appearance resembles the thing perceived through it, and the picture resembles the thing depicted. This makes it natural to say: "When my eyes are wide open, I see a sharper and brighter *picture* of the room than I see when my eyes are almost shut." Or: "When I look at this Rorschach ink-blot, I see a butterfly." Such manners of speaking are perfectly intelligible and, in daily life, they are harmless. But they will not do if we are attempting to distinguish and describe the phenomena accurately. If this is our aim, we do better to say: "When my eyes are wide open, the *appearance* through which I see the room itself is brighter and sharper than it is when my eyes are almost shut." And: "When I look at this ink-blot, I take it to be an image of a butterfly, which I do not see."

And the like is true of our everyday talk about memory-images. Strictly speaking, I do not ordinarily see or quasi-see a reality or a phantom which I take to be an image of my grandmother. On the contrary, I clearly remember my *grandmother, herself,* as I once saw her.

Despite all analogies between perceiving or remembering and image-awareness, there is this important difference between them: Perceiving or remembering is *presentive* awareness of the thing perceived or remembered; image-awareness is non-presentive awareness of the thing depicted.

BIBLIOGRAPHY OF THE WRITINGS OF
DORION CAIRNS

1. "Mr. Hook's Impression of Phenomenology," *The Journal of Philosophy*, XXVII (July 17), 1930, pp. 393–396.
2. "The Philosophy of Edmund Husserl," unpublished Harvard doctoral dissertation, 1933.
3. "Some Results of Husserl's Investigations," *The Journal of Philosophy*, XXXVI (April 27), 1939, pp. 236–238. [Reprinted in Joseph J. Kockelmans, editor, *The Philosophy of Edmund Husserl and Its Interpretation* (New York: Doubleday & Company, Inc., 1967), pp. 147–149.]
4. "An Approach to Phenomenology," *Essays in Memory of Edmund Husserl* (Cambridge, Mass.: Harvard University Press, 1940), edited by Marvin Farber, pp. 3–18. [A revised version of the essay appears in the appendix to this volume of essays, with the revised title, "An Approach to Husserlian Phenomenology."]
5. Review of Edmund Husserl, "Die Frage nach dem Ursprung der Geometrie als intentional-historisches Problem" in *Philosophy and Phenomenological Research*, I (1940), pp. 98–109.
6. Review of E. Parl Welch, *Edmund Husserl's Phenomenology* in *Philosophy and Phenomenological Research*, I (1940), pp. 232–237.
7. "Concerning Beck's 'The Last Phase of Husserl's Phenomenology'," *Philosophy and Phenomenological Research*, I (1940), pp. 492–498.
8. Review of Harald Lassen, *Beiträge zur Phänomenologie und Psychologie der Anschauung* in *Philosophic Abstracts*, Winter 1940–41, pp. 21 f.
9. "The Ideality of Verbal Expressions," *Philosophy and Phenomenological Research*, I (1941), pp. 453–462. [A revised version of the essay appears in the appendix to this volume of essays.] Paper read at the meeting of the Eastern Division of the American Philosophical Association. University of Pennsylvania, December 27, 1940.
10. "Phenomenology" (pp. 231–234) and other entries in *The Dictionary of Philosophy*, edited by Dagobert D. Runes (New York: The Philosophical Library, 1942).
11. "The world as a Phenomenological Problem," by Ludwig Landgrebe. A translation by Dorion Cairns, *Philosophy and Phenomenological Research*, Volume I, Number 1, September, 1944.
12. "Phenomenology" (pp. 353–364) in *A History of Philosophical Systems*, edited by Vergilius Ferm (New York: The Philosophical Library, 1950).
13. *Cartesian Meditations. An Introduction to Phenomenology*, by Edmund

Husserl. A translation by Dorion Cairns (The Hague: Martinus Nijhoff, 1960).

14. *Formal and Transcendental Logic*, by Edmund Husserl. A translation
by Dorion Cairns (The Hague: Martinus Nijhoff, 1969).

15. "The Many Senses and Denotations of the Word *Bewusstsein* ("Consciousness") in Edmund Husserl's Writings," *Life-World and Consciousness. Essays for Aron Gurwitsch*, edited by Lester E. Embree
(Evanston: Northwestern University Press, 1972), pp. 19–31.

16. "Perceiving, Remembering, Image-Awareness, Feigning Awareness."
This previously unpublished manuscript of Dorion Cairns was delivered as a lecture at, among other places, the Philosophy Seminar,
McGill University, 21 February, 1962. The manuscript was revised
by Dorion Cairns in November, 1970, for publication in the appendix
to this volume of essays.

17. *Guide for Translating Husserl* (The Hague: Martinus Nijhoff, in
press).

18. *Conversations with Husserl and Fink* (The Hague: Martinus Nijhoff,
in hands of publisher).

19. *Briefe Edmund Husserls an Dorion Cairns*, herausgegeben von Dorion
Cairns. (Den Haag: Martinus Nijhoff, in hands of publisher).

20. *Ideas Pertaining to a Pure Phenomenology and to a Phenomenological
Philosophy*, "Introduction," "Book One" and "Epilogue," by Ed-
mund Husserl. A new translation by Dorion Cairns. (Currently in
progress and accepted in advance for publication in London by
George Allen and Unwin Ltd. and in New York by the Macmillan
Company.)

21. Projected publication of four essays:
a. "Some Criticisms of Husserl's Fifth Cartesian Meditation." (The
main points of this essay were presented orally at the 1971 meeting
of the Husserl Circle, De Paul University.)
b. "Universal Transfer of Intentional Object-Senses." (Elaboration
of a paper read at the General Seminar of the Graduate Faculty at
the New School.)
c. "Unbuilding (*Abbau*) and Building (*Aufbau*): Two Husserlian
Phenomenological Procedures." (Based on lectures given in the
course, "Husserl's Theory of Intentionality," given at the New
School under the auspices of the Graduate Faculty.)
d. "Philosophy as a Universal Striving towards Sophia in the Integral Sense of This Word." (Based on lectures first given in a course,
"Introduction to Philosophy," at Rockford College).

22. Projected publication of book: "A Husserlian Account of Minds."
(To be based largely on courses of lectures given under the auspices
of the Graduate Faculty at the New School for Social Research.
Many of these courses have undergone thorough revision since they
were last presented.)

LIST OF CONTRIBUTORS

CHAPMAN, Harmon (Ph.D., Harvard, 1933). Professor of Philosophy at New York University. In addition to Harvard, he studied at the Universities of Bern, Munich and Freiburg. Recent publications include "Realism and Phenomenology," in *The Return to Reason* (1953), edited by John Wild, and *Sensations and Phenomenology* (1966).

EMBREE, Lester (Ph.D., Graduate Faculty, The New School, 1972). Assistant Professor of Philosophy at Northern Illinois University. He is co-translator of Paul Ricoeur, *Husserl: An Analysis of His Phenomenology* (1967), and translator of Suzanne Bachelard, *A Study of Husserl's Formal and Transcendental Logic* (1968). Dr. Embree is also editor of Aron Gurwitsch, *Phenomenology and the Theory of Science* (1972).

FARBER, Marvin (Ph.D., Harvard, 1925). Professor of Philosophy SUNY at Buffalo. In addition to Harvard, he studied at the Universities of Berlin, Freiburg and Heidelberg. Docteur de l'Université de Lille, 1955. President of the International Phenomenological Society, editor of *Philosophy and Phenomenological Research*. Recent publications include the second edition of *The Foundations of Phenomenology* (1962), *Husserl* (1956), *Naturalism and Subjectivism* (1959), *The Aims of Phenomenology* (1966), and *Phenomenology and Existence* (1967).

GURWITSCH, Aron (Ph.D., Göttingen, 1928). Professor of Philosophy at the Graduate Faculty, The New School for Social Research. He is an editor of the series Phaenomenologica, Northwestern Studies in Phenomenology, Conscientia. His most recent publications include *The Field of Consciousness* (1964), *Studies in Phenomenology and Psychology* (1966), and *Phenomenology and the Theory of Science* (1972).

HARTSHORNE, Charles (Ph.D., Harvard, 1923). Professor of Philosophy, University of Texas, Austin. He has been President of the American Philosophical Association (1948/49), President of the Metaphysical Society of America (1954/1955), and President of the Peirce Society (1950/51). Recent publications include *The Logic of Perfection* (1962), *Anselm's Discovery* (1965), and *A Natural Theology for Our Times* (1967).

KERSTEN, Frederick (Ph.D., The Graduate Faculty, The New School, 1964). Associate Professor of Philosophy, The University of Wisconsin-Green Bay. Recent publications include "Franz Brentano and William James," *The Journal of the History of Philosophy* (1969), and "Phenomenology, History and Myth," *Phenomenology and Social Reality*, edited by Maurice Natanson (1970).

McGILL, V. J. (Ph.D., Harvard, 1925). Professor of Philosophy, San

Francisco State College. In addition to Harvard, he has studied at the Universities of Cambridge and Freiburg. He was President of the American Philosophical Association (1968), Pacific Division. His most recent publications include *Emotions and Reason* (1954), and *The Idea of Happiness* (1967).

NATANSON, Maurice (Ph.D., Nebraska, 1950; D.S.Sc., Graduate Faculty, The New School, 1953). Professor of Philosophy and Fellow of Cowell College at the University of California, Santa Cruz. His writings include *A Critique of J-P. Sartre's Ontology* (1951), *The Social Dynamics of George Herbert Mead* (1959), *Literature, Philosophy and the Social Sciences* (1962), and *The Journeying Self* (1970). Dr. Natanson has edited Alfred Schutz, *Collected Papers*, Vol. I (1962); *Philosophy of the Social Sciences* (1963), and *Essays in Phenomenology* (1966).

JORDAN, Robert W. (Ph.D., The Graduate Faculty, The New School, expected 1973). Assistant Professor of Philosophy, Colorado State University. He has published "Husserl's Phenomenology as an 'Historical' Science," *Social Research* (1968).

SPIEGELBERG, Herbert (Ph.D., Munich, 1928). Professor of Philosophy, Washington University. His most recent publications include *The Phenomenological Movement* (2 Vols., 1960), *Alexander Pfänder's Phänomenologie* (1963), and *Phenomenology, Psychology, Psychiatry* (1971). He is editor and translator of *Pfänder's Phenomenology of Willing and Motivation* (1967).

ZANER, Richard (Ph.D., The Graduate Faculty, The New School, 1961). Professor of Philosophy, SUNY at Stony Brook. His most recent publications include *The Problem of Embodiment* (1964), *The Way of Phenomenology* (1970). He has edited Alfred Schutz, *Reflections on theProblem of Relevance* (1970).